FAB!

THE SOUNDS OF THE SIXTIES

Tony Jasper

BLANDFORD PRESS
POOLE · DORSET

First published in the UK 1984 by Blandford Press,
Link House, West Street, Poole, Dorset, BH 15 1LL

Copyright © 1984 Tony Jasper

Distributed in the United States by
Sterling Publishing Co., Inc.,
2 Park Avenue, New York, N.Y. 10016

British Library Cataloguing in Publication Data

Jasper, Tony
  Fab!
  1. Music, Popular (Songs, etc)—History
  and criticism
  I. Title
  780'.42'09046   ML3470

     ISBN 0 7137 1518 9

Typeset by Asco Trade Typesetting Limited, Hong Kong

Printed in U.K. by Richard Clay (Chaucer Press) Ltd
Bungay, Suffolk

Contents

To
Jean, George, Florence, Rosemary and Jimmy
of the Barrett household, Penzance and London.

Introduction

This volume looks at the Sixties music scene. It brings
together thousands of facts and names and acts as both an
introduction for more serious study and as an overall
generalised view of the period. I am conscious that more
could have been said on enclosed subjects and on many
others of interest but somewhere a line has to be drawn,
especially when faced with the limited length of a book. A
further volume on the 1950s is now in preparation.

The writer thanks *Music Week* for the reproduction of
certain chart data (and reminds readers that this material
is strictly the copyright of that music industry journal).

Care has been taken to ensure accuracy, but in a work
of this kind – where there are thousands of facts – error
can occur at various stages of writing and production.
The compiler welcomes notification of any errors found
so that in any subsequent edition they may be corrected.

Blandford Press also publish *The Top Twenty Book –
The British Record Charts 1955–1983* which is a useful
companion volume to this book since it carries the weekly
charts of the Sixties. Those wishing to test their knowledge of the decade should try the 500 questions set in
this book, and also those found in *Rock Mastermind*, set
by me and again published by Blandford Press.

T. J.

Main Features of the Decade

This was a 'happening' decade. Some would say it was pop's greatest time.

Yet when the Sixties dawned it was a brave person who would have made such a claim or forecast.

Record-Mirror editor in the Sixties, Peter Jones, wrote in the paper's first issue of 1970 when he and others looked back at the past decade, 'The Sixties *did* swing. But not immediately. At first it was Adam Faith and Russ Conway and Cliff Richard and Tommy Steele and Marty Wilde.'

For Jones and others, the early Sixties were rather twee. 'Fresh-faced balladeers like Mark Wynter, Craig Douglas. No guts, just pleasantness. Ever-so-naice. But where was the hard individuality? The Americans such as The Shirelles, Brenda Lee, The Everly's had us licked. Rick Nelson, Del Shannon, mighty Roy Orbison, Connie Francis, the old twanger Duane Eddy. That's where pop was. But it was all horribly predictable for the most part.'

Jones was of course speaking of the popular musical scene, for beneath the material marketed for mass consumption was some stirring music from black quarters Stateside, from Memphis, Stax and Gospel areas.

Cliff was the one who lasted out of the British stars that Jones named.

Cliff and others, utilised the media of the time, but recorded music was hardly regarded as a friend in broadcasting quarters. A great amount of popular airtime was taken by dance bands who played the hits of others. For black music there was almost no airplay outside Radio Luxembourg. No-one at this period thought teens and twenties should have their own music service, even if Haley and Presley had caused generation gaps.

However, there was clubland and in the early part of the decade enthusiastic DJs and club-owners provided

8

the music that caught young people's attention and eventually filtered into the early recordings of groups like the Beatles and Stones. This music came from the likes of Marvelettes, early Aretha Franklin, Clarence Henry, Sam Cooke, Drifters, Maurice Williams and among the many more, Carla Thomas.

The popular diversion, away from the best music coming out of America and the clubs, came with 'the Twist'. This rather laboured musical idiom merely produced a few pleasant discs from Chubby Checker and thankfully didn't last. It was Soul, R&B and early rock 'n' roll which were being utilised, adopted – perhaps even molested – by a whole bevy of groups who were just waiting for time and attention.

Once the Beatles had been discovered, and eventually signed to a major, the light was green and in 1963 the first invasion of the British music scene by home-grown British groups was underway. American artists, with a few exceptions such as Orbison and the Beach Boys, were pushed aside. Suddenly it was good to be British: it was the first happening of the decade and it came on the back of the Beatles – and later also via other major world groups, such as The Rolling Stones and The Who – with all three's music lasting into the next decade and beyond.

1964 saw the next major happening, for this was the year when America stopped being foolish and insular. In 1963 she had refused the Beatles, and so-called moguls had gazed across the Atlantic and treated Beatlemania as some kind of sad British disease. They turned a blind eye toward the 'fab four' and went their own way. Presumably they hoped the British home-grown nonsense would cease and they could once again fill their own coffers by liberally exporting their artists.

However, capitalistic pragmatism won the day and after considerable hype the Beatles were launched Stateside and showed quite clearly that they were multi-talented. The Beatles carved a big slice of the popular US music for themselves, and with American kids deciding British was best a whole host of British acts found that

9

they too could sell thousands and thousands of records across the Altantic. White American pop would yet have its say, but that was later on in the decade.

At home the Beatles became relatively respectable, once the shock of their mop hair-styles had died down and mothers had given up trying to dissuade their offspring from copying. The real raucous noise came from The Rolling Stones. They seemed rude, uncouth, unkempt. They were led by a leering thick-lipped lead vocalist by the name of Mick Jagger and next to him was the dead-pan, somewhat feminine-looking Brian Jones. Both competed for the girls' attention.

Once the Stones departed from recording the songs of their black musical heroes they launched into lyrics that pilloried the surface of respectable Britain. The Stones were favourites of the tabloids who told with some glee of their life-styles.

Both Stones and Beatles, and later others, popularised American artists they had heard or met during their Stateside travels, so it wasn't entirely one-way traffic, although no record company had engaged Britain's musical heroes to tell of Dylan, James Brown, Bo Diddley, the Isley Brothers and others.

Beatles, Stones and later The Who helped bring into being the new phenomenon of a pop world that would replace film-land for supplying popular heroes; a world where companies would make their monies from record sales rather than at the movie box-office.

Radio and television were improving. The advent of the 'pirate' ships brought a new style of DJ to British ears, and the music presented in this lively style seemed fresh. Television meant shows like *Thank Your Lucky Stars* and the tops of them all *Ready Steady Go* where music and teen culture became aligned.

In the mid-Sixties, music was happening everywhere with at least 1,000 beat groups noted in Merseyside, London and the provinces. Many of them had at least one record issued, but not all by any means became well-known. Chris May and Tim Phillips in their *British Beat* book (Sociopack, 1974) divide Liverpool's bands into two divisions. The first had the Beatles, The Big Three, Fourmost, Gerry and the Pacemakers, Billy J Kramer and the Dakotas, The Merseybeats, The Mojos, Scaffold, The Searchers and The Swinging Blue Jeans. The duo listed second division Liverpool as The Chants, The Dennisons, The Escorts, Faron's Flamingos, The Koobas, Beryl Marsden, Tommy Quickly and the Remo 4, The Riot Squad, Rory Storme and the Hurricanes, Kingsize Taylor and the Dominoes and the deadly-titled The Undertakers. Probably The Big Three's inclusion in the top division is the only questionable choice for the first division, as they had no real hit of any consequence, with just *Some Other Guy* (37) and *By The Way* (22) telling their chart story – but two hits are better than none – and the Brian 'Griff' Griffiths, Johnny 'Gus' Gustafson and Johnny 'Hutch' Hutchinson trio were most respected in the Merseyside area. Known bands from elsewhere included Freddie and the Dreamers, The Nashville Teens, Graham Bond Organisation, The Easybeats, The Honeycombs, Small Faces, The Applejacks and The Rockin' Berries. Less remembered outfits include The Cherokees, The Pack, The Mike Cotton Sound, The Mark Leeman Five, The Naturals and The Roulettes.

The mid-Sixties was a great time, and soon would come another major group revival with a host of mighty names that would fetch global attention: Jethro Tull, Pink Floyd, Emerson Lake & Palmer, Black Sabbath, Led Zeppelin, Humble Pie, Fairport Convention, The Incredible String Band, Tyrannosaurus Rex (later plain T Rex), Traffic, Blind Faith and Deep Purple.

But America had not been completely overtaken by Brits and with Dylan preparing the way – along with the likes of The Byrds, plus the drug culture and student political-social awakening – there came the acid rockers, psychedelics and blues people. Hippie culture hit the States, and the US West Coast in particular experienced a veritable panoply of groups often with weird and wonderful names. I must admit now that I was a child of the late Sixties for, outside of the British names mentioned, the US provided Flock, It's A Beautiful Day, Grateful Dead, Jefferson Airplane, Big Brother and the Holding Company with Janis Joplin, Al Kooper, Tim Buckley, The Doors, Earth Opera, Blood Sweat & Tears, Canned Heat, Love, Crosby Stills & Nash (and then the trio with Neil Young for a fourth), Country Joe, Electric Prunes, Clear Light, Iron Butterfly, Hendrix and new ladies with vision and power, Joni Mitchell, Laura Nyro, Roberta Flack, with favourites Joan Baez and Judy Collins lasting through the new music era. Perhaps having lived in the States during this music explosion colours my feeling, for these were the people who made the music I heard at the Fillmore, San Francisco and elsewhere, on the Berkeley campus, on KSAN, San Francisco: music mostly relating to a social and political context that I knew, but because I was a foreign student I would not find myself part of Nixon's lottery to decide who might have the honour of going to die in Vietnam. The music was powerful. People felt committed to it, and on the US West Coast many of the new big British bands were seldom heard outside of Beatles, Moody Blues and anything that seemed to involve Stevie Winwood, Ginger Baker and Clapton.

Obviously much was happening in Britain but I was not part of it. The music press, the charts, the release schedules partly tell the excitement, and I had caught the first light shows of Floyd, the all-nighters at the Round House and King's Cross. The Pirate ships had, of course, gone by 1967 and Radio One had dawned as had *Top Of The Pops* on BBC-TV but neither really reflected the underground scene. John Peel did and his radio show was listened to avidly.

Soul, R&B also became very important on the British scene during the decade's last few years, although again – and true of all decades – black music had poor airplay amongst the music of the time. Many a gem found itself in the R&B charts of *Record Mirror* but not in the general pop Top 50.

The decade finished in less than pleasant manner for

the heroes of the Sixties, the Beatles were rent with dissention in the ranks and it was obvious that they would never see the Seventies except for unreleased or re-issued recorded material. And with no 'live' gigs (outside of filming for *Let It Be*) for many years, they departed as a studio band, albeit magnificent, yet lacking real contact with the people who had bought their records and shouted their names. Lennon was the most energetic of the four and soon gave notice that he would be producing more than interesting material.

But perhaps what made the Sixties a 'special' happening was the music's alignment with much else that was happening in society. The Sixties spawned numerous groups that questioned traditional values and, even more so, society's conventional behavioural patterns. Feminist, ecological, and peace movements were amongst the growth areas, and the music of the times caught some of this momentum even if it was more often than not spelt out in the assumed simplicity of the hit song *San Francisco (Wear Some Flowers in Your Hair)*. Many really believed that there was a new generation with a new explanation and a new way of living, and for many it seemed that way until the aftermath of Woodstock.

Year by Year

Some of the happenings and promises. The main events are summarised in subject heading and list form in the following section.

1960

London's cabaret club Talk Of The Town features the faithful but disobedient Louis, the first time a dog has been the main attraction. Louis comes with owner Bob Williams. Three offers from Hollywood are turned down by Tommy Steele. 'Groaner' Bing visits London's Decca studios and records four songs. The *New Musical Express* tells its readers that in 1958 108 artists appeared in the Top 30, a year later it was 113 and for the first year of the Sixties, 139. Derek Johnson – their ace reporter – thinks it proves the public is becoming more experimental in its record buying. Sinatra hosts a 'Welcome Home, Elvis' US-TV Special. *Sixteen Reasons* from Connie Stevens, *Way Down Yonder* from Freddy Cannon and Frankie Avalon's *Why* are some of the years million sellers. Malcolm Allison, Pete Murray, Anthony Newley and Jess Conrad are among those who turn out for the TV All Stars XI. Liberty announce that they have a stockpile of 20 Eddie Cochran titles which they consider up to the standard Eddie would have insisted on (Cochran died on 27 April.

A son is born for Diana Dors and husband Dickie Dawson. Pat Hebble marries Russ Hamilton, Evy Norfund marries James Darren and Ann Donoughue marries Tommy Steele. *Bad Boy* is Marty Wilde's first taste of US success, Colin Hicks tries Italy for fame and fortune rather than follow brother Tommy Steele's footsteps at home. Pat Boone has his own film and TV company Cooga Mooga. Jess Conrad is hailed as 'the face' of 1960. Robert Horton, star of *Wagon Train*, comes to sing for his supper in Britain. Jackie Rae and the delectable Janette Scott team up for the album *We Love Life*. Derek Johnson tips Della Reese, Matt Monroe, Dick Jordan, Danny Rivers, Danny Williams and Mary Wynter for real success in the UK 1961. Among *NME*'s albums of the week are Marty Wilde *Marty Wilde Showcase* (Philips), Johnny and the Hurricanes *Stormsville* (London), Doris Day *What Every Girl Should Know* (Philips), Kingston Trio *Sold Out* (Capitol) and Perry Como *Como Swings* (RCA). Decca thinks Alex Murray is for the charts with *Teen Angel* and believe he will be a teen girl hearthrob. *Date* is launched and they say 'smart young women everywhere are rushing for *Date*'. Frankie Vaughan sings his own composition *I Was A Fool*. Sammy Davis, 34 years old, arrives at London's Pigalle. Some see Guy Mitchell hitting the Sixties with *Silver Moon Upon Golden Sands* (Philips) while the *Original Cast of Oliver* is issued by Decca in September. Judy Garland spellbinds her audience at the Palladium.

1961

Anthony Newley stars with Anna Quayle in *Stop The World I Want To Get Off*. People learn the Allisons are not brothers but Brian Allford and Colin Day. And not even Pete Murray is Pete Murray for really he's Pete Murray James. In this year of amazing revelations Vera Lynn is really Margaret Walsh, Marty Wilde is Reg Smith, Ronnie Hilton is Adrian Hill, Robert Earl is Monty Leigh and among other shocks we learn that Craig Douglas is really Terence Perkins. A million-dollar question keeps being asked, 'when will he come to Britain?' The *he* is, of course, Elvis. Birmingham promotor Brian Delorme offers 'the King' £89,000 and jet transport so Elvis need not be away for more than 24 hours. People ask why 1961 is a lean year for artists like Dennis Lotis, Al Saxon, Roy Castle, Lita Roza, Dickie Valentine and Edmund Hockridge and say it seems a waste of fine talent. Sinatra says Monty Babson is one of the most promising singers to come out of Britain and critics say *Utopia* is the hit that is going to establish him.

Adam Faith has his autobiography published. Petula Clarke survives two car crashes with only bruising as a result. Cliff has a record-breaking tour in South Africa. Tony Bennett headlines at the Pigalle, London, for a month's season. Pye begin Nonesuch Records, featuring the spoken word, which gives hope to people with 16 rpm on their turntable speed-choice dial. Max Bygraves accepts the Phil Silvers role in the musical *Do Re Mi*.

Frank Sinatra pays a million dollars for the film rights of musical *Subways Are For Sleeping*. Cliff and the Shadows appeal in the press for a good film story. Peter Jones predicts a future for Shane Fenton. In *Record Mirror*, Jones says he's impressed with Shane's first disc *I'm A Moody Guy*, a song penned by Jerry Lordan. Big future is predicted for Suzy Cope, a 16-year-old singer-songwriter. Rosemary Clooney's *Rosie Solves The Swingin' Riddle* gets a rave album review. *Juke Box Jury* pans *Midnight In Moscow* from Kenny Ball but he takes it high into the charts. Cliff and the Shadows go to Australia and Singapore. Britain hears plumpish-fortyish house-wife Mrs Mills of Loughton in Essex, and her piano medleys become something of a rage. *The Young Ones* from you know who is described as 'Joyous, Jumping, Jubilant'. Mick Mulligan Band breaks up. The Confederates Jazz Band record *Brigitte Bardot* for their second Decca release. Mind disturbing Jill Browne, or 'Nurse Carol Young' of ITV's *Emergency Ward 10*, joins Doctor Ray Barrett on Oriole for the song *Cure For Love*. Oh dear, there is a row over a suggestion that Jess Conrad might play Elvis in a film version of the great singer's life. *Souvenir* is a warmly-reviewed Sinatra album. Presley goes to the top straight-away with *Surrender*. 100,000 dollars spent by US comedian Stan Freberg to make a four-LP set. The US has 'Brenda Lee Day' and 125,000 copies of her new album *Emotions* are sold.

1962
Teenage Millionaire starring Chubby Checker goes out on

general release, 14 January. Hancock's masterpiece *The Blood Donor* is released on record by Pye. Cliff's *The Young Ones* album is released. *Tender Is The Night* sings Tony Bennett during February while *Mama Do The Twist* comes from Susan Maughan and much tipped is *Tell Me What He Said* from Helen Shapiro. Anka record tapes of *Love Me, Warm And Tender* fail to arrive in London and are located in Amsterdam. Anka arrives in Britain, 22 February. Joan Regan has New York cabaret for the first time at the Maisonette Room, St Regis Hotel, Fifth Avenue. Three pretty girls – Janet Buckingham, Melanie Hampshire and Judy Jason – pop up regularly on *Thank Your Lucky Stars*.

The Raymonde Singers, four girls, eight men and run by Ivor Raymonde issue *O Willow Wally* from the film *The Innocents*. Raymonde was the man responsible for the background of Billy Fury hits. Johnny Mathis rates one of the top ten best dressed American men in a listing compiled by Custom Tailors Guild. Equity TV strike deprives many of visual promotion but once everyone is back some artists get massive push – one was John Leyton who's disc *Lonely City* nets *All That Jazz*, *Thank Your Lucky Stars*, *Disc-A-Go-Go*, *One O'Clock Show* (Border TV), *Swingalong* (Westward), *Rendevous* (Ulster), *Tuesday Rendevous* (AR-TV).

Schoolgirl 12-year-old Susan Hayward from Hanley, in the Potteries, lands a recording contract with Fontana and she sings *You Bet I Would*. Critics are astonished. Sinatra is at the Royal Festival Hall, London and meets Princess Margaret. Don Lang's new group debut with him on record via *Wicked Woman* (Decca). Disaster hits ATV-TV showing of *Dan Farson Meets Joe Brown*. First a rehearsal tape that ended abruptly then a minute's silence followed and another tape took up the action. *A Picture Of You*, Joe's hit, was stopped after four bars and instead of ending it ran into the commercials. The upshot was a feature re-filmed and shown properly. Apparently Brown was shattered. Singer Carol Deene begins a Radio Luxembourg series Carol Deene Presents, for EMI. It co-incides with her hit *Some People* and the contract is signed on her eighteenth birthday. Chubby Checker celebrates his twenty-first backstage at East Ham, Granada. London's Talk Of The Town features Shirley Bassey as her *What Now My Love* is in the Top 20. Mathis is in Britain from 24 November. The Beatles are described by Little Richard as one of Britain's best two rock groups and they appear in the Top 50 with *Love Me Do*. Some Cliff fans bemoan his straying from rock. Beatles win the Mersey Beat Popularity Poll again. EMI throw a twenty-fifth birthday party for Frank Ifield and give him a gold disc for *I Remember You*. *Rockin' Around The Christmas* is the first Yuletide Top 50 charting record though Brenda Lee recorded it back in 1959.

1963

Chariot gave Petula Clark a French hit and it appears in Britain translated as *I Will Follow Him*. Frankie Vaughan is announced as a co-star in a film with Doris Day. The Springfields visit Nashville, and Mike Pickworth replaces Tim Feild in the line-up. Fans attack Beatle taxis, in London they wrench a door and in Manchester they remove mirrors and an aerial. Frustrated by Elvis's *No* to live work in Britain *Record Mirror* writer Wesley Laine asks, 'Is Elvis becoming a Hermit?' Jimmy Savile records *The Bossa Nova* coupled with *Don't Do Anything I Like* for Decca. 20-year-old brunette Jill Jackson and 22-year-old Ray Hildebrand emerge as Paul and Paula and hit the charts with *Hey Paula*. Duffy Power says he's really Raymond Howard to his mates in Fulham. Brenda Lee marries a year-older Nashvillian Charles Shoklett and to some it's the surprise of the year, considering that 18-year-old Brenda had put across a tomboy image. Presley says he'll eventually marry but the 28-year-old continues acting with devastating girls in his films. Jim Reeves sings in Britain, and the Blue Boys come with him. In June Brian Epstein sees three of his groups in the chart 1-2-3 order: *From Me To You* (Beatles), *I Like It* (Gerry & The Pacemakers), *Do You Want To Know A Secret* (Billy J

Kramer & The Dakotas). Cliff and Carol Gray star in the Blackpool show Holiday Carnival. *Beggar In Love* is debut single from Clinton Ford. Kenny Ball is made an honorary citizen of New Orleans during July and there's news of former Beatles drummer Pete Best playing with Lee Curtis and the All Stars. An American 11-year-old Lana Jean has her disc *It Hurts To Be Sixteen* released in Britain by Pye. Police help Heinz leave *Thank Your Lucky Stars* studio but he is upset by losing his 'Good Luck Heinz' inscribed pen in the mêlée.

Frank Ifield records the old Frankie Laine smash *Mule Train*. Joe Brady from popular TV series *Z Cars* records *The Great Train Robbery* for Pye. The critics are not impressed. A 60-nighter package show of The Tornados, Billy Fury, Joe Brown and the Bruvvers, The Karl Denver Trio, Marty Wilde and the Wildecats, Dickie Pride, Daryl Quist with Ilford beat group The Ramblers backing, opens on 4 October at the ABC, Croydon. Four stars on *JBJ* for *Yesterday's Gone* from Chad Stuart and Jeremy Clyde. Bruce Welch, a mere twenty-one, makes his last British TV appearance with the Shadows – on *Sunday Night At The London Palladium* during September. Mickie Most records *The Feminine Look* for Columbia. Cliff is 23, a 'fabulous' Beatle sweater in 100 per cent botany wool is offered for 35 shillings. By October 1963 all Beatle A sides and flip sides have included either 'you' or 'me' in their title. Brian Poole is told to rest his voice by a throat specialist. Peter Paul & Mary have three albums in the Stateside Top 5. *With The Beatles* is out in November and gets an advance order of 250,000.

1964

'New New New' shouted Decca as they issued what they described as a 'terrific' EP – it came from Bern Elliott & The Fenmen and contained *Please Mr Postman*, *Shake Sherry Shake* and *Mashed Potatoes* amongst its tracks. Freddie of the Dreamers stunned everyone by saying he and the group would be taking life more seriously. New on the scene was Rochdale lady Lorraine Gray who recorded *Your Little Toy*. It turned out she had backed the Allisons on their *Are You Sure* biggie and been on the Caravelles first *You Don't Have To Be A Baby To Cry*. Dusty hit the US charts at 94 first week in with *I Only Want To Be With You*. Billy J Kramer went to Sweden without the Dakotas. A blue-beat craze began with Prince Buster alias Buster Campbell, born 24 May, 1938 and Jamaican singer Derrick Morgan was doing well. *Love In Las Vegas* with Elvis and Ann Margret opened on 11 March at the Empire Theatre, Leicester Square, London. Del Shannon began his Stateside release schedule with *Mary Jane*. New group on Decca, Johnny Milton and the Condors claimed they had travelled 175,000 miles around Britain. Dave Kaye debuted with El's hit *A Fool Such As I* and sounded rather like the 'King', and he was managed by Albert Hand, publisher and boss-man of Elvis's fan-club but no-one seemed to mind. The Dykons were Dave's backing group.

Johnny Burnette's death through a boating accident upset many. He and Elvis had been teenagers in Memphis. The Wild Ones became the new backing group of Heinz. Dionne Warwick, Little Richard and Chuck Berry paid a visit to Britain. Police in Denmark banned two scheduled Beatle performances after watching a film of the four's performance and observing the reaction of young people as hysterical. Fortunately for kids the Minister Of Justice reversed the police ban. Polydor, the German label, said they would record in Britain. Ringo was hospitalised with tonsils. Jimmy Savile topped *Record Mirror's* DJ poll and was followed in the pecking order by David Jacobs and Alan Freeman. The Crickets came to Britain and co-inciding with this Liberty released *(They Call Her) La Bamba*. 'Miss my mum,' said hit-lady Millie as her *Sweet William* record shot into the charts. Top Ten Discs issued top ten tunes on disc for 10 shillings. They said 'our musicians, almost without exception, have played on the original recordings.' The Bachelors played college dates in America.

Billy J Kramer was 'beat-up' by two men who gate-crashed his Sydney hotel room. 16-year-old Peter Noone landed the lead role in Dick Whittington, at Chester Royalty Theatre. Meantime they topped the charts and pop fans and journalists said Manchester was taking over from Liverpool. The Supremes recorded an album of Liverpool songs, issued in the US as *A Little Bit Of Liverpool*. Epstein said he was representing US super-hero Johnny Rivers for Britain, Europe and Australasia. Johnny Gustafson left the Merseybeats.

1965

'Rubbish,' said Ringo to rumours that he might quit the Beatles. The five Manfred Mann members produced the debut disc *Portland Town* of the Mark Leaman Five. Kathy Kirby sang 'A Song For Europe' contest in Naples on the 20th of March with Decca issuing the six song EP from which the year's entrant was chosen. Ringo married Maureen Cox and it was asked, 'will Ringo's marriage harm the Beatles?' A Welsh lad called Tom Jones had *It's Not Unusual* issued by Decca. People wondered whether The Searchers were changing their style after they recorded *Goodbye, My Love*, but the group said they had heard the song Stateside and simply wanted to record it. CBS issued Dylan's *The Times They Are A Changin'* in March. Parlophone trumpeted *The Hucklebuck* from Brendan Bowyer and The Royal Showband. The Konrads toured with The Stones. On 27 April The Who ended their weekly residency spot at London's Marquee and they said they had hopes of appearing just once a month in future. Joan Baez toured with Dylan and had her own solo concert at the Albert Hall on 23 May. July the 29th saw the premiere of *Help* at London Pavilion. Burt Bacharach married Angie Dickinson. JS954 is the number of J Savile's Rolls Royce.

New magazine *Beat Instrumental* is launched in June. The Seekers find a fantastic welcome on a return to Melbourne, their home town. A fan complained to *Record Mirror* that *Ready Steady Go's Kathy* says 'super' too much and co-presenter Patrick Kerr was always saying 'too much!' Shirley Ellis sang *The Puzzle Song* for Decca. Savile again won *RM*'s DJ section in their annual poll. *Pick Of The Pops* was the most popular radio show, with *Saturday Club* second. The Byrds were in Britain and seemed to have a desire for shopping in Carnaby Street. Mick Jagger and Keith Richard said they would produce discs for their manager's new label Immediate. Decca issued *Hark* from Unit Four Plus Two. A new company is launched called Music For Pleasure which will release EMI back-catalogue material for 12/6d. Them disbanded. Granada TV screened a 'day in the life of' Billy J Kramer. Lack of security led to the Walker Brothers cancelling any further ballroom dates. Larry Adler's son Peter had a debut disc *Love And Not Hate* for Decca. Cliff hit his 25th birthday. Tom McGuinness replaced Mike Vickers in the Manfred Mann line-up. Donald Leach, dad of Donovan, took over the management of his son. Jonathan King flew to US for an appearance on the prestigious *Ed Sullivan Show*. The British boxer Johnny Prescott part co-wrote *Whole Lotta Love* for The Cheetahs. Beatles toured and opened in Glasgow, December. Fordyce was announced for a return on a special New Years' *RSG* in 1966. Honey Lantree forsook her drums at London Palladium and for the evening Pretty Things man Vic Prince substituted. Honey sang vocals with Dennis D'Ell. Hollies released George Harrison penned *If I Needed Someone*.

1966
There is a new look and a new sound for Pinkerton's Colours – so say Decca and they issue *Mirror Mirror*. Sinatra completes 25 years in the business. The Fortunes tell of how their US tour lost them £10,000. NEMS take over the Vic Lewis Organisation. Tony Rivers and the Castaways sign with Brian Epstein. *Sound Of Music* sale figure in February given as 700,000 since release 12 months previously. Donovan dislikes the release of *Josie* as a single. BBC-1 transmits *The Beatles At Shea Stadium*

with 12 camera crews filming the great occasion. Doris Troy says she's fed up with people saying only Negro people can sing soul, 'I say everybody's got a soul – it's just a question of whether or not they choose to use it.'

The Who record *Waltz For A Pig* as B-side to *Substitute* and do so as The Who Orchestra. Genial Roy Orbison hits Britain with a new tour kicking off on 20 March. Three new announcers join Radio Luxembourg: Tommy Vance, Tony Brandon and Don Wardell. Orbison arrives but the motor-bike enthusiast goes to the Hawkstone Park Scramble, borrows a bike and falls off into a sandpit and breaks a bone in his foot. By 1966 Duggie Reece is only original left with The Echoes, backing group to Dusty. *Aftermath* is announced as new Stones album in April and both David and Jonathan contract tonsilitis. Gene Vincent has a leg operation. *Sorrow* comes from The Merseys.

A group name change for The Troglodytes and they become The Troggs and are tipped for a hit with their *Wild Thing*. Tito Burns Productions is taken over by Harold Davison Ltd, a division of the Grade Organisation. Beatles single *Paperback Writer* coupled with *Rain* is released two weeks before originally planned. *Saturday Club* is 400 on 4 June and the Beatles are booked. Gene Pitney comes in June. Soul and Blues fans lap up Mike Raven. The Fortunes battle with Manfred Mann over *You Gave Me Somebody To Love*. Presley starts work on his 23rd film – *Double Trouble*. Eric Haydock quits The Hollies with 23-year-old Bern Calvert replacing. Cliff says he is a Christian.

The Cavern re-opens with the Prime Minister Harold Wilson at the opening ceremony. Otis Redding visits in October. Cilla buys a luxury £2,000 plus Mini Cooper with lambswool carpeting, reclining seats upholstered in hide, a record player, twin speakers and of course tinted windows. Stones issue *Have You See Your Mother Baby Standing In The Shadows* and pill-popping prescription-approved adults dislike the insinuation. The four Shads write Cliff's disc *Time Drags By*. Eric Burdon has first

23

solo single for Decca released entitled *Mama Told Me Not To Come*. Ike Turner says he didn't like the 26 voices and strings that Spector pushed behind *River Deep Mountain High*. The Dixie Cups say Manchester is their favourite city. Cliff stars in *Cinderella*. Britain's most prolific hit-maker Shel Talmy, 28, says he is quitting pop for films. *Green Green Grass Of Home* is the Xmas chart-topper.

1967

Monkees have their first album released in January and they are due in February for a tour. Their TV show gains plaudits and a huge audience. National Theatre invites McCartney to write songs for Shakespeare's *As You Like It* but he declines. Jagger says 'panto' is not for him. Sonny & Cher have Atlantic single *The Beat Goes On*. Hollies spend considerable time overseas at San Remo, Italian tour and Germany. Pye issue huge stack of R&B discs, *January–February*. Dusty waxes number for Warner-Bros film *The Corrupt Ones* starring Elke Sommer. She had recently recorded *The Look Of Love* for *Casino Royale* movie. Jagger sues *The News of The World* for giving a misleading and untrue picture of his ac-tivities. 1,000 teddy boys wearing 1950-style zoot suits, winkle pickers and beetle crushers riot at London's Savile Theatre with curtains coming down only 25 minutes into Chuck Berry's act: Beatles attended as did Savile licensee Epstein. *Record Mirror* – often first with predicting stars of tomorrow – tells of up and coming Jimi Hendrix and Hendrix's first album is issued in March, and a cracker it was. Stevie Winwood quits Spencer Davis Group with last performance on 2 April at Liverpool Empire. After fan reaction to Davy Jones of Monkees arrival at Heathrow the Airport Authority review facilities. 20-year-old Sharon Tandy gets backing from Booker T & MGs and says she is the first white artist to record in Stax Studios, Memphis. Sharon is from South Africa. Fats Domino with 55 million disc sales behind him arrives in Britain for the first time. Bobby Elliott falls ill and Hollies cancel world tour. In May it's announced that Beatle record sales have passed 200 million.

Elvis weds Priscilla Beaulieu. Monkees have Wembley concerts. British Rail arranges 'beat' cruises from Portsmouth. Beatles write *All You Need Is Love* for *Our World* television broadcast. 400,000,000 see them (and others) as show is screened in 24 countries. Polydor complete deal to market US, Elektra product in Britain. Tony Hatch and Jackie Trent marry. Pink Floyd say they are planning 'spectaculars' with 100-piece choir, small chamber orchestra. Radio One begins. New Cliff book from David Winter, *New Singer New Song*. *Flowers* is new Julie Felix album. Growing interest in Stax material. Ex-Beatle producer Tom Wilson says Zappa's Mothers Of Invention 'biggest talent I have ever come across.' *Nights In White Satin* from The Moody Blues is issued on Deram. Tony Macaulay becomes 'hot' producer with hits for Long John Baldry and Foundations. Otis Redding and four members of Bar-Kays die in plane crash. Bee Gees sing in Liverpool Cathedral. BBC announces showing of *Magical Mystery Tour* from the Beatles will be on BBC-2, 5 January, 1968. At the end of December it's announced that the album has sold 1,600,000 copies in three weeks. Captain Beefheart is announced for January 1968 visit.

1968

George Harrison agrees to write music for *Wonderwall* film. Shadows man John Rostill falls ill and 'Licorice' Locking steps in. Ian McClagan of the Small Faces weds Sandy Sargeant. Presley fan-club magazine lambasts Tony Blackburn. The Herd get mobbed in Brussels as they record TV show *Then Klienken*. New label MCA opens up. Bee Gees get million dollar US tour. Beatles win four categories in US Grammy Awards. New single *She's My Girl* from Tony Blackburn on MGM. Luxembourg announces a 'new look'. Philips issue *I'm Gonna Make You Love Me* from Madeline Bell. Roger Miller injures a hand in US shooting incident and cancels UK tour. Mike Vickers Orchestra is backing group on

Hollies – Paul Jones tour. Mickie Most produces Seekers disc. Johnny Cash says Dylan is the best songwriter around. Lennon-McCartney write four new songs for animated feature film *Yellow Submarine*. Move release 'mini-album' at EP price but with playing time of 18 minutes. Andy Williams sings the song *(In The Summertime) You Don't Want My Love* seven times (once in Japanese) at London concert. Great packaging for new *Ogden's Nut Gone Flake* album from Small Faces, which is fold-out round in shape. Dusty lands Atlantic record contract. Gordon Mills announces another great discovery – Steve Montgomery. He bows in with *What's Good About Goodbye* but doesn't become another Tom or Engelbert.

Harrison says the four new Beatle songs for *Yellow Submarine* were recorded twelve months before. Leonard Bernstein is peeved by The Nice recording of *West Side Story* number *America*. Jefferson Airplane arrive in Britain with both themselves and Doors booked for the Roundhouse, Chalk Farm, London, on 6 and 7, September, with Granada TV filming. Massive September arrival of Elektra artists – with Doors, David Ackles, Judy Collins and Tim Buckley amongst them. Fleetwood Mac point out that they have three lead guitarists. *Milk Train* is late August Everly Brothers single and hopes for revival.

Girl On A Motorcyle with Marianne Faithfull looking marvellous is issued by British Lion. Paul Jones appears in *The Committee*. After a nine-month lay-off Cat Stevens returns with predicted hit *Here Comes My Wife*. Jagger films *Performance*, co-starring with James Fox. Mike Love of the Beach Boys says he likes cars but 'my passion is reserved for women.' Tiny Tim performs at the Royal Albert Hall. Humperdinck says he wants a 'Western', while after three years of waiting the *Wednesday Morning 3 am* album from Simon and Garfunkel gets British release. Masterful Stones on *Beggars Banquet* while Scott and John (of the Walkers) co-produce John's single *Woman*. Doris Henderson joins excellent Eclection.

More rumours of Move split. John Peel says personality cult built around him is scary. *RM* readers say *Little Arrows* from Leapy Lee most disliked disc of the year.

1969

They call it *Pop World*, it's described as 'the biggest happening of 1969' and the date is Sunday 16 March, two performances. The British Polio Fellowship bring together a host of big pop names for the event. A medium tells Barry Rylan that Elvis is coming to Britain. The Nice visit Prague. Marmalade, Gene Pitney, Joe Cocker and the Grease Band, Iveys, the Mike Cotton sound and compere Mike Quinn go off on UK tour. Elvis records in Memphis for the first time since early Sun days. Mike Lennox is host at Ronnie Scott's Soho discotheque. *Sister Morphine* is B-side of Decca Marianne Faithfull single. Bee Gee Maurice says Lulu is quite prepared to give up singing when they marry. A new magazine *Record Buyer* is launched and costs 2/6d, which contrasts with weekly 6d for *Record Mirror*. MGM issue another Tony Blackburn single *It's Only Love*. Hendrix charms at the Royal Albert Hall. Much touting for new group Harmony Grass. David Symonds the DJ says Moody Blues album *On The Threshold of A Dream* is better than *Sgt Pepper*. Lulu is the Eurovision lady with the song *Boom Bang-A-Bang*. The Rascals say 'we're a damned good group', while it seems Diana Ross is leaving Supremes. John Lee Hooker says, 'I don't go for psychedelic crap!'

Decca issue 50 years of music on five albums and introduce all via five singles and do so through the orchestrations of Ivor Raymonde. Raymonde makes a reasonable statement, 'we're not aiming for a teenage market.' New Midlands band is Cooperfield. *Get Back* is new Beatles Spring release. So marvellous *Dusty In Memphis* album appears. Social lyrics from Supremes with *I'm Livin' In Shame* and it seems natural follow-up to *Love Child*. EMI launch Harvest Records to take in 'underground' music scene. Label begins with Edgar Broughton Band and Michael Chapman. Stones say they are lost

27

without Mick as the golden boy is filming in Australia. Elvis makes first live appearance in seven years at America's International Hotel Show Room, Las Vegas.

Decca advertise The Kingly Band and Malcolm's All Stars. Bee Gees have television *Cucumber Castle* series. Elvis fan-club is asked not to buy Presley's *Clean Up Your Own Back Yard* but to request other side *The Fair Is Moving On*. Dylan plays Isle of Wight pop festival. Radio One strengthens Saturday programme fare. Paul and Linda have baby 6lb 8 oz, named Mary. Vertigo is new Philips label for progressive rock. For a while Elvis' *Suspicious Minds* is available only on import at 14s 6d. Diana Ross does quit Supremes. Fleetwood Mac have double album *Blues Jam At Chess* released by old company Blue Horizon. John 'Polli' Palmer joins Family from Eclection, Jim King is the departing one. US buzzes to news of Paul McCartney's death, Capitol denies but some fans then (as now) insist Paul has a double. James Hamilton says Stevie Wonder discs are becoming too 'white' slanted.

Festivals

Festivals – many of them attracting 50,000 or more people and running for several days – became the norm in Britain and the States during the second half of the decade, although there were earlier gatherings. Major bands and artists played the festival circuit. Although many events were successful even the best like Monterey and Woodstock had their problems. At worst, festivals attracted the get-rich quickly promotor whose overall planning left much to be desired. Violence was often seen at events supposedly illustrating peace, love and freedom, of youth with a new way of life, for often the 'new way' was merely comprised of kids who could not handle alcohol and dope.

This brief summary gives data on the major events in both Britain and America.

Altamont, Livermore, California, America, 6 December, 1969. The Stones headlined and the event was filmed, but the festival turned sour when halfway through *Sympathy For The Devil* an 18-year-old black from Berkeley, Meredith Hunter, was stabbed to death by Hell's Angels who had been hired as security by The Rolling Stones. 300,000 attended.

Ann Arbor Blues Festival, Michigan, America 1969. BB King, Arthur Crudup, Big Mama Thornton and Son House starred. Drink was banned, with police keeping constant watch.

Beaulieu, Hampshire, England. The Beaulieu festival had begun in the Fifties, partly under the patronage of Lord Montagu.

10,000 attended the 1960 event and heard some trad jazz bands and other jazz artists. Rioting marred the event and Montagu said it would be the last, but it was held again in 1961, when numerous security measures were taken to forestall trouble but sadly there was still trouble in the village. It heralded the end.

Godshill, Isle of Wight, England. In 1968 the first rather tentative Isle of Wight Festival was held. 8,000 attended and heard among others The Pretty Things and Tyrannosaurus Rex.

Hyde Park, London, England. London's sprawling Hyde Park, best-known to many for its Speakers Corner, was the scene of various free festivals, and audiences went as high as 250,000 people. The best remembered was on 5 July, 1969, with The Rolling Stones starring. Jagger wore his frilly frock over trousers and excited the popular press, while for the more serious there was his tribute to Brian Jones who had died on 3 July at his Cotchford Farm home, Hartfield, Sussex.

Isle of Wight, England (see also Godshill festival). The Isle of Wight Festival of 1969 bore little resemblance to the Godshill event of 1968. The attendance rose to 180,000, a 2,000 Watt PA ensured it was heard over a wide area and many of rock's best-known came, including The Nice, Who, Stones, Tom Paxton and less predictably Françoise Hardy. The star was Bob Dylan. He sang after The Band had played an hour long set and opened with *She Belongs to Me*. He sang two encores, *Who's Gonna Let It Roll* and *Rainy Day Women Nos 12 & 35*. The crowd wanted much more but he never re-appeared. Compere Rikki Farr came on stage and said, 'He's gone . . . He's gone. He came here to do what he had to do, he did it for you and now he's gone. Really, there is no more.' This festival moment was captured by the British press in differing fashion. The tabloid *Daily Sketch* screamed 'Dylan Cuts It Short After Midnight Flop', while respectable *Daily Telegraph* headlined '150,000 Go Wild As Dylan Rocks Isle.' The latter seemed more true by far. Dylan left in a privately-hired hovercraft with a fleet of limousines (Rolls for the Dylan family and Daimlers and Austin Princesses for The Band) to continue his land journey.

Memphis Country Blues Festivals, Memphis, America. The first was held in 1966, a two-day event drawing together some of the best known blues stylists. In 1969 the line-up included some names better known to the total music fraternity – Canned Heat, The Bar-Kays as well as respected blues people Bo Diddley, Muddy Waters, Howlin' Wolf, Albert Collins and a host of those termed 'the good old-time blues men' with ages between 65 and 95. Johnny Winter, a later rock star, played for fifty bucks. On the last night Rufus Thomas and daughter Carla sang.

Monterey International Pop Festival, America, 16–18 June, 1967. It was held at the Monterey County Fairgrounds, a capacity crowd of 7,100 swelled by at least 50,000 others who just came. The non-profit festival netted $200,000. An excellent documentary was shot by movie-maker D A Pennebaker. Music, love and flowers (the Haight-Ashbury hippie ethic) reigned. The festival was envisaged as an annual event but never became so. It was the forerunner of endless festivals Stateside.

The performers were The Association, Booker T and the MGs, Buffalo Springfield, Eric Burdon and the Animals, The Paul Butterfield Blues Band, The Byrds, Canned Heat, Country Joe and the Fish, The Electric Flag, Aretha Franklin, The Grateful Dead, Jimi Hendrix Experience, Jefferson Airplane, Janis Joplin and Big Brother and the Holding Company, Al Kooper, Mamas and Papas, Hugh Masekela, Steve Miller Band, Moby Grape, Laura Nyro, The Paupers, Quicksilver Messenger Service, Otis Redding, Johnny Rivers, Ravi Shankar, Simon and Garfunkel, The Who.

It was a line-up dreamed of, dreamt of and it became reality.

Newport Folk Festival, Freebody Park, California, America. The first had been held in 1959, and the festivals continued through the Sixties bringing to the fore the best known and loved artists, who broadly fitted the billing of 'folk'. Owing to violence at the companion Jazz Festival in 1960 organiser George Wein stepped down and 1961 and 1962 saw no Folk Festival. However, in 1963 Judy Collins and Bob Dylan were new voices when the Folk Festival recommenced. 40,000 attended in 1963, 70,000 the following year, and 80,000 in 1965 when Dylan introduced himself in an electric guitar context and found himself almost hounded off-stage. In 1969 there was Pete Seeger, Jesse Fuller, Joni Mitchell, Doug Kershaw, James Taylor, Jack Elliott, Big Mama Thornton, Johnny Cash and many others.

Newport '69, Northbridge, California, America, 20–22 June, 1969. This festival was dubiously distinguished, for fans who caused massive damage to property, hospitalised at least 15 police and wounded others. 75 fans were arrested and 300 injured. Brutal tactics by the police were witnessed. 150,000 people attended, a number far above expectations. The sound system was inadequate, the stage too low and small. Music artists numbered 33 and included Jimi Hendrix, Edwin Hawkins Singers, Love, Flock, Spirit, the Tina Turner Revue, Eric Burdon and Taj Mahal.

Newport '69 had nothing to do with the real Newport Folk Festival that was held in Freebody Park.

Richmond Festivals, England. National Jazz Federation member Harold Pendleton had helped Lord Montagu organise the Beaulieu Festival, and had run the Marquee Club, Soho. In 1961 and for the next five years he put together a series of festivals at Richmond.

In 1963 he featured The Rolling Stones, along with Long John Baldry, Georgie Fame and Acker Bilk. Once titled a Jazz Festival it became Jazz and Blues in 1964 with 27,000 hearing the groups. The Stones took top billing.

In 1965 the festival further broadened its appeal with over 30,000 attending and the event attracting many more general music fans. For the first time the festival became security conscious, there was local outcry at the area being invaded by so-called less desirables.

Pendleton moved to Windsor Racecourse in 1966 with Spencer Davis, The Who, Yardbirds, Eric Clapton, Small Faces, The Action and Georgie Fame appearing. The same site was utilised for the '67 festival when flower-power made its presence felt. Donovan sang his medley of romantic songs, while 'doves of peace' were released by The Nice. Ten Years After and Eric Clapton were amongst the other stars. Less expected for those attending was the arrival of Arthur Brown who made his appearance on a crane with hair ablaze. Much less pleasing was the non-appearance of Pink Floyd.

Kempton Park, Sunbury was the venue for Pendleton's '68 festival. Arthur Brown again starred although his act of considerable proportion and verve was somewhat dampened by the collapse of a canopy.

Plumpton Racecourse provided the setting of the 1969 event. Among those appearing were The Who, Chicken Shack, Peter Hammill, Roy Harper, Family, the cast of *Hair*, Dry Ice, The Bonzo Dog Doo Dah Band, Jo Ann Kelly, Pentangle, Keef Hartley, Hard Meat, Chris Barber and the Blossom Toes. The Nice starred and came last.

Woodstock, Bethel, New York, 15¬17, August, 1969. 400,000 (some say more) traipsed to Max Yasgur's farm at Bethel, New York. The *New York Times* said it was a 'Nightmare in the Catskills' and asked, 'What kind of culture is it that can produce so colossal a mess?' Many who went disagreed. The event was captured in film, on record, and given one major journalistic review in *Barefoot In Babylon – The Creation of the Woodstock Music Festival, 1969* by Robert Stephen Spitz (Viking Press, New York). Artists appearing were Joan Baez, The Band, Blood Sweat & Tears, The Paul Butterfield Blues Band, Canned Heat, Joe Cocker, Country Joe and the

Fish, Creedence Clearwater Revival, Crosby, Stills, Nash and Young, The Grateful Dead, Arlo Guthrie, Tim Hardin, The Keef Hartley Band, Richie Havens, Jimi Hendrix, The Incredible String Band, Jefferson Airplane, Janis Joplin, Melanie, Mountain, Quill, Santana, John Sebastian, Sha Na Na, Ravi Shankar, Sly and the Family Stone, Bert Sommer, Sweetwater, Ten Years After, The Who, Johnny Winter.

Of all rock festivals this and Monterey are arguably the best known and remembered.

The Main Headlines

1960

1 ABC TV axe *Boy Meets Girl*.
2 Cliff Richard makes his pantomime debut.
3 Gene Vincent calls it a day.
4 BBC say 7,000,000 watch *Juke Box Jury*.
5 Presley's *Stuck On You* coupled with *Fame And Fortune* has advance order of 100,000. Army service had not harmed him.
6 Eddie Cochran is killed in a car crash.
7 ABC-TV kill off Jack Good's *WHAM!*
8 Media goes wild over 'death' disc *Tell Laura I Love Her* from Ray Peterson and say it should be banned.
9 Row in the States over a book *Operation Elvis*. US fans appeal to British fellow Elvis lovers to ignore it.
10 Chris Barber loses Monty Sunshine.
11 Terry Dene makes a come-back.
12 MU says artists must avoid South Africa.
13 Judy Garland plays at the London Palladium.
14 Shirley Bassey and Eartha Kitt find themselves fighting for audiences as Bassey plays the Pigalle, and Kitt is at Talk of the Town.
15 Ken Dodd has Top 20 smash with his first record and silences critics who say he is a comedian and no more.
16 Pete Murray pre-dates a 'Mike Reid' of 1984 and refuses to play *Royal Date* from Russ Conway considering it bad taste.
17 Cliff Richard hits America and makes great impression, and for a while it looks as though he could be a major Stateside star.
18 Frankie Vaughan goes filming in Hollywood.
19 Cliff's backing group The Shadows find they too can be stars.
20 Adam Faith lands prestigious Royal Variety Show.

1961

1 Presley gets a million seller with *It's Now Or Never*.

2 Helen Shapiro hits the record scene and people take notice of a teenager with plenty of talent.

3 Eurovision votes Britain's Allisons second, but the duo who turned out not to be brothers after all, just miss the chart top spot with *Are You Sure*.

4 The Shadows and Cliff say they will film *The Young Ones*.

5 Veteran Jo Stafford says she will make British TV series.

6 Bing Crosby spends three months here filming.

7 Tony Meehan leaves the Shads and Brian Bennett is the new drummer.

8 Trad people get call for the Royal Variety Performance so tripping the floorboards go Kenny Ball, Acker Bilk, The Temperance Seven.

9 Vic Lewis says Presley is coming to Britain and he will play for charity. But then it doesn't happen.

10 A pirate radio ship theatens to operate from just outside the Thames estuary.

11 Susan Maughann is discovered by Ray Ellington.

12 Pye Records sent Russian boss Mr Kruschev a copy of *Midnight In Moscow* by Kenny Ball.

13 The first British album recorded at EMI's soon to be famous Abbey Road studios, London NW8 is by Kay Starr.

14 Twelve Sammy Davis concerts cancelled without explanation.

15 Songwriters Guild tell everyone that in their opinion DJs are getting too powerful.

16 EMI says Russ Conway is shifting a phenomenal number of albums and they give him a silver disc.

17 Jimmy Savile flies to America and meets Elvis and the Colonel.

18 Adam Faith is 21, so is Cliff Richard.

19 Johnny Mathis makes British TV debut.

20 Back on the music scene Gene Vincent falls ill and returns to the States.

1 Manx Radio for the Isle of Man is announced.

2 *Maigret* TV series on the BBC spawns hit for the Joe Loss Band.

3 Billy Fury, Adam Faith, Cliff Richard and Helen Shapiro maintain their grip and score in the year's Top 10 of major pop papers.

4 Cliff Richard has 500,000 advance for *The Young Ones* and announces he and the Shads will star in *Summer Holiday*.

5 A 19-year-old son of a Bournemouth doctor Tony Blackburn is heard singing with Ian Ralfini's Band at the town's Pavilion.

6 The amazing and most individualistic Mrs Mills is offered a 28-week series.

7 Chubby Checker of Twist fame flies in for a tour and finds he is the subject of record company wrangling over who should have or has the right to his material.

8 Frank Sinatra pays a visit and sings for his supper very successfully. He meets Princess Margaret. And records.

9 Most unexpected is the disc *Christmas With The Everly Brothers & Boystown Choir*.

10 Joe Meek emerges as a top producer, thanks to recordings and hits with the likes of John Leyton, The Tornados, Anne Shelton, Gary Miller, Frankie Vaughan, Marty Wilde, Emile Ford, Lance Fortune, Mike Berry and Michael Cox.

11 Pat Boone is back in favour and sells a million plus overall with *Speedy Gonzales*.

12 Claims of 2,000,000 world sales for *Stranger On The Shore*, and UK sheet music 40,000.

13 *NME* says more and more pop stars are making films while *MM* tells of its first transatlantic phone call by satellite Telstar.

14 Judy Garland, Bobby Darin, Ray Charles and Shirley Bassey named by *NME* as the artists with the year's top four albums.

15 Pre-Beatle invasion, 1963 record observers note that

Acker Bilk, Kenny Ball, Frank Ifield, Springfields, Tony Newley, Hayley Mills finding US success as well as familiar dance band people Mantovani, Ted Heath, Stanley Black and Edmundo Ross.

16 November sees the first Beatle single in the chart – *Love Me Do* is the title.

17 In the yearly *NME* compilation of artists – on the basis of points according to chart position – Presley took first place, Cliff second, and with almost half the Elvis total scoring came third position Acker Bilk.

18 Ed Sullivan has Helen Shapiro on his famed US show and she gets rave notices.

19 Johnny Mathis speaks his mind on *Juke Box Jury* and many people are upset. And speaking in its own style TV show *That Was The Week That Was* hammers Norrie Paramor but many spring to his defence.

20 Jet Harris and Tony Meehan form a recording team for Decca.

1963

1 Beatles, Beatles everywhere. In January they make historic first major TV appearance on *Thank Your Lucky Stars*.

2 Craig Douglas has a tonsils operation and learns it may be the end of his singing career that until then had seen 17 singles.

3 20 years in the music business for Nat King Cole who announces he will tour the UK with Ted Heath band accompanying.

4 Buddy Holly mania breaks out once more, and that's four years on from his death.

5 New band The Rolling Stones announced as support for Everlys.

6 There may be the Beatles, but the first Liverpool group to have their own series on Luxembourg is the Swinging Blue Jeans.

7 A Miss X has a disc entitled *Christine* and the Christine is presumed by many to be Ms Keeler.

Melody Maker says Miss X is Joyce Blair, sister of Lionel.

8 Beatles debut on the famous *Sunday Night at the London Palladium*. Later they get booked for Royal Variety Performance.

9 Cavern stage is for the chopping and the bits sold as souvenirs.

10 Shadows shock when it's learnt that Bruce Welch is in ill-health and says he's for the leaving. But all's well by November.

11 US nominate Acker Bilk for a Grammy.

12 November and December not good months: in the former 34 year-old Michael Holliday dies, the latter sees Dinah Washington (39) dying.

13 US chases after surfing music and the Twist seems on the wane.

14 A Southern TV pop show *Dad, You're A Square* has a panel voting on discs – to buy or break – and, if the latter, then their 'disc-cruncher' comes into operation.

15 *Mersey Beat* becomes 'the' Liverpool music mag, edited by Bill Harry.

16 Peter Jones, Norman Jopling and *Record Mirror* tell the world about The Rolling Stones and say *RM* first told everyone about Beatles, Marty Wilde, Gerry and the Pacemakers, Billy Fury, etc.

17 Little Stevie Wonder gets British press -he's 12!

18 Americans go for the 'Hootenanny', a kind-of folk affair in which the audience are expected to sing or clap hands.

19 £1,000 a week incomes but the Springfields say they are breaking up.

20 Second UK visit for Gene Pitney.

1964

1 *Billboard*, the US music magazine giant, tots up the chart positions and says Cliff was the world's top recording artist of 1963.

2 Eurovision entry is Matt Monroe singing *I Love The Little Things. You Do* by Tony Hatch.

3 600,000 people place advance order for Beatles single *Can't Buy Me Love*. Later Ella records her version in London.

4 *In His Own Write* by John Lennon is published.

5 Bob Dylan is at the Royal Albert Hall.

6 Beach Boys come to Britain and stun.

7 South Africa tells Dusty Springfield she can leave – the ex-Springfield's lead vocalist had refused to play segregated halls.

8 Supremes in Britain for first-ever tour.

9 Harold Wilson finds he is opposed by pop singer Screaming Lord Sutch in his held Liverpool constituency.

10 Rolling Stones cause a commotion on *Juke Box Jury*.

11 New era dawns for UK groups Stateside.

12 In 1957 Bill Haley's arrival caused uproar – he returns in '64 but not so much excitement by far.

13 Tamla Motown finally happens.

14 Beatles are the kings of albumland, U.K. and everywhere.

15 Freddie of Freddie and the Dreamers says the comedy is over and he is about serious things in future.

16 A new, vivacious, stunning Marianne Faithfull arrives with *As Tears Go By*.

17 Chuck Berry visits the UK for the first time.

18 Peter, Paul and Mary perform in the UK.

19 The French dig the Bachelors as they perform in Paris' Olympia.

20 Jim Reeves is killed in an air crash.

1965

1 Beatles reign – still!

2 ABC and Rank theatre circuits ban P J Proby, and say he is obscene. His pants keep splitting.

3 Seekers hit the top with *I'll Never Find Another You* and arouse record companies to look for commercial pop-folk.

4 The man reputed to be the first ever DJ, Christopher Stone dies at the age of 82.

5 Beatles play historic concert at Shea Stadium, New York before 55,000.

6 People talk about a new group from London – *The Who*.

7 Jonathan King refused entry to the States.

8 Brian Wilson has problems and Glen Campbell steps into the Beach Boy line-up.

9 Beatle marriage as Ringo weds Maureen Cox.

10 The Yardbirds lose Eric Clapton.

11 *RSG* grab Roy Orbison for his first ever UK TV appearance.

12 Top US star Johnny Rivers refuses to sing 'live' on *Gadzooks*.

13 US 'class' singers Johnny Mathis, Buddy Green, Tony Bennett and Jack Jones arrive in Britain during the Spring.

14 Hollies manager Norman Petty flies into Britain and helps Brian Poole and Tremeloes in their recording.

15 Who record their first album but manager Kit Lambert stuns fans by saying it's only for America and France. He says it's not the right time for group album release in UK.

16 Jonathan King releases *Everyone's Gone To The Moon* and signs a contract with Decca as a producer.

17 New cheap priced album company formed called Music For Pleasure. They release records for 12s 6d.

18 Them disband.

19 ABC-TV says 'out' go the long-haired groups and in come the entertainers with family appeal, as they launch new TV show *Lucky Stars*. But it is nowhere near the standard of *Thank Your Lucky Stars*.

20 The Beatles: MBEs.

1966

1 £1,000,000 is Decca's figure for a new five year deal with Rolling Stones.

2 Mamas and Papas surprise by coming, but delight many British fans.

3 British Government lines up plans to kill-off the pirate ships.

4 US outrage over Lennon's comment that Beatles more popular than Jesus.

5 A new group called Cream is announced and their debut is for the Windsor Festival.

6 Psychedelia hits London – a huge event at London's Roundhouse brings Floyd, Move, Who and Suzie Creamcheese together.

7 The Monkees scamper and clamber for affection.

8 Electric guitar Dylan meets considerable abuse on UK tour.

9 Beach Boys issue *Pet Sounds* and most of the record world doffs the cap.

10 The folk world gets a real boost with success for The Dubliners.

11 America goes wild – rumours of Mick Jagger's death. But then they said Paul McCartney was dead, some still maintain it.

12 Cliff and Shadows make history – it's the first time that an act of their kind appears at London's Talk Of The Town.

13 Famed British radio pop show *Saturday Club* has its 400th edition on 4 June. Appropriately the Beatles star. Brian Matthew the DJ-mastermind behind the show interviews them.

14 Adverts for the Billy Graham evangelistic crusade at London's Earls Court appear in the music press!

15 June 25th, 1966 the last edition of *Thank Your Lucky Stars* and who should star but the Beatles!

16 Beatles hit trouble in US as cover for *Yesterday and Today* gets thumbs down. It carried a picture of the Beatle members in butcher's aprons and surrounded by pieces of meat and dolls in bits and pieces.

17 Dusty Springfield lands her own BBC TV series.

18 Sick records get a big lift with the release of *They're Coming To Take Me Away* from Napoleon XIV.

19 Battle rages between pirate ship Caroline and Andrew Loog Oldham with the result the ship refuses to play Immediate Records or anyone associated with ALO. The Stones are one.

20 Scott Walker found unconscious in gas-filled flat.

1967

1 Birmingham Cathedral rejects Move plan to chop up an effigy of the Devil and Move turn down offer of playing at venue.

2 Beatles produce *Sgt Pepper's Lonely Hearts Club Band*. BBC doesn't like *A Day In The Life*.

3 Stevie Winwood departs from Spencer Davis Group.

4 Beatles get eight US Grammy Award nominations.

5 *Melody Maker* say there is chart fiddling – to counteract they say their chart will feature only a 30, not a 50. *MM* say low sales 30 to 50 encourages irregular practices.

6 In the US, Monkee tour organisers drop Jimi Hendrix because he is not so family oriented. They say his act is not for the well-heeled.

7 Paul McCartney says he has taken the drug LSD.

8 Radio One is launched by the BBC with many 'pirate ship' DJs on land.

9 Graham Nash proclaims 'flower-power' is dead but it seems rather premature.

10 London's Alexandra Palace has a 'love-in'.

11 Brian Epstein, manager of the Beatles dies.

12 Woburn Abbey has a three-day Festival Of Flower Children.

13 Mama Cass says Mamas and Papas splitting – it means London concert is cancelled.

14 Mick Jagger gets jail sentence of three months for possessing four pep pills. *The Times*, no less, springs to his defence. On appeal the sentence is quashed.

15 All-nighter with Pink Floyd and lights at London's Roundhouse.

16 The Walker Brothers split.

17 States have marvellous Monterey Festival on the West Coast.

18 Gerry Dorsey becomes Engelbert Humperdinck. He has a chart-topper with *Release Me*.

19 The Sinatras, Frank and Nancy, find themselves a massive hit with *Something Stupid*.

20 Ructions in British press as Stones release *Let's Spend The Night Together*. The Stones seen as suggesting young people should have pre-marital sex.

1968

1 Uproar breaks over honest statement from Love Affair that session musicians helped out. Later MU discusses a ban to stop this terrible state of affairs.

2 Dylan film *Don't Look Back* gets showing at London Film Festival.

3 Hollies lose Graham Nash: Traffic split: Burdon leaves Animals: Mick Abraham departs from Jethro Tull.

4 Lennon is fined for possessing cannabis. Yoko cleared.

5 Hyde Park scene of a free festival during July. Floyd, Roy Harper, T-Rex and Jethro Tull appear.

6 New Beatle company Apple is promised as the means of changing the music biz.

7 Small Faces cause uproar with their exquisitely packaged album *Ogden's Nut Gone Flake* for parodying the Lord's Prayer.

8 The Bee Gees get a million dollar US tour.

9 Lulu gets launched in the fashion world by Lenbry, she gives various clothing ideas, there's Lulu boutiques and all for the younger girl in mind.

10 Mick Jagger lands major film role along with James Fox in *Performance*.

11 Micky Dolenz of Monkees fame marries chief record spinner of *Top Of The Pops*, Samantha.

12 Easybeats gate-crash Buckingham Palace garden party in full morning dress.

13 Isle of Wight Pop Festival announced for 31 August.

Jefferson Airplane, Move, T-Rex among listed participants.

14 Marianne Faithfull stuns in film *Girl On A Motorcycle*.
15 America produces Tiny Tim.
16 250th edition of *Top Of The Pops*.
17 Keith Skues book *Radio Onederland* is published by Landmark for 10 shillings (50p).
18 The 'original' Animals, including Burdon, get-together at Newcastle City Hall.
19 Joh Peel says 'it's very scary this whole personality cult' – he's talking about DJs. But *Record Mirror* readers vote him tops.
20 Sly and Family Stone dropped from *Top Of The Pops* after London drug charge.

1969

1 Brian Jones is dead.
2 Mick and Marianne are arrested and accused of possessing cannabis.
3 EMI establish a progressive label called Harvest.
4 FBI arrest Jim Morrison for lewd behaviour.
5 The Shadows finish after ten years.
6 Someone called Elton John has a single *Lady Samantha*.
7 Deep Purple team up with the Royal Philharmonic.
8 US has massive Woodstock Festival.
9 The Royal Albert Hall is venue of Pom Proms.
10 Crane and Palmer quit from Arthur Brown; Julie Driscoll from Brian Auger; Redding from Jimi Hendrix Experience.
11 The Who stun with *Tommy*.
12 Wedding album from new couple John and Yoko.
13 *Je T'Aime* causes uproar, no ban from Beeb but it's not played. Disc gets dropped while at the top and Major Minor take over from Philips/Fontana.
14 Stones play massive free concert in London's Hyde Park. Jagger pays his tribute and reads from Shelley.

15 Isle Of Wight goes ahead even though protest groups try to prevent.
16 Brief but so splendid Blind Faith life.
17 Janis Joplin in Britain.
18 Jagger lands film *Ned Kelly* as the main character.
19 Jonathan King says he's too old at 25 for pop. It's retirement.
20 UNICEF concert at Lyceum brings together John, Yoko, Clapton and George Harrison.

Top Artists

This section looks at how British acts fared during the Sixties and concerns itself with artists who entered the Top 20 charts. It should be remembered that an artist who had more hits than someone else may not have sold more records; sales always have varied considerably according to season and indeed the sound itself.

Singles

1 Cliff Richard. Record company – *Columbia (EMI)*. Hits   43, including the *Expresso Bongo* EP.
2 The Shadows. Record company – *Columbia (EMI)*. Hits   25.
3 Billy Fury. Record company – *Decca*. Hits   24.
4 Adam Faith. Record company – *Parlophone (EMI)*: Beatles. Record company – *Parlophone (EMI)*. Hits   23
6 Hollies. Record company – *Parlophone (EMI)*. Hits   20.
7 Petula Clark. Record company – *Pye*. Hits   19, including 2 for *Polygon*, 1 for *Nixa (PYE)*, 3 for *Pye Nixa (Pye)*.
7 Dave Clark Five. Record company – *Columbia (EMI)*. Hits   19.
9 Cilla Black. Record company – *Parlophone (EMI)*. Hits   17.
9 Herman's Hermits. Record company – *Columbia (EMI)*. Hits   17.
9 Bachelors. Record company – *Decca*. Hits   17.
9 Sandie Shaw. Record company – *Pye*. Hits   17.
9 Manfred Mann. Record company – *HMV* (9 hits), *Fontana* (8 hits). Hits   17. *HMV (EMI) Fontana (Philips)*.
9 Tom Jones. Record company – *Decca*. Hits   17.

15 Shirley Bassey. Record company – *Columbia (EMI)*. Hits 16. 1 for *United Artists*.

15 Dusty Springfield. Record company – *Philips*. Hits 16.

17 Rolling Stones. Record company – *Decca*. Hits 15.

17 Frank Ifield. Record company – *Columbia (EMI)*. Hits 15.

17 Kinks. Record company – *Pye*. Hits 15.

20 Kenny Ball. Record company – *Pye*. Hits 14.

20 Ken Dodd. Record company – *Columbia (EMI)*. Hits 14.

20 The Who. Record company – *various*. Hits 14, 5 for *Brunswick*, 3 for *Reaction*, 6 for *Track*.

Cliff Richard was already well versed in chart success by the time the decade dawned. He had already gathered eight hits in the 1950s with the first coming in the Autumn of 1958 – his recording of the classic Ian Samwell composition *Move It*. His first 'proper' hit of the Sixties decade was *Expresso Bongo*, although a summer hit of 1959 entitled *Living Doll* was into its second re-entry for the first week only of 1960. His influence continued through the Sixties.

His longevity as a hit artist is, of course, common lore – but what is not so often expressed or realised is how well he survived so many powerful onslaughts during the Sixties, a decade which more than any other was to produce huge "supergroups' and famous names, and be tugged into teen-mania, R&B, blues, soul, psychedelic, folk-rock, endless varieties of electronic rock and heavy music. Yet he calmly chugged along with nothing overtly dramatic, nor political or social with only his Christian conversion to cause a real rumpus and partly lead to the Shads going their own way. He survived while virtually all his contemporaries fell by the wayside. But then, with a few stutters, it was to be the same career speech in the next decade and seemingly so in the Eighties as well.

Top of the Charts: *Please Don't Tease* (1960), *I Love You*

(1960), *The Young Ones* (1962), *The Next Time/ Bachelor Boy* (1963), *Summer Holiday* (1963), *The Minute You're Gone* (1965), *Congratulations* (1968).

The Shadows backed Cliff Richard, but from the beginning of this decade proved they could be hit-makers in their own right. And the eventual trio of Bruce Welch, Hank Marvin and Brian Bennett survives into the Eighties, albeit with times of non-activity, rumoured group wind-ups over and the years, and mixed fortunes in these latter days as far as the chart is concerned.

It would seem invidious, and ultimately pointless, to suggest that The Shadows as such changed the face of British music. They played throughout the Sixties friendly tuneful melodies in a deceptively casual manner. Their power to influence came more in persuading would-be guitarists to persevere. Marvin particularly attracted his devotees, and many famous guitarists have said that it was he who gave them first love for the sound of a guitar.

Top of the Charts: *Apache* (1960), *Kon-Tiki* (1961), *Dance On* (1962), *Wonderful Land* (1962), *Foot Tapper* (1963).

Billy Fury came into the Sixties with two minor hits to his name – *Maybe Tomorrow* (18) and *Margot* (28). Other records were to be in their teens and even further down, but there were eleven Top 10 hits in his tally of 23. Fury was from Liverpool, real name Ron Wycherley, a familiar face on TV pop shows like *Oh Boy*, *Wham* and *Boy Meets Girl*. He was screened from his waist up because he moved sensuously at a time when it was not regarded as seemly. As with many artists he had subtle changes along the way. For his classic *Halfway To Paradise* (3, 1961) he had an orchestra for the first time. He vied with Cliff Richard and Adam Faith for the hearts of the girls. Now sadly no longer with us.

Top of the Charts: *none.*

Adam Faith had proved himself a one-hit star late in 1959 as the catchy *What Do You Want*, sung in his inimitable way, reached number one. But would he last? The answer was clearly 'yes', as his next six records all made the Top 10. There were many hits to follow, though things were erratic at times; for instance, during the period between December 1962 and the Summer of 1963 *Baby Take A Bow* reached only 22, *What Now* fared badly (in his terms) in going no further than 31, and *Walkin' Tall* stopped at 23. Another bad period was between December and June 1963–64. But overall he accumulated hits and made himself one of the most popular figures around. Both his chart-toppers had originally been written for Johnny Kidd.

Top of the Charts: *What Do You Want* (first two weeks of 1960), *Poor Me* (1960).

The Beatles. No-one can dispute that the Sixties in terms of actual hit records means first and foremost Cliff Richard. But it must also be said that the Beatles were world stars, and they changed the face of popular music in the two great music countries of the world; Britain – and even more so, in terms of sales potential and financial reward – the United States. Outside of some very early times, the Beatles meant John Lennon, Paul McCartney, George Harrison and Ringo Starr. They came from Liverpool and they put Liverpool on the world map. Other big names were to came from the city once the fab four had bulldozed their way through a world music scene that had been traditionally dominated by the Americans, whatever the type of music. The Beatles sold EPs and albums in the same quantity as others sold singles. And in keeping with the times, they made films, became TV personalities and lent themselves to radio-land either on disc or in person. They had two records before gaining their first chart-topper (although one music trade paper did list *Please Please Me* as a number one) but then, outside of an oldie issued by Polydor, they had an eleven number-one hit run, and if *Penny Lane* coupled with *Strawberry Fields Forever* plus the double EP *Magical Mystery Tour* had not unaccountably stopped at two then it would have been 19 chart-toppers in a row. Quite remarkable.

Top of the Charts: *From Me To You* (1963), *She Loves You* (1963), *I Want To Hold Your Hand* (1963), *Can't Buy Me Love* (1964), *A Hard Day's Night* (1964), *I Feel Fine* (1964), *Ticket To Ride* (1965), *Help* (1965), *Day Tripper/We Can Work It Out* (1965), *Paperback Writer* (1966), *Yellow Submarine/Eleanor Rigby* (1966), *All You Need Is Love* (1967), *Hello Goodbye* (1967), *Lady Madonna* (1968), *Hey Jude* (1968), *Get Back* (1969), *Ballad Of John And Yoko* (1969).

Hollies. After an indifferent chart start with (*Ain't That*) *Just Like Me* reaching only 25 the Hollies were to find themselves with 19 consecutive Top 20 hits in this decade, and of these only the George Harrison composed *If I Needed Someone* (20), *King Midas In Reverse* (18) and *Listen To Me* (11) failed to make the upper rungs of the Top 10. The Hollies came from Manchester, very much in the vanguard of groups that began to come from provincial cities once Mersey-mania was underway, opening the doors to all sorts and kinds. Yet for all their chart consistency – and variety of music, while retaining an individualistic vocal style – the Hollies never grabbed the world's music markets in the same as, say, The Kinks, Stones or Who. They paid their first visit to the States in 1965. One curiosity lies in the group's seeming unwillingness to record their own songs other than as B-sides, although from 1966 there was a change. At times they casually embraced the prevailing pop image but overall the Hollies then – and in subsequent years – never veered far from a recognisable approach and sound, even if important members left and like Alan Clarke would return and go as the years progressed.

Top of the Charts: *I'm Alive* (1965).

Petula Clark. By the time the Sixties dawned Petula Clark – one-time child-star – had made her name in the pop world, but from April 1958 to January 1961 the charts saw an absence of her name. She returned to hit-parade favour in the best way possible, with a number one entitled *Sailor*. Her hits through the decade were a mixed bag with eight between 39 and 50 but among better moments came *Romeo* (3), *My Friend The Sea* (7), the atmospheric *Downtown* (2) which was a global smash, *My Love* (4), *I Couldn't Live Without Your Love* (6), and another chart-topper *This Is My song*.

The Epsom, Surrey, 1933-born artist was by now far, far from the child who sang the *Teddy Bears' Picnic* and *When Alice Goes To Buckingham Palace*. And by the early 1960s she was living in France and had married a Frenchman so it was not suprising to see her opening the Sixties with a French tune and English lyrics – *Sailor*.

Top of the Charts: *Sailor* (1961), *This Is My Song* (1967).

Dave Clark Five. In common with some of the other artists who accumulated quite a score of hits during the 1960s this group had a mixture of fairly highly placed records and others below the 20. The group's best moments came from the chart-topper, the stomping *Glad All Over*, the even more footbanging *Bits And Pieces* (2), *Everybody Knows* (2) and *Catch Us If You Can* (5). At the other extreme there was *Everybody Knows* (37), *Over And Over* (45), *Look Before You Leap* (50), *Live In The Sky* (39) and *Put A Little Love In Your Heart* (31). Originally the group was into skiffle but two years after their formation they veered into pop with several companies offering terms. Prior to their minor hit *Do You Love Me* (30) they had issued *Mulberry Bush* coupled with *Chaquita*. The group found considerable acclaim Stateside.

Top of the Charts: *Glad All Over* (1963).

Cilla Black, alias Priscilla White from Liverpool, arrived with Beatle commendation and indeed the

Lennon & McCartney team had penned her first hit, the rather brash *Love Of The Loved* which surprisingly went no further than 35. It was, though, a taster of success to come, and a very good cover of the US Dionne Warwick recorded *Anyone Who Had A Heart* was enough to see her career leap forward.

Along the way there were some lowish chart positions, especially with *I Only Live To Love You* (26) and *Where Is Tomorrow* (40) but of the very good there was another number one thanks to the poignant yet forceful *You're My World*, second position with another cover of a US hit *You've Lost That Lovin' Feelin'* and *Surround Yourself With Sorrow* (3). There were six other records that made the Top 10. She was much seen on television, toured often and always seemed to have the right kind of quip for the music writer and journalist. In early times she was a typist but spent much of her time at the famous Cavern, haunt of the Beatles. She sang without attracting too much attention but when the Fourmost found themselves booked on the TV pop show *Ready Steady Go* she supported the Beatles instead, at their Southport concert. It created interest and soon she was projecting herself on the highly successful TV show *Thank Your Lucky Stars* and a career blossomed.

Top of the Charts: *Anyone Who Had A Heart* (1964), *You're My World* (1964).

Herman's Hermits. People either loved or disliked this Manchester group which was led by buck-teethed Peter Noone who had been an actor in the television soap opera *Coronation Street*. He was 'little boy lost' and was prone to stick his fingers in his mouth but he had vim and fizz, a personality, and producer Mickie Most found for him and the group a series of uncomplicated bouncy pure-pop numbers. The group was more visual than musically proficient for only three singles *Mrs Brown*, *I'm Into Something Good* (a Goffin-King song, and a US hit for Earl Jean) and *Henry VIII* saw their playing imprimateur. Much of the guitar work was by Big Jim

Sullivan, Jimmy Page and John Paul Jones, the latter two eventually forming part of the legendary Led Zeppelin.

Their chart record was patchy, a seeming short run of two Top 10 singles, followed by a lowish positioning. But their pop-style lasted against the blasts from elsewhere and they were always popular on TV pop shows while Noone won himself a place of affection from many a girl.

Top of the Charts: *I'm Into Something Good* (1964).

Bachelors. It would be wrong to suggest that the Bachelors had no teenage support, but they were largely for older people with their always tuneful, tasteful songs and an overall image that was safe. They were a singing trio, born out of a harmonica threesome with the two brothers Clusky, Con and Declan, and Sean James Stokes. As the surname Clusky might suggest they were Irish, from Dublin; folkish with a modern pop air, good-looking and possessed of the knack of choosing commercial numbers. They were a reminder of past times, but, then not all former musical territory was wished lost. They found themselves popular in concert, never short of cabaret bookings and often adorning the guest spot in show-biz oriented TV shows. They commenced their chart career briskly with *Charmaine* (6) but might have wondered a little when their next *Faraway Places* spent three weeks only in the chart and never went above 36. But this was the only early blockage, for the next six records all made the Top 20. Once past 1965 things were not so easy, save for *Marie* (9, 1965) and their version of the classic Simon and Garfunkel hit *The Sound of Silence* (3, 1966). Five other records could not make the 20. Hits or no hits their future was assured, for the MOR market doesn't necessarily expect from its sons and daughters current chart placings.

Top of the Charts: *Diane* (1964).

Sandie Shaw was born in Dagenham, Essex. Alias Sandra Goodrich, she attracted record buyers generally. While her music was pop, the girl's demeanour received applause from many in the rock fraternity. Her first chart placing *(There's) Always Something There To Remind Me* was her second record and a number one. A catchy trombone start, choral backing and a vocal texture that wavered, ever so slightly uncertain (which added to the overall attractiveness) played their part in its success. It was the beginning of a fine run which saw none of her first five records lower than position six for *Message Understood*. There were some problems coming, with a number of records outside the 20 including a rather disastrous reception for *I Don't Need Anything* which had an insulting one-week ride at 50. But there was something major coming her way – Eurovision. Her contest entry song *Puppet On A String* gave her a third number one. Her last hit was at the decade's end as *Think It Over* charted to 42. A decade or so later she resurfaced in the company of modern pop practitioners.

Top of the Charts: *(There's) Always Something There To Remind Me* (1964), *Long Live Love* (1965), *Puppet On A String* (1967).

Manfred Mann. For good quality catchy pop material Manfred Mann must take group honours. Just two records *You Gave Me Somebody To Love* (36, 1966) and *Sweet Pea* (36, 1967) cause slight blemish, for no other record amongst the remaining 15 hits was lower than 11. The group gave two major record companies a stream of hits. On the HMV recordings Paul Jones provided the vocals, on Fontana it was Mike D'Abo. Both suited the group well. Manfred Mann is also a person, a South African, a jazz pianist who first ran the Mann-Hugg Blues Brothers, with an addition in 1963 of Tom McGuinness.

An instrumental *Why Should We Not* (HMV) was issued. Then they added Paul Jones on vocals and a greater response came to the next release *Cock A Hoop*. The breakthrough came with the catchy *5-4-3-2-1* and it was helped on its way by becoming the theme tune of the popular TV pop show *Ready Steady Go*. When Jones left Manfred Mann he tried a solo career but outside of two major hits and a couple of low charting records little came of it, though since then Jones has become known in film and theatre circles. When Manfred thought of a replacement all kinds of names were bandied about with Rod Stewart, Long John Baldry and Wayne Fontana tipped. In the event Mike D'Abo from the little known Band Of Angels received the summons and the group success continued. Among the hits were two Dylan compositions *Just Like A Woman* and *Mighty Quinn*. The Mann-Dylan association would continue in the next decade.

Top of the Charts: *Do Wah Diddy Diddy* (1964), *Pretty Flamingo* (1966), *Mighty Quinn* (1968).

Tom Jones came from Treforest, Glamorgan. Alias Thomas J Woodward, one-time Tom Scott for the bar-rooms of South Wales, he utilised the mid-1960s onwards to ensure his place in show-biz musical history. Jones, discovered by Gordon Mills, turned down by Joe Meek in 1963, hit the British music scene with a classic pop song *It's Not Unusual*. He was to chart four times in both 1965 and 1966 with mixed success save for his second number one with the emotive *Green Green Grass of Home*. This record began his career's purple patch – as far as chart hits and performances were concerned. Ten discs (including the latter) made the 20 consecutively and only *A Minute Of Your Time* (14, 1968) failed the Top 10. Three records *I'll Never Fall In Love Again*, *I'm Coming Home* and the raunchy cheeky *Delilah* settled for number two. Jones was booked for big things and eventually he was to charm the major cabaret spots of the US and be given major television specials. As time progressed, in the Seventies decade his visits to Britain became less and sales correspondingly decreased, though his fans remain.

Top of the Charts: *It's Not Unusual* (1965) *Green Green Grass Of Home* (1966).

Dusty Springfield was arguably the heroine of most pop music fans – the number one female singer of the decade. Formerly with The Springfields – they had five hits between 1961 and 1963, with Dusty on lead vocals – she was destined for big things from the moment she decided on a solo career. To many people it was a patently obvious move. For the most part her chart-hit record was comprised of Top 20 discs, 13 of the 16 did so. The poor showings came for *Am I The Same Girl* (43, 1969), *Give Me Time* (surprisingly low at 24, 1967) and again surprising, the relative failure of *Your Hurtin' Kind of Love* (37, 1965). But these pale against the success and charm of such gems as *I Just Don't What To Do With Myself* (3), *I Close My Eyes And Count To Ten* (4), her first hit *I Only Want To Be With You* (4), and the chart-topper *You Don't Have To Say You Love Me*, She also produced one real stunner of an album – *Dusty In Memphis*. But while the Sixties display a rampant and gorgeous Dusty, subsequent happenings outside of a few stage and record moments tell only a sad story of a great artist lost to music.

Top of the Charts: *You Don't Have To Say You Love Me* (1966).

Shirley Bassey entered the 1960s on the heels of a late 1950s chart-topper *As I Love You* which had on its first release a year earlier meant little. She had five hits in the previous decade and they were enough to establish her as an international star in the making. For her the new decade posed only the problem of finding the right songs to suit her fiery dramatic vocal style. Sometimes she was given major hit material, at other moments she had good songs, with these two elements well illustrated in the topsy-turvy fortunes of her records in the charts. There was only one brief purple patch when *As Long As He Needs Me* charted to second position, to be followed by the number six *You'll Never Know* and then a number one, thanks to the double-sided tour-de-force of *Climb Every Mountain* coupled with *Reach For The Stars*. The three hits covered the period from the second week of May 1961 until almost the end of November, the same year. Eight of her hits in the Sixties failed to make the Top 30. *I(Who Have Nothing)* (6, 1963) was one of the more successful. Several numbers *Goldfinger* (21, 1964) and *Big Spender* (21, 1967) never charted to the heights yet have become major songs associated with her. Of her 16 hits only two came after 1964.

Top of the Charts: *Climb Every Mountain/Reach For The Stars* (1961).

The Rolling Stones had big hits but numerically their quantity doesn't thrust them forward. Though, yes, they were a supergroup of the decade (and the two following), and international stars. And when they had records released their chart performance bettered most, if not all, save for the Beatles. In the early days *Come On* made only 21 and the Beatle composition *I Wanna Be Your Man* reached 12. No record, after the latter left the chart early in 1964, failed to make the Top 10. The Sixties saw The Stones achieve eight chart-toppers with only *We Love You* coupled with *Dandelion* not making the top five. It was a remarkable run. The first of the seven number one's came mid-summer of 1964 with the punchy *It's All Over Now*. It was a number written by Bobby Womack and a minor hit for the US group Valentinos. It co-incided with a monster Stones UK tour that was described as the most sensational ever put on the road. The Stones story is history and the actual happenings either get revised or else fresh revelation alters the state of play as a new Stones book hits the market. Some say the Mick Jagger authorised biography will tell all, others wait for the Bill Wyman detailed description, for it's Wyman who has faithfully kept the minute detail of the Stones history. But whatever the case nothing can detract from The Stones and their remarkable hit run of the Sixties, even if they never had enough records released to establish sufficient hits to ensure a higher place in this table of artists with the most chart successes.

Top of the Charts: *It's All Over Now* (1964), *Little Red Rooster* (1964), *The Last Time* (1965), *[I Can't Get No] Satisfaction* (1965), *Get Off Of My Cloud* (1965), *Paint It*

Black (1966), *Jumping Jack Flash* (1968), *Honky Tonk Women* (1969).

Frank Ifield was brought to England from Australia and managed by Peter Gormley, manager of Cliff Richard and at one time the man behind other hit-makers like The Shadows and Olivia Newton-John. Ifield's first foray was tentative. *Lucky Devil* charted to 22 in 1960. His second hit of the year *Gotta Get A Date* scraped a miserable 49 and spent not suprisingly a mere one week in the 50. But then things changed. 1961 was bereft of anything – the ensuing year was not. *I Remember You* began a hat-trick of chart-toppers with *Nobody's Darlin' But Mine* (4, 1963) coming in the way of another chart-topper. *I Remember You* had a staggering run of 28 weeks in the chart and this included a remarkable placing in the Top 20 from 14 July until 1 December. This kind of success did not continue, for once the Top 10 hit *Don't Blame Me* (8, 1964) left the charts in early April no other hit of his made the Top 20. It was a rather unexpected reversal of fortune. Ifield sang ballads and did so with a distinctive voice. He had good looks. He last charted with *Call Her Your Sweetheart* (24, 1966).

Top of the Charts: *I Remember You* (1962), *Lovesick Blues* (1962), *Wayward Wind* (1963), *Confessin'* (1963).

The Kinks. British pop music would not be the same without the long-lasting Kinks – a group formed around the two Davies brothers, Ray and Dave. For many people The Kinks chart successes in the Sixties fall into two categories.

The second phase is considered to have begun with the March 1966 hit *Dedicated Follower Of Fashion*. Proponents of this view say the Kinks song-writing qualities assumed a new depth from this point. They describe the ensuing hits as impregnated with satire and tragi-comic observations, 'sub-consciously tapping music hall traditions'. Prior to *Dedicated Follower Of*

Fashion (4, 1966) their hits had been good strong driven-pop material, often the beat was raw and tingling, sharp and incisive. Before arriving on the British pop scene with a chart-topper, The Kinks had made no impact with two singles, *Long Tall Sally* (a rather lack-lustre version of the oldie) and *You Do Something To Me*.

Top of the Charts: *You Really Got Me* (1, 1964), *Tired Of Waiting For You* (1965), *Sunny Afternoon* (1966).

Kenny Ball's hit career was effectively between February 1961 and July 1964. There was a three year break following *Hello Dolly* (30, 1964), before just one other hit in the decade *When I'm 64* (43, 1967) which was a lively toe-tapping version of the Beatle classic from *Sgt Pepper's Lonely Hearts Club Band*. Ball's purple patch came with three hits commencing the second week of November, 1961 – *Midnight In Moscow* (2), *March Of The Siamese Children* (4, 1962) and *The Green Leaves Of Summer* (7, 1962). Ball was a trad-jazz man who could dress a tune with that musical idiom and make it most acceptable to the general public.

Top of the Charts: *none*.

Ken Dodd was a comedian who utilised his popularity in that field to make hit records. But his was no voice that needed covering by back-up vocalists, choirs and instrumentation. The man could sing and in the MOR market of the 1960s he was immensely popular. Dodd and his 'Knotty Ash' characters made the nation laugh and the voice charmed. His peak was the record *Tears* (1965). It was a song from the late Twenties, then sung by Rudy Vallee. Dodd's re-recording shot to number one and stayed there the five chart weeks of October. All in all he had a 24 week run in the Top 50. His success was not universally popular, with *Tears* derided by many famous stars who kindly gave their acid comments an airing in the popular music press of the time. *Tears* was his eighth chart hit and before this only his chart debut *Love Is Like*

A Violin had made the Top 10. The success of *Tears* enabled him to have a number three follow-up *The River* and then in 1966 *More Than Love* reached number fourteen. One other record *Let Me Cry On Your Shoulder* (11, 1967) made the 20.

Top of the Charts: *Tears* (1965).

The Who with The Stones and Beatles became the major UK acts during the 1960s in the States and, of course, into the next decade. Although more of an album-oriented act The Who none-the-less produced a number of fine singles, which came with a rather cheeky air to the lyric, and a commercial catchiness in tune. Their third hit *My Generation* became an anthem for many young people in the mid-1960s. The Who's singles generally made the Top 30, most in the 20 but, surprising to many, there was a meagre position of 44 for the double-sided hit *The Last Time* coupled with *Under My Thumb*. The Who's predilection for songs revolving around sexual gender is illustrated in chart terms by such records as *Substitute*, *I'm A Boy* and *Happy Jack*. Others appear on various early Who albums. Their late 1960s hits like *I Can See For Miles*, *Magic Bus* and *Pinball Wizard* caught the flower-power feeling of the time. Although best heard live, The Who did capture much of their splendour on record with all their singles worth possessing.

Top of the Charts: *none*.

The Top 20 Hit Artist file (chart toppers)
1   Beatles 17
2   The Rolling Stones 8
3   Cliff Richard 7
4   The Shadows 5
5   Frank Ifield 4

Obviously tabulating on the basis of hits can hide a great deal of what actually happened in the British charts during any decade. At the same time, it does throw up names which consistently made the news and were featured on the chart radio and TV programmes of the time.

However, a mere tabling of the Top 20 and no more would hide the success rate of other artists with hits who made a profound impression on the decade's music scene: The Animals (9), Gerry and the Pacemakers (9), The Tremeloes (13), The Troggs (9), Dave Dee Group (13), Spencer Davis (10), Small Faces (12), the mighty Who (14); and even ignore some of the previous decade's stars who made some impression on the Sixties chart, as did Frankie Vaughan (13). Again the balladeers and instrumentalists would be overlooked, since most music writers (myself included) tend to overlook that aspect of the market simply because it never represented us as teenagers, and here names like Matt Monroe (12), Anthony Newley (9), Acker Bilk (10) and Val Doonican (12) must be mentioned. It would be a brave person who would argue they influenced the overall pop scene but, nonetheless, they represented, and in some cases still do, the preferences of millions who turn askance at the gyrations of the more popular, usually more noisy elements of popular music.

A full and detailed list of artists and their total number of hits, with highest and last charting records, can be found later in this volume.

ALBUMS

The British album charts of the 1960s reveal the following as the successful charting stars of the decade: in terms of individual album entries

1   Frank Sinatra 29
2   Elvis Presley 27
3   Cliff Richard 23
4   Jim Reeves 19
5   The Beach Boys 13
5   The Beatles 13

7	Boy Dylan 11
8	Andy Williams 10
8	Roy Orbison 10
8	The Rolling Stones 10
11	Otis Redding 9
11	John Mayall 9
11	Ray Conniff 9
11	Tom Jones 9
15	Bert Kaempfert 8
15	James Last 8
15	Gene Pitney 8
15	The Crickets with Buddy Holly 8
15	Shirley Bassey 8
20	Kinks 7
20	Mantovani 7
20	Bachelors 7

The album chart more than the 'singles' listing tells of overall age-buying and is not so confined to a younger set. Thus there is place for Sinatra, Williams, Conniff, Last, Reeves and Mantovani. But album chart entry is also dependent on releases and many famed artists and groups of the decade recorded no more than a handful of albums.

The Sinatras of the quality song market found ready audiences, as did many of the band leaders who developed their own individualistic style of musical presentation. They recorded existing classic material from past decades, show and film scores and unlike Beatles and Stones were not reliant upon 'in-house' material. Again there is a vast difference in recording time and costs between a quality singer and orchestra and a band with the later studio technicalities of say *Revolver*, *Sgt Pepper's Lonely Hearts Club Band* or the double record *White Album* set. The latter can and did take months.

But how otherwise did single and album compare? In price structure this way:

	7 inch singles	7 inch EP	12 inch pop LP
1960	6s. 3d (31p)	10s. 11d (54½p)	£1.14s. 3d (£1.71p)
1961	6s. 4d (31½p)	10s. 11d (54½p)	£1.14s. 3d (£1.71p)
1962	6s. 6d (33p)	11s. 3d (56p)	£1.14s. 6d (£1.72½p)
1963	6s. 8d (33½p)	11s. 6d (57½p)	£1.12s. 3d (£1.61p)
1964	6s. 8d (33½p)	11s. 6d (57½p)	£1.12s. 3d (£1.61p)
1965	6s. 8d (33½p)	11s. 6d (57½p)	£1.12s. 3d (£1.61p)
1966	7s. 2d (36p)	11s. 6d (57½p)	£1.12s. 3d (£1.61p)
1967	7s. 3d (36p)	11s. 6d (57½p)	£1.12s. 6d (£1.62½p)
1968	8s. 0d (40p)	12s. 11d (64½p)	£1.16s. 9d (£1.83½p)
1969	8s. 6d (42½p)	13s. 3d (66p)	£1.17s. 6d (£1.87½p)

In general production terms: all figures in thousands

	78s	7 inch singles	12 inch pop LP
1960	3.803	51.811	17.057
1961	2.181	54.757	19.388
1962	1.944	55.239	20.361
1963	1.846	61.342	22.267
1964	.587	72.841	27.829
1965	.475	61.809	31.462
1966	.400	51.196	33.275
1967	.308	51.576	37.275
1968	.206	49.161	49.184
1969	.173	46.618	59.565

From the vantage point of the 1980s it seems hard to
realise that just 20 years or so ago albums were regarded as
new and exciting. And indeed at the commencement of
the decade commentators could exclaim that there was
now a steady stream of long-playing records being issued.
It was remarked that we were following the lead of
America where the album had become more important
than the single. Indeed album production between 1955
and 1960 doubled, and doubled once more when figures
are compared between 1960 and 1965. This growth was
maintained until – by the mid-1970s, for instance – album
production was just over six times the level of 1960.

But in the earlyish days, stage, film and general music
albums sold most. In 1960 the number of stereophonic
(another new vogue which is now taken for granted)

albums sold, compared with monophonic, had increased by fifty percent. It was reported with a little excitement and incredulity that 15 percent of all albums sold were in stereo. The *NME* noted albums like *Flower Drum Song*, *Most Happy Fella*, *Oliver*, *Vagabond King*, *Fin's Ain't Wot They Used T'be*, *Can-Can*, *The Bells Are Ringing*, *Let's Make Love* and *G I Blues*. They picked out the selling rockers as Elvis, Cliff and Eddie Cochran, but their survey as for the next few years covered much ground and endless artists.

In 1964 it was 'Beatles Are Kings Of Albumland' with only Jim Reeves and The Stones causing the 'fab four' to relinquish their top album placing for either *With The Beatles* or *A Hard Day's Night*.

A more radical change in album perception was to come with the development of the 'concept' album where instead of a number of loosely slotted songs, a sustained theme was traced, track by track. In the case of the 1960s most celebrated album *Sgt Pepper's Lonely Hearts Club Band* it was an approach that extended into album sleeve design, printing of lyrics, appropriate meaningful inside group pictures and a record surface that for all intents and purposes (unless viewed at close range) lacked the normal bands. Tracks fell into each other. The same year as *Pepper*, 1967, saw The Who's *The Who Sell Out* where one side had tracks linked by pirate ship jingles and advertising spoofs. *I Can See For Miles* pre-dated much later British psychedelia. The Who also recorded an ambitious album project entitled *Tommy*, termed a rock opera and lasting 90 minutes. As the *NME Encyclopedia Of Rock* rightly points out The Pretty Things had already attempted something similiar with *S F Sorrow* but *Tommy* was one of the masterpieces of rock in the 1960s.

The growth of flower-power, of social and political awareness by groups, and the influence of acid-oriented music led to many exciting stereo records. For good or for bad it became a popular practice for pot to be smoked and acid taken, in dark rooms with the music left to waft its path through the air aiding and abetting a so-called 'drug-high'. Groups denied their music was either made under the influence of drugs or for the enhancing of the 'drug trip experience' but often their denials seemed designed more to offset criticism from powerful 'straight' sections of the community than as expressions of truth. Album tracks lengthened, records became longer overall and, in some instances, a complete side was given over to one song. One of the most famous was located on the first album of Iron Butterfly where the second side was occupied with *In-A-Gadda-Da-Vida*.

There grew an album culture,* much as singles gave verbal parlance to generally younger buyers.

People waited at the record store with as much excitement for the arrival of a new album from Dylan, Joan Baez, Beach Boys (especially their great album of the decade, *Pet Sounds*), Grateful Dead, Tim Buckley, Love, Jefferson Airplane and the Beatles, as others waited for singles by Monkees, Cliff Richard or Troggs in 1967.

These were exciting times.

* See end of this volume for my attempted listing of the decade's best albums.

Chart People

This section lists all the people who made the singles chart during the decade.

The year of the first hit is given before the name. Then comes the number of hits achieved.

This is followed by the title, chart position and year of the most successful record (A).

The final note gives the last chart record of the decade (B). Where this is the same as the previous entry then the word *ditto* is used.

1960 Cliff Adams (1). *A) Lonely Man Theme* (39), 1968. *B) ditto*

1965 Jewel Akens (1). *A) The Birds And The Bees* (29), 1965. *B) ditto*

1963 Herb Alpert (6). *A) Spanish Flea* (3), 1965; *This Guy's In Love With You* (3), 1968. *B) Without Her* (36), 1969

1960 Richard Allan (1). *A) As Time Goes By* (44), 1960. *B) ditto*

1961 Allisons (3). *A) Are You Sure* (2), 1961. *B) Lessons In Love* (30)

1967 Amen Corner (6). *A) (If Paradise Is) Half As Nice* (1), 1969. *B) Hello Suzie* (4), 1969

1968 American Breed (1). *A) Bend Me Shape Me* (24), 1968. *B) ditto*

1969 Moira Anderson (1). *A) Holy City* (43), 1969. *B) ditto*

1965 Chris Andrews (5). *A) Yesterday Man* (3), 1965. *B) Stop That Girl* (36)

1961 Bobby Angelo and the Tuxedos (1). *A) Baby Sittin'* (30), 1961. *B) ditto*

1963 Angels (1). *A) My Boyfriend's Back* (50), 1963. *B) ditto*

1964 Animals (9). *A) House Of The Rising Sun* (1),

1964. *B) Don't Bring Me Down* (6), 1966

1960   Paul Anka (5).   *A) Love Me Warm And Tender* (19), 1962.   *B) A Steel Guitar And A Glass Of Wine* (41), 1962

1963   Richard Anthony (2).   *A) Walking Alone* (37), 1963.   *B) If I Loved You* (re-entry, 18), 1964

1968   Aphrodite's Child (1).   *A) Rain and Tears* (30), 1968.   *B) ditto*

1964   Applejacks (3).   *A) Tell Me When* (7), 1964.   *B) Three Little Words* (23), 1964

1969   Archies (1).   *A) Sugar Sugar* (1), 1969.   *B) ditto*

1964   Louis Armstrong (3).   *A) What A Wonderful World/Cabaret* (1), 1968.   *B) Sunshine Of Love* (41), 1968

1966   Eddy Arnold (3).   *A) Make The World Go Away* (8), 1966.   *B) If You Were Mine Mary* (49), 1966

1967   P P Arnold (4).   *A) First Cut Is The Deepest* (18), 1967.   *B) Angel Of The Morning* (29), 1969

1968   Association (1).   *A) Time For Living* (23), 1968.   *B) ditto*

1960   Chet Atkins (1).   *A) Teensville* (46), 1960.   *B) ditto*

1960   Frankie Avalon (2).   *A) Why* (20), 1960.   *B) Don't Throw Away All Those Teardrops* (37), 1960

1960   Avons (3).   *A) Rubber Ball* (30), 1961.   *B) ditto*

1963   Alice Babs (1).   *A) After You've Gone* (43), 1963.   *B) ditto*

1965   Burt Bacharach (1).   *A) Trains And Boats And Planes* (4), 1965.   *B) ditto*

1963   Bachelors (17).   *A) Diane* (1), 1964.   *B) Marta* (20)

1965   Joan Baez (5).   *A) There But For Fortune* (8), 1965.   *B) Pack Up Your Sorrows* (50), 1966

1967   Long John Baldry (4).   *A) Let The Heartaches Begin* (1), 1967.   *B) It's Too Late Now* (21), 1969

1961   Kenny Ball and his Jazzmen (14).   *A) Midnight In Moscow* (2), 1961.   *B) When I'm 64* (43), 1967

1968   Band (1).   *A) The Weight* (21), 1968. *B) ditto*

1962   Chris Barber's Jazz Band (1).   *A) Revival* (43),

1962. *B) ditto*

1967 Bar-Kays (1). *A) Soul Finger* (33), 1967. *B) ditto*

1964 Barron Knights (6). *A) Call Up The Groups* (3), 1964. *B) An Olympic Record* (35), 1968

1961 Joe Barry (1). *A) I'm A Fool To Care* (49), 1961. *B) ditto*

1960 John Barry (10). *A) Hit And Miss* (10), 1960. *B) From Russia With Love* (39), 1963

1965 Len Barry (2). *A) 1–2–3* (3), 1965. *B) Like A Baby* (10), 1966

1965 Fontella Bass (2). *A) Rescue Me* (11), 1965. *B) Recovery* (32), 1966

1960 Shirley Bassey (16). *A) Reach For The Stars/Climb Every Mountain* (1), 1961. *B) Big Spender* (21), 1967

1963 Beach Boys (19). *A) Good Vibrations* (1), 1966: *Do It Again* (1), 1968. *B) Breakaway* (6), 1969

1962 Beatles (23). *A) From Me To You* (1), 1963; *She Loves You* (1), 1963; *I Want To Hold Your Hand* (1), 1963; *Can't Buy Me Love* (1), 1964; *A Hard Day's Night* (1), 1964; *I Feel Fine* (1), 1964; *Ticket To Ride* (1), 1965; *Help!* (1), 1965; *Day Tripper/We Can Work It Out* (1), 1965; *Paperback Writer* (1), 1966; *Yellow Submarine/ Eleanor Rigby* (1), 1966; *All You Need Is Love* (1), 1967; *Hello Goodbye* (1), 1967; *Lady Madonna* (1), 1968; *Hey Jude* (1), 1968; *Get Back* (1), 1969; *Ballad Of John And Yoko* (1), 1969. *B) Something/Come Together* (4), 1969

1967 Jeff Beck (3). *A) Hi-Ho Silver Lining* (14), 1967. *B) Love Is Blue* (23), 1968

1968 Bedrocks (1). *A) Ob-La-Di Ob-La-Da* (20), 1968. *B) ditto*

1967 Bee Gees (7). *A) Massachusetts* (1), 1967; *I've Gotta Get A Message To You* (1), 1968. *B) Don't Forget To Remember* (2), 1969

1961 Harry Belafonte and Odetta (1). *A) Hole In The Bucket* (32), 1961. *B) ditto*

1968 William Bell (1). *A) Tribute To A King* (31), 1968. *B) ditto*

1964   Cliff Bennett and the Rebel Rousers (3).   *A) Got To Get You Into My Life* (6), 1964.   *B) ditto*

1961   Tony Bennett (5).   *A) The Very Thought Of You* (21), 1965.   *B) ditto*

1960   Brook Benton (3).   *A) Kiddio* (42), 1960.   *B) Boll Weevil Song* (30), 1961

1963   Chuck Berry (7).   *A) No Particular Place To Go* (3), 1964.   *B) Promised Land* (26), 1965

1963   Dave Berry (8).   *A) The Crying Game* (5), 1964; Little Things* (5), 1965; *Mama* (5), 1965.   *B) Mama* (5)

1961   Mike Berry (3).   *A) Don't You Think It's Time* (6), 1963.   *B) My Little Baby* (34), 1963

1960   Beverley Sisters (1).   *A) Green Fields* (29), 1960.   *B) ditto*

1963   Big Three (2).   *A) By The Way* (22), 1963.   *B) ditto*

1960   Mr Acker Bilk (10).   *A) Stranger On The Shore* (2), 1960.   *B) A Taste Of Honey* (16), 1963

1960   Umberto Bindi (1).   *A) Il Nostro Concerto* (47), 1960.   *B) ditto*

1965   Birds (1).   *A) Leaving Here* (45), 1965.   *B) ditto*

1969   Jane Birkin and Serge Gainsbourg (1).   *A) Je T'aime.... Moi Non Plus* (1), 1969.   *B) ditto*

1963   Cilla Black (17).   *A) Anyone Who Had A Heart* (1), 1964; *You're My World* (1), 1961.   *B) If I Thought You'd Ever Change Your Mind* (20), 1969

1960   Jeanne Black (1).   *A) He'll Have To Stay* (41), 1960.   *B) ditto*

1968   Tony Blackburn (2).   *A) So Much Love* (31), 1968.   *B) It's Only Love* (42), 1969

1960   Bill Black's Combo (2).   *A) Don't Be Cruel* (32), 1960.   *B) ditto*

1961   Blackwells (1).   *A) Love Or Money* (46), 1961.   *B) ditto*

1960   Billy Bland (1).   *A) Let The Little Girl Dance* (15), 1960.   *B) ditto*

1969   Blood Sweat & Tears (1).   *A) You've Made Me So Very Happy* (35), 1969.   *B) ditto*

1965   Babbity Blue (1).   *A) Don't Make Me* (48), 1965.

B) ditto

1969 Blue Mink (1). *A) Melting Pot* (3), 1969. *B) ditto*

1969 Bob and Earl (1). *A) Harlem Shuffle* (7), 1969. *B) ditto*

1961 Gary 'US' Bonds (2). *A) Quarter To Three* (7), 1961. *B) ditto*

1966 Graham Bonney (1). *A) Supergirl* (19), 1966. *B) ditto*

1968 Bonzo Dog Doo-Dah Band (1). *A) I'm The Urban Spaceman* (5), 1968. *B) ditto*

1968 Booker T & the M Gs (3). *A) Time Is Tight* (4), 1969. *B) Soul Clap '69* (35), 1969

1960 Pat Boone (7). *A) Speedy Gonzales'* (2), 1962. *B) The Main Attraction* (12), 1962

1969 David Bowie (1). *A) Space Oddity* (5), 1969. *B) ditto*

1967 Box Tops (3). *A) The Letter* (5), 1967. *B) Soul Deep* (22), 1969

1960 Jacqueline Boyer (1). *A) Tom Pillibi* (33), 1960. *B) ditto*

1963 Wilfred Brambell and Harry H Corbett (1). *A) At The Palace* (25). *B) ditto*

1966 Los Bravos (2). *A) Black Is Black* (2). *B) I Don't Care* (16), 1966

1961 Rose Brennan (1). *A) Tall Dark Stranger* (31). *B) ditto*

1962 Walter Brennan (1). *A) Old Rivers* (38). *B) ditto*

1960 Teresa Brewer (1). *A) How Do You Know It's Love* (21). *B) ditto*

1961 Brook Brothers (5). *A) Warpaint* (5), 1961. *B) Trouble Is My Middle Name* (38), 1963

1960 Brothers Four (1). *A) Greenfields* (40). *B) ditto*

1968 Crazy World of Arthur Brown (1). *A) Fire* (1). *B) ditto*

1965 James Brown (3). *A) It's A Man's Man's Man's World* (13), 1966. *B) ditto*

1960 Joe Brown (10). *A) A Picture Of You* (2), 1962.

71

B) With A Little Help From My Friends (32), 1967

1961   Dave Brubeck Quartet (3). *A) Take Five* (6), 1961. *B) Unsquare Dance* (14), 1962

1960   Tommy Bruce (3). *A) Ain't Misbehavin'* (3), 1960. *B) Babette* (50), 1962

1963   Bruisers (1). *A) Blue Girl* (31). *B) ditto*

1963   Dora Bryan (1). *A) All I Want For Christmas Is A Beatle* (20), 1963. *B) ditto*

1962   B Bumble and the Stingers (1). *A) Nut Rocker* (1). *B) ditto*

1966   Eric Burdon (6). *A) San Franciscan Nights* (7), 1967. *B) Ring Of Fire* (35), 1969

1960   Johnny Burnette (6). *A) You're Sixteen* (3), 1961. *B) Clown Shoes* (35), 1962

1967   Prince Buster (1). *A) Al Capone* (18). *B) ditto*

1960   Max Bygraves (4). *A) You're My Everything* (34). *B) ditto*

1965 Byrds (5). *A) Mr Tambourine Man* (1), 1965. *B) You Ain't Goin' Nowhere* (45), 1968

1960   Edward Byrnes and Connie Stevens (1). *A) Kookie Kookie (Lend Me Your Comb)* (27). *B) ditto*

1967   Bystanders (1). *A) 98.6* (45). *B) ditto*

1966   Roy 'C' (1). *A) Shotgun Wedding* (6), 1966. *B) ditto*

1965   Cadets (1). *A) Jealous Heart* (42). *B) ditto*

1961   Al Caiola (1). *A) The Magnificent Seven* (34). *B) ditto*

1969   Glen Campbell (2). *A) Wichita Lineman* (7), 1969. *B) Galveston* (14), 1969

1961   Jo-Anne Campbell (1). *A) Motorcycle Michael* (41). *B) ditto*

1969   Pat Campbell (1). *A) The Deal* (31). *B) ditto*

1965   Ian Campbell Folk Group (1). *A) The Times They Are A-Changin'* (42). *B) ditto*

1968   Canned Heat (2). *A) On The Road Again* (8), 1968. *B) Going Up The Country* (19), 1969

1960   Freddy Cannon (6). *A) Way Down Yonder In New Orleans* (3), 1960. *B) Palisades Park* (20), 1962

1963   Caravelles (1). *A) You Don't Have To Be A*

Baby To Cry (6).   *B) ditto*

1961   Pearl Carr and Teddy Johnson (1).   *A) How Wonderful To Know* (23).   *B) ditto*

1967   Vikki Carr (3).   *A) It Must be Him (Suel Sur Son Etoile)* (2), 1967.   *B) With Pen in Hand* (40), 1969

1960   Ronnie Carroll (5).   *A) Roses Are Red* (3), 1962.   *B) Say Wonderful Things* (6), 1963

1965   Johnny Cash (2).   *A) A Boy Named Sue* (4), 1969.   *B) ditto*

1968   Mama Cass (2).   *A) It's Getting Better* (8), 1969.   *B) ditto*

1960   Roy Castle (1).   *A) Little White Berry* (40).   *B) ditto*

1968   Casuals (2).   *A) Jesamine* (2), 1968.   *B) Toy* (30), 1968

1969   Cats (1).   *A) Swan Lake* (48).   *B) ditto*

1962   Chakachas (1).   A) Twist Twist (48).   *B) ditto*

1960   George Chakiris (1).   *A) Heart Of A Teenage Girl* (49).   *B) ditto*

1962   Richard Chamberlain (4).   *A) Theme From Dr Kildare (Three Stars Will Shine Tongiht)* (12), 1962.   *B) True Love* (30), 1963

1960   Champs (1).   *A) Too Much Tequila* (49).   *B) ditto*

1968   Gene Chandler (1).   *A) Nothing Can Stop Me* (41).   *B) ditto*

1962   Bruce Channel (2).   *A) Hey! Baby* (2), 1962.   *B) Keep On* (12), 1968

1963   Chantays (1).   *A) Pipeline* (16).   *B) ditto*

1960   Chaquito (1).   *A) Never On Sunday* (50).   *B) ditto*

1962   Don Charles (1).   *A) Walk With Me My Angel* (39).   *B) ditto*

1960   Ray Charles (16).   *A) I Can't Stop Loving You* (1), 1962.   *B) Eleanor Rigby* (36), 1968

1961   Dick Charlesworth and his City Gents (1).   *A) Billy Boy* (43).   *B) ditto*

1960   Chubby Checker (7).   *A) Let's Twist Again* (2), 1961.   *B) What Do Ya Say* (37), 1963

1962 Chubby Checker and Bobby Rydell (2). *A) Jingle Bell Rock* (40), 1962. *B) ditto*

1969 Checkmates Ltd (1). *A) Proud Mary* (30). *B) ditto*

1964 Cheetahs (2). *A) Mecca* (36), 1964. *B) Soldier Boy* (39), 1965

1965 Cher (4). *A) Bang Bang (My Baby Shot Me Down)* (3), 1966. *B) Sunny* (32), 1966

1964 Cherokees (1). *A) Seven Daffodils* (33). *B) ditto*

1969 Chicken Shack (2). *A) I'd Rather Go Blind* (14), 1969. *B) Tears In The Wind* (29), 1969

1963 Chiffons (3). *A) He's So Fine* (16), 1963. *B) Sweet Talkin' Guy* (31), 1966

1964 Gigliola Cinquetti (1). *A) Non Ho L'Eta Per Amarti* (17). *B) ditto*

1960 Jimmy Clanton (1). *A) Another Sleepless Night* (50). *B) ditto*

1961 Petula Clark (19). *A) Sailor* (1), 1961; This Is My Song* (1), 1967. *B) Kiss Me Goodbye* (50), 1968

1963 Dave Clark Five (19). *A) Glad All Over* (1), 1963. *B) Good Old Rock'n Roll* (7), 1969

1968 Classics IV (1). *A) Spooky* (46). *B) ditto*

1968 Judy Clay and William Bell (1). *A) Private Number* (8). *B) ditto*

1969 Jimmy Cliff (1). *A) Wonderful World Beautiful People* (6). *B) ditto*

1961 Buzz Clifford (1). *A) Baby Sittin' Boogie* (17). *B) ditto*

1962 Patsy Cline (2). *A) Heartaches* (31), 1962. *B) ditto*

1962 Clyde Valley Stompers (1). *A) Peter And The Wolf* (25). *B) ditto*

1960 Eddie Cochran (7). *A) Three Steps To Heaven* (1), 1960. *B) My Way* (23), 1963

1968 Joe Cocker (3). *A) With A Little Help From My Friends* (1), 1968. *B) Delta Lady* (10), 1969

1960 Alma Cogan (2). *A) Train Of Love* (27), 1960. *B) Cowboy Jimmy Joe* (37), 1961

1960   Shaye Cogan (1).   *A) Mean To Me* (43).   *B)*
ditto

1960   Nat 'King' Cole (10).   *A) Ramblin' Rose* (5),
1962.   *B) Dear Lonely Hearts* (37), 1962

1960   Perry Como (2).   *A) Delaware* (3), 1960.   *B)*
Caterina (37), 1962

1967   Arthur Conley (2).   *A) Sweet Soul Music* (7),
1967.   *B) Funky Street* (46), 1968

1960   Jess Conrad (3).   *A) Mystery Girl* (18), 1961.
B) Pretty Jenny (50), 1962

1969   Consortium (1). *A) All The Love In The World*
(22), 1969.   *B) ditto*

1960   Russ Conway (10).   *A) Toy Balloons* (7), 1961.
B) Always You and Me (33), 1962

1965   Peter Cook (1).   *A) The Ballad of Spotty*
Muldoon (34).   *B) ditto*

1965   Peter Cook and Dudley Moore (1).   *A) Goodbye-*
ee (18).   *B) ditto*

1960   Sam Cooke (6).   *A) Twistin' The Night Away* (6),
1962.   *B) Frankie and Johnny* (30), 1963

1963   Cookies (1).   *A) Chains* (50).   *B) ditto*

1961   Tommy Cooper (1).   *A) Don't Jump Off The*
Roof Dad (40), 1961.   *B) ditto*

1961   Frank Cordell (1).   *A) Black Bear* (44).   *B) ditto*

1962   Louise Cordet (1).   *A) I'm Just A Baby* (13).
B) ditto

1960   Lynn Cornell (1).   *A) Never On Sunday* (30).
B) ditto

1960   Don Costa (1).   *A) Never On Sunday* (27).   *B)*
ditto

1963   Mike Cotton's Jazzmen (1).   *A) Swing That*
Hammer (36).   *B) ditto*

1963   Cougars (1).   *A) Saturday Nite At The Duck*
Pond (33).   *B) ditto*

1962   Countrymen (1).   *A) I Know Where I'm Going*
(45).   *B) ditto*

1960   Michael Cox (2).   *A) Angela Jones* (7), 1960.
B) Along Came Caroline (41), 1960

1961   Floyd Cramer (3).   *A) On The Rebound* (1),

1961.   *B) Hot Pepper* (46) 1962

1961   Jimmy Crawford (2).   *A) I Love How You Love Me* (18), 1961.   *B) ditto*

1969   Crazy Elephant (1).   *A) Gimme Gimme Good Lovin'* (12).   *B) ditto*

1966   Cream (7).   *A) I Feel Free* (11), 1966.   *B) Badge* (18), 1969

1966   Creation (2).   *A) Painter Man* (36), 1966.   *B) ditto*

1969   Creedence Clearwater Revival (3).   *A) Bad Moon Rising* (1), 1969.   *B) Green River* (19), 1969

1962   Bernard Cribbins (3).   *A) Hole In the Ground* (9), 1962.   *B) Gossip Calypso* (25), 1962

1960   Crickets (6).   *A) Don't Ever Change* (5), 1962.   *B) (They Call Her) La Bamba* (21), 1964

1969   Crosby, Stills and Nash (1).   *A) Marrakesh Express* (17).   *B) ditto*

1966   Cryin' Shames (1).   *A) Please Stay* (26).   *B) ditto*

1962   Crystals (4).   *A) Then he Kissed Me* (2), 1963.   *B) I Wonder* (36), 1964

1969   Cuff-Links (1).   *A) Tracy* (4).   *B) ditto*

1964   Larry Cunningham and the Mighty Avons (1).   *A) Tribute To Jim Reeves* (40).   *B) ditto*

1968   Cupid's Inspiration (2).   *A) Yesterday Has Gone* (4), 1968.   *B) My World* (33), 1968

1967   Adge Cutler and the Wurzels (1).   *A) Drink Up Thy Zider* (45).   *B) ditto*

1963   Johnny Cymbal (1).   *A) Mr Bass Man* (24).   *B) ditto*

1963   Dakotas (1).   *A) The Cruel Sea* (18).   *B) ditto*

1964   Dale and Grace (1).   *A) I'm Leaving It Up To You* (42).   *B) ditto*

1961   Dale Sisters (1).   *A) My Sunday Baby* (36).   *B) ditto*

1966   Kenny Damon (1).   *A) While I Live* (48).   *B) ditto*

1961   Johnny Dankworth (1).   *A) African Waltz* (9).   *B) ditto*

1960 Bobby Darin (14). *A) Lazy River* (2), 1961;
Things (2), 1962. *B) If I Were A Carpenter* (9), 1966
1960 James Darren (4). *A) Goodbye Cruel World* (28),
1961. *B) Conscience* (30), 1962
1966 David and Jonathan (2). *A) Lovers Of The
World Unite* (7), 1966. *B) ditto*
1967 Dave Davies (2). *A) Death Of A Clown* (3),
1967. *B) Susannah's Still Alive* (20), 1967
1963 Billie Davis (3). *A) Tell Him* (10), 1963. *B) I
Want You To Be My Baby* (33), 1968
1962 Sammy Davis Jr (1). *A) What Kind Of Fool Am
I?/Gonna Build A Mountain* (26), 1962. *B) ditto*
1960 Sammy Davis Jr and Carmen McRae (1). *A)
Happy To Make Your Acquaintance* (46), 1960. *B) ditto*
1963 Skeeter Davis (1). *A) End Of The World* (18).
B) ditto
1964 Spencer Davis Group (10). *A) Keep On
Running* (1), 1965; *Somebody Help Me* (1), 1966. *B) Mr
Second Class* (35), 1968
1964 Doris Day (1). *A) Move Over Darling* (8). *B)
ditto*
1961 Jimmy Dean (2). *A) Big Bad John* (2), 1961.
B) Little Black Book (33), 1962
1965 Dave Dee, Dozy, Beaky, Mick and Tich (13). *A)
Legend Of Xanadu* (1), 1968. *B) Snake In The Grass*
(23), 1969
1962 Joey Dee and the Starliters (1). *A) Peppermint
Twist* (33). *B) ditto*
1961 Carol Deene (4). *A) Norman* (24), 1962. *B)
Some People* (25), 1962
1967 Desmond Dekker and the Aces (3). *A) Israelites*
(1), 1969. *B) It Miek* (7), 1969
1969 Delaney and Bonnie and Friends, featuring Eric
Clapton (1). *A) Comin' Home* (16). *B) ditto*
1969 Dells (1). *A) I Can Sing A Rainbow-Love Is
Blue* (15). *B) ditto*
1963 Dennisons (2). *A) Walkin' The Dog* (36), 1964.
B) ditto
1961 Karl Denver (11). *A) Wimoweh* (4), 1962. *B)*

Love Me With All Your Heart (37), 1964

1961   Dick and Deedee (1).   *A) The Mountain's High* (37). *B) ditto*

1965   Charles Dickens (1).   *A) That's The Way Love Goes* (37). *B) ditto*

1969   Neville Dickie (1).   *A) Robin's Return* (33). *B) ditto*

1963   Bo Diddley (2).   *A) Pretty Thing* (34), 1963. *B) Hey Good Lookin'* (39), 1965

1960   Mark Dinning (1).   *A) Teen Angel* (37). *B) ditto*

1961   Dion (3).   *A) The Wanderer* (10), 1962. *B) ditto*

1964   Dixie Cups (2).   *A) Chapel Of Love* (22), 1964. *B) Iko Iko* (23), 1965

1960   Ken Dodd (14).   *A) Tears* (1), 1965. *B) Tears Won't Wash Away My Heartache* (22), 1969

1969   Joe Dolan (2).   *A) Make Me An Island* (3), 1969. *B) Teresa* (20), 1969

1960   Fats Domino (8).   *A) Be My Guest* (19), 1960, Country Boy* (19), 1960. *B) Red Sails In The Sunset* (34), 1963

1960   Lonnie Donegan (10).   *A) My Old Man's A Dustman* (1), 1960. *B) Pick A Bale Of Cotton* (11), 1962

1961   Ral Donner (1).   *A) You Don't Know What You've Got* (25). *B) ditto*

1965   Donovan (9).   *A) Sunshine Superman* (3), 1966. *B) Atlantis* (23), 1968

1969   Donovan, with the Jeff Beck Group (1).   *A) Goo Goo Barabajagal (Love Is Hot)* (12). *B) ditto*

1964   Val Doonican (12).   *A) What Would I Be* (2), 1966. *B) Ring Of Bright Water* (48), 1969

1967   Doors (2).   *A) Hello I Love You* (15), 1968. *B) ditto*

1966   Lee Dorsey (4).   *A) Holy Cow* (6), 1966. *B) ditto*

1960   Craig Douglas (9).   *A) Pretty Blue Eyes* (4), 1960. *B) Town Crier* (36), 1963

1964   Dowlands (1).   *A) All My Loving* (33). *B) ditto*

1960   Charlie Drake (2).   *A) Mr Custer* (12), 1960.

B) My Boomerang Won't Come Back (14), 1961

1960   Rusty Draper (1).   *A) Mule Skinner Blues* (39).
B) ditto

1963   Alan Drew (1).   *A) Always The Lonely One* (48).
B) ditto

1960   Drifters (9).   *A) Save The Last Dance For Me* (2),
1960.   *B) Baby What I Mean* (49), 1967

1968   Julie Driscoll, Brian Auger and the Trinity
(1).   *A) This Wheel's On Fire* (5).   *B) ditto*

1960   Frank D'Rone (1).   *A) Strawberry Blonde* (24).
B) ditto

1967   Dubliners (3).   *A) Seven Drunken Nights* (7),
1967.   *B) Never Wed An Old Man* (43), 1967

1967   Simon Dupree and the Big Sound (2).   *A) Kites*
(9), 1967.   *B) For Whom The Bell Tolls* (43), 1968

1967   Judith Durham (1).   *A) Olive Tree* (33).   *B)
ditto*

1965   Bob Dylan (11).   *A) Like A Rolling Stone* (4),
1965.   *B) Lay Lady Lay* (5), 1969

1966   Easybeats (2).   *A) Friday On My Mind* (6), 1966.
B) Hello How Are You (20), 1968

1969   Billy Eckstine and Sarah Vaughan (1).   *A)
Passing Strangers* (20).   *B) ditto*

1960   Duane Eddy (15).   *A) Because They're Young*
(2), 1960; *Pepe* (2), 1961.   *B) Your Baby's Gone Surfin'*
(49), 1963

1967   Electric Prunes (2).   *A) Get Me To The World
On Time* (42), 1967.   *B) ditto*

1962   Ray Ellington (1).   *A) The Madison* (36).   *B)
ditto*

1963   Bern Elliott and the Fenmen (2).   *A) Money* (4),
1963.   *B) New Orleans* (24), 1964

1965   Shirley Ellis (1).   *A) The Clapping Song* (6).
B) ditto

1969   Dick Emery (1).   *A) If You Love Her* (32).   *B)
ditto*

1960   England Sisters (1).   *A) Heartbeat* (33).   *B)
ditto*

1968   Equals (7).   *A) Baby Come Back* (1), 1968.   *B)*

Rub A Dub Dub (34), 1969

1964   Escorts (1).   *A) The One To Cry* (49).   *B) ditto*

1963   Essex (1).   *A) Easier Said Than Done* (41).   *B) ditto*

1967   Ethiopians (1).   *A) Train To Skaville* (40).   *B) ditto*

1960   Maureen Evans (5).   *A) Like I Do* (3), 1962.   *B) I Love How You Love Me* (50), 1964

1965   Betty Everett (2).   *A) Getting Might Crowded* (29), 1965.   *B) It's In His Kiss* (34), 1968

1960   Everly Brothers (21).   *A) Cathy's Clown* (1), 1960; Walk Right Back* (1), 1961; *Temptation* (1), 1961. *B) It's My Time* (39), 1968

1963   Exciters (1).   *A) Tell Him* (46).   *B) ditto*

1962   Shelley Fabares (1).   *A) Johnny Angel* (41).   *B) ditto*

1960   Fabian (1).   *A) Hound Dog Man* (46).   *B) ditto*

1969   Fairport Convention (1).   *A) Si Tu Dois Partir* (21).   *B) ditto*

1960   Adam Faith (23).   *A) Poor Me* (1), 1960.   *B) Cheryl's Goin' Home* (46), 1966

1960   Percy Faith (1).   *A) Theme From A Summer Place* (2).   *B) ditto*

1964   Marianne Faithfull (6).   *A) Come And Stay With Me* (4), 1965.   *B) Is This What I Get For Loving You* (43), 1967

1964   Georgie Fame (12).   *A) Yeh Yeh* (1), 1964; *Get Away* (1), 1966; *Ballad Of Bonnie And Clyde* (1), 1967. *B) Seventh Son* (25), 1969

1969   Family (1).   *A) No Mule's Fool* (29).   *B) ditto*

1969   Family Dogg (1).   *A) Way Of Life* (6).   *B) ditto*

1966   Chris Farlowe (6).   *A) Out Of Time* (1), 1966. *B) Handbags And Gladrags* (33), 1967

1968   José Feliciano (2).   *A) Light My Fire* (6), 1968. *B) And The Sun Will Shine* (25), 1969

1960   Fender men (1).   *A) Mule Skinner Blues* (32). *B) ditto*

1966   Peter Fenton (1).   *A) Marble Breaks Iron Bends* (46).   *B) ditto*

1961   Shane Fenton and the Fentones (4).   *A) Cindy's Birthday* (19), 1962.   *B) ditto*

1962   Fentones (2).   *A) The Mexican* (41), 1962.   *B) The Breeze & L* (48), 1962

1960   Ferrante and Teicher (2),   *A) Theme From Exodus* (6), 1961.   *B) ditto*

1969   Fifth Dimension (1).   *A) Aquarius/Let The Sunshine In* (11).   *B) ditto*

1961   Fireballs (1).   *A) Quite A Party* (29).   *B) ditto*

1960   Ella Fitzgerald (5).   *A) Mack The Knife* (19), 1960.   *B) Can't Buy Me Love* (34), 1964

1969   Flamingos (1).   *A) Boogaloo Party* (26).   *B) ditto*

1967   Lester Flatt and Earl Scruggs (1).   *A) Foggy Mountain Breakdown* (39).   *B) ditto*

1968   Fleetwood Mac (5).   *A) Albatross* (1), 1968.   *B) Oh Well* (2), 1969

1967   Flowerpot Men (1).   *A) Let's Go To San Francisco* (4).   *B) ditto*

1967   Eddie Floyd (3).   *A) Knock On Wood* (19), 1967.   *B) Things Get Better* (31), 1967

1965   Wayne Fontana (4).   *A) Game Of Love* (2), 1965.   *B) She Needs Love* (32), 1965

1960   Bill Forbes (1).   *A) Too Young* (29).   *B) ditto*

1961   Clinton Ford (3).   *A) Fanlight Fanny* (22), 1962.   *B) Run To The Door* (25), 1967

1960   Emile Ford and the Checkmates (7).   *A) On A Slow Boat To China* (3), 1960.   *B) I Wonder Who's Kissing Her Now* (43), 1962

1960 George Formby (1).   *A) Happy Go Lucky/Banjo Boy* (40).   *B) ditto*

1960   Lance Fortune (2).   *A) Be Mine* (4), 1960.   *B) This Love I Have For You* (26), 1960

1965   Fortunes (3).   *A) You've Got Your Troubles* (2), 1965.   *B) ditto*

1967   Foundations (6).   *A) Baby Now That I've Found You* (1), 1967.   *B) Born To Live And Born To Die* (46), 1969

1960   Four Lads (1).   *A) Standing On The Corner* (34),

1960. *B) ditto*

1964 Four Pennies (6). *A) Juliet* (1), 1964. *B) Trouble Is My Middle Name* (32), 1966

1960 Four Preps (2). *A) Got A Girl* (2), 1960. *B) More Money For You And Me* (39), 1961

1962 Four Seasons (10). *A) Rag Doll* (2), 1964. *B) Tell It To The Rain* (37), 1967

1965 Four Tops (14). *A) Reach Out I'll Be There* (1), 1966. *B) Do What You Gotta Do* (11), 1969

1963 Fourmost (6). *A) A Little Loving* (6), 1964. *B) Girls Girls Girls* (33), 1965

1964 Inez Foxx (1). *A) Hurt By Love* (40). *B) ditto*

1969 Inez and Charlie Foxx (1). *A) Mockingbird* (36). *B) ditto*

1960 Connie Francis (14). *A) Mama/Robot Man* (2), 1960. *B) Jealous Heart* (44), 1966

1967 Aretha Franklin (6). *A) I Say A Little Prayer* (4), 1968. *B) ditto*

1968 John Fred and the Playboy Band (1). *A) Judy In Disguise (With Glasses)* (3). *B) ditto*

1963 Freddie and the Dreamers (9). *A) I'm Telling You Now* (2), 1963. *B) Thou Shalt Not Steal* (44), 1965

1966 Bobby Fuller Four (1). *A) I Fought The Law* (33). *B) ditto*

1960 Billy Fury (24). *A) Jealousy* (2), 1961. *B) Give Me Your Word* (27), 1966

1966 David Garrick (2). *A) Dear Mrs Applebee* (22), 1966. *B) ditto*

1964 Marvin Gaye (4). *A) I Heard It Through The Grapevine* (1), 1969. *B) Too Busy Thinking About My Baby* (5), 1969

1968 Marvin Gaye and Tammi Terrell (6). *A) Onion Song* (9), 1969. *B) ditto*

1964 Marvin Gaye and Mary Wells (1). *A) Once Upon A Time* (50). *B) ditto*

1967 Marvin Gaye and Kim Weston (1). *A) It Takes Two* (16). *B) ditto*

1961 G-Clefs (1). *A) I Understand* (17). *B) ditto*

1966 Genevieve (1). *A) Once* (43). *B) ditto*

1967   Bobbie Gentry (2).   *A) I'll Never Fall In Love Again* (1), 1969.   *B) Raindrops Keep Fallin' On My Head* (40), 1970

1969   Bobbie Gentry and Glen Campbell (1).   *A) All I Have To Do Is Dream* (3).   *B) ditto*

1963   Gerry and the Pacemakers (9).   *A) How Do You Do It* (1); *I Like It* (1); *You'll Never Walk Alone* (1), all 1963.   *B) Walk Hand In Hand* (29), 1965

1962   Stan Getz and Charlie Byrd (1).   *A) Desafinado* (11).   *B) ditto*

1964   Stan Getz and Joao Gilberto (1).   *A) The Girl From Ipanema* (29).   *B) ditto*

1969   Robin Gibb (1).   *A) Saved By The Bell* (2).   *B) ditto*

1961   Don Gibson (2).   *A) Sea Of Heartbreak* (14), 1961.   *B) Lonesome Number One* (47)

1964   Don Gibson (1).   *A) Kelly* (48).   *B) ditto*

1963   Jimmy Gilmer and the Fireballs (1).   *A) Sugar Shack* (45).   *B) ditto*

1963   James Gilreath (1).   *A) Little Band of Gold* (29).   *B) ditto*

1965   Goldie and the Gingerbreads (1).   *A) Can't You Hear My Heart Beat?* (25).   *B) ditto*

1968   Bobby Goldsboro (1).   *A) Honey* (2).   *B) ditto*

1963   Lesley Gore (2).   *A) It's My Party* (9), 1963.   *B) Maybe I Know* (20), 1964

1963   Julie Grant (3).   *A) Count On Me* (24), 1963.   *B) Come To Me* (31), 1964

1968   Grapefruit (2).   *A) Dear Delilah* (21), 1968.   *B) C'Mon Marianne* (31), 1968

1965   Dobie Gray (1).   *A) The In Crowd* (25).   *B) ditto*

1968   Dorian Gray (1).   *A) I've Got You On My Mind* (36), 1968.   *B) ditto*

1960   Buddy Greco (1).   *A) Lady Is A Tramp* (26).   *B) ditto*

1964   Lorne Green (1).   *A) Ringo* (22).   *B) ditto*

1962   Ian Gregory (1).   *A) Can't You Hear The Beat Of A Broken Heart* (39), 1962.   *B) ditto*

1967   Guess Who (1).   *A) His Girl* (45).   *B) ditto*

1968   Gun (1).   *A) Rave With The Devil* (8), 1968.   *B)*
ditto

1967   Happenings (2).   *A) I Got Rhythm* (28), 1967.
B) My Mammy (34), 1967

1967   Tim Hardin (1).   *A) Hang On To A Dream* (50).
B) ditto

1964   Françoise Hardy (3).   *A) It's All Over The World*
(16), 1965.   *B) ditto*

1967   Harpers Bizarre (2).   *A) Anything Goes* (33),
1967.   *B) ditto*

1967   Anita Harris (4).   *A) Just Loving You* (6), 1967.
B) Dream A Little Dream Of Me (33), 1968

1962   Jet Harris (2).   *A) Main Title Theme From The*
Man With The Golden Arm (12), 1962.   *B) ditto*

1963   Jet Harris and Tony Meehan (3).   *A) Diamonds*
(1), 1963.   *B) Applejack* (4), 1963

1960   Max Harris (1).   *A) Gurney Slade* (11), 1960.
B) ditto

1968   Richard Harris (1).   *A) Macarthur Park* (4),
1968.   *B) ditto*

1960   Rolf Harris (5).   *A) Two Little Boys* (1),
1969.   *B) ditto*

1969   Noel Harrison (1).   *A) Windmills Of your Mind*
(8), 1969.   *B) ditto*

1969   Harry J All Stars (1).   *A) Liquidator* (1).   *B)*
ditto

1962   Tony Hatch (1).   *A) Out Of This World* (50).
B) ditto

1969   Edwin Hawkins Singers (1).   *A) Oh Happy Day*
(2).   *B) ditto*

1965   Roy Head (1).   *A) Treat Her Right* (30).   *B)*
ditto

1961   Ted Heath (1).   *A) Sucu Sucu* (36).   *B) ditto*

1966   Bobby Hebb (1).   *A) Sunny* (12).   *B) ditto*

1965   Hedgehoppers Anonymous (1).   *A) It's Good*
News Week (5).   *B) ditto*

1963   Heinz (5).   *A) Just Like Eddie* (5), 1963.   *B)*
Diggin' My Potatoes (49), 1965

1960   Joe 'Mr Piano' Henderson (1).   *A) Ooh La La* (46).   *B) ditto*

1967   Jimi Hendrix Experience (6).   *A) Purple Haze* (3), 1967.   *B) Crosstown Traffic* (37), 1969

1961   Clarence 'Frogman' Henry (3).   *A) But I Do* (3), 1961.   *B) Lonely Street/Why Can't You* (42), 1961

1967   Herd (3).   *A) I Don't Want Our Lovin' To Die* (5), 1968.   *B) ditto*

1964   Herman's Hermits (17).   *A) I'm Into Something Good* (1), 1964.   *B) Here Comes The Star* (33), 1969

1961   Highwaymen (2).   *A) Michael* (1), 1961.   *B) Gypsy Rover* (41), 1961

1961   Benny Hill (3).   *A) Gather In The Mushrooms* (12), 1961.   *B) Harvest Of Love* (20), 1963

1962   Vince Hill (10).   *A) Edelweiss* (2), 1967.   *B) Little Blue Bird* (42), 1969

1964   Ronnie Hilton (2).   *A) Don't Let The Rain Come Down* (21), 1964.   *B) A Windmill In Old Amsterdam* (23), 1965

1961   Eddie Hodges (2).   *A) I'm Gonna Knock On Your Door* (37), 1961; *Made To Love (Girls Girls Girls)* (37), 1962.   *B) as latter*

1960   Michael Holliday (3).   *A) Starry Eyed* (1), 1960.   *B) Little Boy Lost* (50), 1960

1963   Hollies (20).   *A) I'm Alive* (1), 1965.   *B) He Ain't Heavy, He's My Brother* (3), 1969

1960   Buddy Holly (10, plus 4 re-issues).   *A) Brown-Eyed Handsome Man* (3), 1963.   *B) Love's Made A Fool Of You* (39), 1964. *Peggy Sue* charted as a re-issue (32), 1968

1960   Hollywood Argyles (1).   *A) Alley Oop* (24).   *B) ditto*

1968   Honeybus (1).   *A) I Can't Let Maggie Go* (8).   *B) ditto*

1964   Honeycombs (4).   *A) Have I The Right* (1).   *B) That's The Way* (4), 1965

1964   John Lee Hooker (1).   *A) Dimples* (23).   *B) ditto*

1968   Mary Hopkin (2).   *A) Those Were The Days* (1), 1968.   *B) Goodbye* (2), 1969

85

1961   Johnny Horton (1).   *A) North To Alaska* (23).
B) ditto
1964   Howlin' Wolf (1).   *A) Smokestack Lightin'* (42).
B) ditto
1969   Humble Pie (1).   *A) Natural Born Boogie* (4).
B) ditto
1967   Engelbert Humperdinck (9).   *A) Release Me* (1);
The Last Waltz (1); both 1967. *B) Winter World Of
Love* (7), 1969
1969   Marsha Hunt (1).   *A) Walk On Gilded Splinters*
(46). *B) ditto*
1960   Brian Hyland (5).   *A) Sealed With Kiss* (3), 1962.
B) Warmed Over Kisses (28), 1962
1960   Frank Ifield (15).   *A) I Remember You* (1);
Lovesick Blues (1); both 1962; *Wayward Wind* (1), 1963;
same year for *Confessin'* (1). *B) Call Her Your
Sweetheart* (24), 1966
1965   In Crowd (1).   *A) That's How Strong My Love Is*
(48), 1965. *B) ditto*
1963   Indios Tabajaras (1).   *A) Maria Elena* (5), 1963.
B) ditto
1963   Isley Brothers (6).   *A) This Old Heart of Mine*
(3), 1968. *B) Put Yourself In My Place* (13), 1969
1962   Burl Ives (2).   *A) A Little Bitty Tear* (9), 1962.
B) Funny Way Of Laughin' (29), 1962
1965   Ivy League (4).   *A) Tossing And Turning* (3),
1965. *B) Willow Tree* (50), 1966
1964   Tony Jackson and the Vibrations (1).   *A) Bye
Bye Baby* (38), 1964. *B) ditto*
1960   Wanda Jackson (3).   *A) Let's Have A Party* (32),
1960. *B) Mean Mean Mean* (40), 1961
1968   Jacky (1).   *A) White Horses* (10), 1968. *B) ditto*
1968   Jimmy James and the Vagabonds (1).   *A) Red
Red Wine* (36), 1968. *B) ditto*
1966   Tommy James and the Shondells (2).   *A) Mony
Mony* (1), 1968. *B) ditto*
1961   Jan and Dean (2).   *A) Heart And Soul* (24), 1961.
B) Surf City (26), 1963
1960   Jan and Kjeld (1).   *A) Banjo Boy* (36), 1960.

B) ditto

1965 Horst Jankowski (1). *A) A Walk In The Black Forest* (3), 1965. *B) ditto*

1962 Peter Jay and the Jaywalkers (1). *A) Can Can 62* (31), 1962. *B) ditto*

1969 Jefferson (1). *A) Colour Of My Love* (22), 1969. *B) ditto*

1969 Jethro Tull (3). *A) Living In The Past* (3), 1969. *B) Sweet Dream* (7), 1969

1960 Johnny and the Hurricanes (4). *A) Rocking Goose* (3), 1960. *B) Old Smokey/High Voltage* (24), 1961

1960 Bryan Johnson (1). *A) Looking High High High* (20), 1960. *B) ditto*

1968 Johnny Johnson and the Bandwagon (3). *A) Breakin' Down The Walls Of Heartache* (4), 1968. *B) Let's Hang On* (36), 1969

1961 Laurie Johnson (1). *A) Sucu Sucu* (9), 1961. *B) ditto*

1960 Marv Johnson (5). *A) You Got What It Takes* (5), 1960. *B) I Miss You Baby* (25), 1969

1966 Janie Jones (1). *A) Witches Brew* (46), 1966. *B) ditto*

1960 Jimmy Jones (5). *A) Good Timin'* (1), 1960. *B) I Told You So* (33), 1961

1966 Paul Jones (4). *A) High Time* (4), 1966. *B) Aquarius* (45), 1969

1965 Tom Jones (17). *A) It's Not Unusual* (1), 1965; *Green Green Grass Of Home* (1), 1966. *B) Without Love* (10), 1969

1960 Dick Jordan (2). *A) Little Christine* (39), 1960. *B) ditto*

1964 Joy Strings (2). *A) It's An Open Secret* (32), 1964. *B) A Starry Night* (35), 1964

1962 Jimmy Justice (3). *A) Ain't That Funny* (8), 1962. *B) Spanish Harlem* (20), 1962

1965 Bert Kaempfert (1). *A) Bye Bye Blues* (24), 1965. *B) ditto*

1964 Gunther Kallman Choir (1). *A) Elisabethan Serenade* (45), 1964. *B) ditto*

1961   Eden Kane (5).   *A) Well I Ask You* (1), 1961.
B) Boys Cry (8), 1964

1968   Kasenetz Katz Singing Orchestral Circus (1).
A) Quick Joey Small (Run Joey Run) (19), 1968. *B) ditto*

1960   Kaye Sisters (1).   *A) Paper Roses* (7), 1960.   *B)
ditto*

1961   Ernie K Doe (1).   *A) Mother-In-Law* (29), 1961.
B) ditto

1962   Johnny Keating (1).   *A) Theme From Z Cars* (8),
1962.   *B) ditto*

1960   Nelson Keene (1).   *A) Image Of A Girl* (37),
1960.   *B) ditto*

1960   Keith Kelly (2).   *A) Tease Me* (27), 1960.   *B)
Listen Little Girl* (47), 1960

1960   Johnny Kidd and the Pirates (8).   *A) Shakin' All
Over* (1), 1960.   *B) Always and Ever* (46), 1964

1961   Ben E King (3).   *A) First Taste Of Love* (27),
1961; *Stand By Me* (27), 1961.   *B) Amor Amore* (38),
1961

1962   Carole King (1).   *A) It Might As Well Rain Until
September* (3), 1962.   *B) ditto*

1965   Jonathan King (1).   *A) Everyone's Gone To The
Moon* (4), 1965.   *B) ditto*

1968   Solomon King (2).   *A) She Wears My Ring* (3),
1968.   *B) When We Were Young* (21), 1968

1960   King Brothers (4).   *A) Standing On The Corner*
(4), 1960.   *B) 76 Trombones* (19), 1961

1964   Kingsmen (1).   *A) Louie Louie* (26), 1964.   *B)
ditto*

1964   Kinks (15).   *A) You Really Got Me* (1), 1964;
Tired Of Waiting For You (1), 1965; *Sunny Afternoon* (1),
1966.   *B) Plastic Man* (31), 1969

1963   Kathy Kirby (5).   *A) Secret Love* (4), 1963.   *B)
I Belong* (36), 1965

1967   Gladys Knight and the Pips (2).   *A) Take Me In
Your Arms and Love Me* (13), 1967.   *B) I Heard It
Through The Grapevine* (47), 1967

1962   Buddy Knox (1).   *A) She's Gone* (45), 1962.   *B)
ditto*

1961   Kokomo (1).   *A) Asia Minor* (35), 1961.   *B)*
ditto

1963   Billy J Kramer and the Dakotas (6).   *A) Bad To*
Me (1), 1963; *Little Children* (1), 1964.   *B) Trains And*
Boats And Planes (12), 1965

1961   Krew-Kats (1).   *A) Trambone* (33), 1961.   *B)*
ditto

1968   Danny La Rue (1).   *A) On Mother Kelly's*
Doorstep (33), 1968.   *B) ditto*

1960   Cleo Laine (2).   *A) You'll Answer To Me* (5),
1961.   *B) ditto*

1961   Frankie Laine (1).   *A) Gunslinger* (50), 1961.
B) ditto

1964   Lancastrians (1).   *A) We'll Sing In The Sunshine*
(47), 1964.   *B) ditto*

1964   Major Lance (1).   *A) Um Um Um Um Um Um*
(40), 1964.   *B) ditto*

1969   Don Lang (1).   *A) Sink The Bismarck* (43), 1960.
B) ditto

1960   Steve Lawrence (2).   *A) Footsteps* (4), 1960.   *B)*
Girls Girls Girls (49), 1960

1960   Brenda Lee (22).   *A) Speak To Me Pretty* (3),
1962.   *B) Too Many Rivers* (22), 1965

1961   Curtis Lee (1).   *A) Pretty Little Angel Eyes* (42),
1961.   *B) ditto*

1968   Leapy Lee (2).   *A) Little Arrows* (2), 1968.   *B)*
Good Morning (47), 1969

1961   Peggy Lee (1).   *A) Till There Was You* (30),
1961.   *B) ditto*

1968   Raymond Lefevre (1).   *A) Soul Coaxing* (46),
1968.   *B) ditto*

1968   Lemon Pipers (2).   *A) Green Tambourine* (7),
1968.   *B) Rice Is Nice* (41), 1968

1969   John Lennon (2).   *A) Give Peace A Chance* (2),
1969.   *B) Cold Turkey* (14), 1969

1962   Ketty Lester (2).   *A) Love Letters* (4), 1962.   *B)*
But Not For Me (45), 1962

1961   Lettermen (1).   *A) The Way You Look Tonight*
(36), 1961.   *B) ditto*

1961   Hank Levine (1).   *A) Image* (45), 1961.   *B) ditto*
1960   Jerry Lee Lewis (3).   *A) What'd I Say* (10), 1961.
B) Good Golly Miss Molly (31), 1963
1961   John Leyton (9).   *A) Johnny Remember Me* (1),
1961.   *B) Make Love to Me* (49), 1964
1961   Terry Lightfoot and his New Orleans Jazzmen
(2).   *A) King Kong* (29), 1961.   *B) Tavern In The
Town* (49), 1962
1966   Bob Lind (2).   *A) Elusive Butterfly* (5), 1966.
B) Remember The Rain (46), 1966
1962   Little Eva (3).   *A) The Loco-Motion* (2), 1962.
B) Let's Turkey Trot (13), 1963
1962   Little Richard (2).   *A) Bama Lama Bama Loo*
(20), 1964.   *B) ditto*
1960   Little Tony (1).   *A) Too Good* (19), 1960.   *B)
ditto*
1960   Hank Locklin (4).   *A) Please Help Me I'm
Falling* (9), 1960.   *B) I Feel A Cry Coming On* (28), 1966
1968   Locomotive (1).   *A) Rudi's In Love* (25), 1968.
B) ditto
1968   Shorty Long (1).   *A) Here Comes The Judge* (30),
1968.   *B) ditto*
1964   Long and the Short (2).   *A) The Letter* (30),
1964.   *B) Choc Ice* (49), 1964
1963   Trini Lopez (4).   *A) If I Had A Hammer* (4),
1963.   *B) Gonna Get Along Without Ya Now* (41), 1967
1960   Jerry Lordan (3).   *A) Who Could Be Bluer* (17),
1960.   *B) Sing Like An Angel* (36), 1960
1961   Joe Loss (5).   *A) The Maigret Theme* (20), 1962;
Must Be The Madison (20), 1962.   *B) March Of The
Mods* (31), 1964
1962   John D Loudermilk (1).   *A) The Language Of
Love* (13), 1962.   *B) ditto*
1968   Love Affair (5).   *A) Everlasting Love* (1), 1968.
B) Bringing On Back The Good Times (9), 1969
1968   Love Sculpture (1).   *A) Sabre Dance* (5), 1968.
B) ditto
1966   Lovin' Spoonful (4).   *A) Daydream* (2), 1966.
B) Darling Be Home Soon (44), 1967

1964 Lulu (12). *A)* *Boom Bang-a-Bang* (2), 1969. *B) Oh Me Oh My (I'm A Fool For You Baby)* (47), 1969

1960 Bob Luman (3). *A) Let's Think About Living* (6), 1960. *B) The Great Snowman* (49), 1961

1960 Kenny Lynch (7). *A) Up On The Roof* (10), 1962; *You Can Never Stop Me Loving You* (10), 1963. *B) I'll Stay By You* (29), 1965

1962 Patti Lynn (1). *Johnny Angel* (37), 1962. *B) ditto*

1969 Neil MacArthur (1). *A) She's Not There* (34), 1969. *B) ditto*

1967 Frankie McBride (1). *A) Five Little Fingers* (19), 1967. *B) ditto*

1966 David McCallum (1). *A) Communication* (32), 1966. *B) ditto*

1965 McCoys (2). *A) Hang On Sloopy* (5), 1965. *B) Fever* (44), 1965

1961 Gene McDaniels (1). *A) Tower Of Strength* (49), 1961. *B) ditto*

1965 Barry McGuire (1). *A) Eve Of Destruction* (3), 1965. *B) ditto*

1966 Kenneth McKellar (1). *A) A Man Without Love* (30), 1966. *B) ditto*

1967 Scott McKenzie (2). *A) San Francisco (Be Sure To Wear Flowers In Your Hair)* (1). 1967. *B) Like An Old Time Movie* (50), 1967

1960 Ken Mackintosh (1). *A) No Hiding Place* (45), 1960. *B) ditto*

1966 Tommy McLain (1). *A) Sweet Dreams* (49), 1966. *B) ditto*

1962 Phil McLean (1). *A) Small Sad Sam* (34), 1962. *B) ditto*

1966 Magic Lanterns (1). *A) Excuse Me Baby* (44), 1966. *B) ditto*

1960 Makadopulos and his Greek Serenaders (1). *A) Never On Sunday* (36), 1960. *B) ditto*

1966 Mamas and the Papas (6). *A) Dedicated To The One I Love* (2), 1967. *B) Creeque Alley* (9), 1967

1961   Henry Mancini (2).   *A) How Soon* (10), 1964.
B) ditto
1964   Manfred Mann (17).   *A) Do Wah Diddy Diddy*
(1), 1964; *Pretty Flamingo* (1), 1966; *Mighty Quinn* (1),
1968.   *B) Ragamuffin Man* (8), 1969
1967   Johnny Mann Singers (1).   *A) Up, Up And
Away* (6), 1967.   *B) ditto*
1960   Manuel and his Music of the Mountains (2).   *A)
Never On Sunday* (29), 1960.   *B) Somewhere My Love*
(42), 1966
1963   Marauders (1).   *A) That's What I Want* (43),
1963.   *B) ditto*
1968   Marbles (2).   *A) Only One Woman* (5), 1968.
B) The Walls Fell Down (28), 1969
1961   Marcels (2).   *A) Blue Moon* (1), 1961.   *B)
Summertime* (46), 1961
1963   Little Peggy March (1).   *A) Hello Heartache
Goodbye Love* (29), 1963.   *B) ditto*
1968   Marmalade (5).   *A) Ob-La-Di Ob-La-Da* (1),
1968.   *B) Reflections Of My Life* (3), 1969
1966   Joy Marshall (1).   *A) The More I See You* (34),
1966.   *B) ditto*
1964   Dean Martin (3).   *A) Gentle On My Mind* (2),
1969.   *B) ditto*
1960   Wink Martindale (1).   *A) Deck Of Cards* (5),
1963.   *B) ditto*
1960   Al Martino (2).   *A) I Love You Because* (48),
1963.   *B) ditto*
1967   Marvelettes (1).   *A) When You're Young And In
Love* (13), 1967.   *B) ditto*
1968   Massiel (1).   *A) La La La* (35), 1968.   *B) ditto*
1966   Master Singers (2).   *A) Highway Code* (25),
1966.   *B) Weather Forecast* (50), 1966
1960   Sammy Masters (1).   *A) Rockin' Red Wing* (36),
1960.   *B) ditto*
1967   Mireille Mathieu (1).   *A) La Derniere Valse* (26),
1967.   *B) ditto*
1960   Johnny Mathis (5).   *A) My Love For You* (9),
1960.   *B) What Will My Mary Say* (49), 1963

1962   Susan Maughan (3).   *A) Bobby's Girl* (3), 1962.
B) She's New To You (45), 1963

1968   Paul Mauriat (1).   *A) Love Is Blue (L'Amour Est
Bleu)* (12), 1968.   *B) ditto*

1964   Mary May (1).   *A) Anyone Who Had A Heart*
(49), 1964.   *B) ditto*

1964   Tony Meehan Combo (1).   *A) Song Of Mexico*
(39), 1964.   *B) ditto*

1966   Tony Merrick (1).   *A) Lady Jane* (49), 1966.
B) ditto

1963   Merseybeats (7).   *A) I Think Of You* (5), 1964.
B) I Stand Accused (38), 1966

1966   Merseys (1).   *A) Sorrow* (4), 1966.   *B) ditto*

1969   Microbe (1).   *A) Groovy Baby* (29), 1969.   *B)
ditto*

1964   Mighty Avengers (1).   *A) So Much In Love* (46),
1964.   *B) ditto*

1964   Migil Five (2).   *A) Mockingbird Hill* (10), 1964.
B) Near You (31), 1964

1960   Miki and Griff (3).   *A) Little Bitty Tear* (16),
1962.   *B) I Wanna Stay Here* (23), 1963

1961   Gary Miller (1).   *A) There Goes That Song
Again/The Night Is Young* (29), 1961.   *B) ditto*

1965   Jody Miller (1).   *A) Home Of The Brave* (49),
1965.   *B) ditto*

1963   Ned Miller (2).   *A) From A Jack To A King* (2),
1963.   *B) Do What You Do Do Well* (48), 1965

1965.   Roger Miller (5).   *A) King Of The Road (1)*,
1965.   *B) Little Green Apples* (19), 1968

1964   Millie (3).   *A) My Boy Lollipop* (2), 1964.   *B)
Bloodshot Eyes* (48), 1965

1960   Garry Mills (3).   *A) Look For A Star* (7), 1960.
B) I'll Step Down (39), 1961

1961   Hayley Mills (1).   *A) Let's Get Together* (17),
1961.   *B) ditto*

1961   Mrs Mills (1).   *A) Mrs Mills' Medley* (18), 1961.
B) ditto

1966   Mindbenders (4).   *A) A Groovy Kind Of Love*
(2), 1966.   *B) The Letter* (42), 1967

1965   Marcello Minerbi (1).   *A) Zorba's Dance* (6),
1965.   *B) ditto*
1968   Willie Mitchell (1).   *A) Soul Serenade* (43),
1968.   *B) ditto*
1964   The Mojos (3).   *A) Everything's Alright* (9),
1964.   *B) Seven Daffodils* (30), 1964
1966   Zoot Money and the Big Roll Band (1).   *A) Big
Time Operator* (25), 1966.   *B) ditto*
1967   Monkees (10).   *A) I'm A Believer* (1), 1967.   *B)
Someday Man* (47), 1969
1960   Matt Monro (12).   *A) Portrait Of My Love* (3),
1960.   *B) Yesterday* (8), 1965
1968   Hugo Montenegro (3).   *A) The Good The Bad &
The Ugly* (1), 1968.   *B) Hang 'Em High* (50), 1969
1962   Chris Montez (4).   *A) Let's Dance* (2), 1962.   *B)
There Will Never Be Another You* (37), 1966
1964   Moody Blues (7).   *A) Go Now* (1), 1964.   *B)
Ride My See-Saw* (42), 1968
1960   Jane Morgan (1).   *A) Romantica* (39), 1960.   *B)
ditto*
1963   Mickie Most (1).   *A) Mister Porter* (45), 1963.
B) ditto
1967   Move (6).   *A) Blackberry Way* (1), 1968.   *B)
Curly* (12), 1969
1964   Nashville Teens (5).   *A) Tobacco Road* (6), 1964.
B) The Hard Way (45), 1966
1964   Naturals (1).   *A) I Should Have Known Better*
(24), 1964.   *B) ditto*
1969   Rick Nelson (9).   *A) Hello Mary Lou/Travellin'
Man* (2), 1961.   *B) For You* (14), 1964
1961   Nero and the Gladiators (2).   *A) Entry Of The
Gladiators* (37), 1961.   *B) In The Hall Of The Mountain
King* (48), 1961
1966   New Vaudeville Band (4).   *A) Winchester
Cathedral* (4), 1966.   *B) Green Street Green* (37), 1967
1960   Anthony Newley (9).   *A) Why* (1), 1960; *Do You
Mind* (1), 1960.   *B) That Noise* (34), 1962
1962   Brad Newman (1).   *A) Somebody To Love* (47),
1962.   *B) ditto*

1968   Sue Nichols (1).   *A) Where Will You Be* (17),
1968.   *B) ditto*
1969   Nilsson (1).   *A) Everybody's Talkin'* (23), 1969.
B) ditto
1960   Nina and Frederick (4).   *A) Little Donkey* (3),
1960.   *B) Sucu Sucu* (23), 1961
1968   1910 Fruitgum Co. (1).   *A) Simon Says* (2),
1968.   *B) ditto*
1968   Nirvana (1).   *A) Rainbow Chaser* (34), 1968.
B) ditto
1966   Dermot O'Brien (1).   *A) The Merry Ploughboy*
(46), 1966.   *B) ditto*
1967   Des O'Connor (7).   *A) I Pretend* (1), 1968.   *B)*
Loneliness (18), 1969
1968   Esther and Abi Ofarim (2).   *A) Cinderella*
Rockefella (1), 1968.   *B) One More Dance* (13), 1968
1968   Ohio Express (1).   *A) Yummy Yummy Yummy*
(5), 1968.   *B) ditto*
1969   Oliver (1).   *A) Good Morning Starshine* (6),
1969.   *B) ditto*
1961   Olympics (1).   *A) I Wish I Could Shimmy Like*
My Sister Kate (45), 1961.   *B) ditto*
1960   Roy Orbison (28).   *A) Only The Lonely* (1),
1960; *It's Over* (1), 1964; *Oh Pretty Woman* (1), 1964.
B) Penny Arcade (27), 1969
1961   Tony Orlando (1).   *A) Bless You* (5), 1961.   *B)*
ditto
1962   Orlons (1).   *A) Don't Hang Up* (39), 1963 (re-
entry).   *B) ditto*
1961   Tony Osborne Sound (1).   *A) Man From*
Madrid (50), 1961.   *B) ditto*
1961   Outlaws (2).   *A) Ambush* (43), 1961.   *B) ditto*
1966   Overlanders (1).   *A) Michelle* (1), 1966.   *B)*
ditto
1960   Reg Owen (1).   *A) Obsession* (43), 1960.   *B)*
ditto
1961   Packabeats (1).   *A) Gypsy Beat* (49), 1961.   *B)*
ditto
1960   Hal Page and the Whalers (1).   *A) Going Back To*

My Home Town (50), 1960.   *B) ditto*

1968   Paper Dolls (1).   *A) Something Here In My Heart (Keeps A-Tellin' Me No)* (11), 1968.   *B) ditto*

1960   Norrie Paramor (2).   *A) Theme From Z Cars* (33), 1962.   *B) ditto*

1964   Paramounts (1).   *A) Poison Ivy* (35), 1964.   *B) ditto*

1966   Robert Parker (1).   *A) Barefootin'* (24), 1966.   *B) ditto*

1963   Paul and Paula (2).   *A) Hey Paula* (8), 1963.   *B) Young Lovers* (9), 1963

1966   Rita Pavone (2).   *A) You Only You* (21), 1967.   *B) ditto*

1965   Peddlers (2).   *A) Birth* (17), 1969.   *B) ditto*

1968   Donald Peers (1).   *A) Please Don't Go* (3), 1968.   *B) ditto*

1969   Pentangle (1).   *A) Once I Had A Sweetheart* (46), 1969.   *B) ditto*

1962   Danny Peppermint and the Jumping Jacks (1).   *A) Peppermint Twist* (26), 1962.   *B) ditto*

1965   Lance Percival (1).   *A) Shame And Scandal In The Family* (37), 1965.   *B) ditto*

1962   Emilio Pericoli (1).   *A) Al Di La* (30), 1962.   *B) ditto*

1960   Steve Perry (1).   *A) Step By Step* (41), 1960.   *B) ditto*

1964   Peter and Gordon (7).   *A) A World Without Love* (1), 1964.   *B) Lady Godiva* (16), 1966

1963   Peter, Paul and Mary (3).   *A) Blowing In The Wind* (13), 1963.   *B) The Times They Are A-Changin'* (44), 1964

1960   Ray Peterson (1).   *A) Corrine, Corrina* (41), 1961.   *B) ditto*

1969   Philharmonia Orchestra, conductor Lorin Maazel (1).   *A) Thus Spake Zarathustra* (33), 1969.   *B) ditto*

1960   Edith Piaf (1).   *A) Milord* (24), 1960.   *B) ditto*

1965   Wilson Pickett (7).   *A) In The Midnight Hour* (12), 1965.   *B) Hey Jude* (16)

1961   Piltdown Men (2).   *A) MacDonald's Cave* (14),

1960; *Piltdown Rides Again* (14), 1961. *B) Goodnight Mrs Flintstone* (18), 1961

1961   Ping Ping and Al Verlaine (1). *A) Sucu Sucu* (41), 1961. *B) ditto*

1967   Pink Floyd (2). *A) See Emily Play* (6), 1967. *B) ditto*

1966   Pinkerton's Assorted Colours (2). *A) Mirror Mirror* (9), 1966. *B) Don't Stop Lovin' Me Baby* (50), 1966

1969   Pioneers (1). *A) Long Shot Kick De Bucket* (21), 1969. *B) ditto*

1961   Gene Pitney (17). *A) I'm Gonna Be Strong* (2), 1964; *Nobody Needs Your Love* (2), 1966. *B) Maria Elena* (25), 1969

1968   Plastic Penny (1). *A) Everything I Am* (6), 1968. *B) ditto*

1960   Platters (1). *A) Harbour Lights* (11), 1960. *B) ditto*

1964   Poets (1). *A) Now We're Thru* (31), 1964. *B) ditto*

1963   Brian Poole and the Tremeloes (8). *A) Do You Love Me* (1), 1963. *B) I Want Candy* (25), 1965

1966   Sandy Posey (3). *A) Single Girl* (15), 1967. *B) What A Woman In Love Won't Do* (48), 1967

1960   Elvis Presley (42). *A) It's Now Or Never* (1), 1960; *Are You Lonesome Tonight/Wooden Heart/Surrender/His Latest Flame* (1), 1961; *Rock A Hula Baby/Good Luck Charm/She's Not You/Return To Sender* (1), 1962; *Devil In Disguise* (1), 1963; *Crying In The Chapel* (1), 1965. *B) Suspicious Minds* (2), 1969

1960   Johnny Preston (5). *A) Running Bear* (1), 1960. *B) Charming Billy* (34), 1960

1960   Mike Preston (4). *A) Marry Me* (14), 1961. *B) ditto*

1964   Pretty Things (7). *A) Don't Bring Me Down* (10), 1964. *B) A House In The Country* (50), 1966

1966   Alan Price (8). *A) Simon Smith And His Amazing Dancing Bear* (4), 1967; *The House That Jack Built* (4), 1967. *B) Don't Stop The Carnival* (13), 1968

1960   Lloyd Price (1).   *A) Lady Luck* (45), 1960.   *B) ditto*

1964   P J Proby (11).   *A) Hold Me* (3), 1964.   *B) It's Your Day Today* (32), 1968

1967   Procol Harum (7).   *A) A Whiter Shade Of Pale* (1), 1967.   *B) Salty Dog* (44), 1969

1961   Dorothy Provine (2).   *A) Don't Bring Lulu* (17), 1961.   *B) Crazy Words Crazy Tune* (45), 1962

1967   Pyramids (1).   *A) Train Tour To Rainbow City* (35), 1967.   *B) ditto*

1966   ? (Question Mark) and the Mysterians (1).   *A) 96 Tears* (37), 1966.   *B) ditto*

1964   Tommy Quickly (1).   *A) Wild Side Of Life* (33), 1964.   *B) ditto*

1965   Quiet Five (2).   *A) Homeward Bound* (44), 1966.   *B) ditto*

1963   Steve Race (1).   *A) Pied Piper (The Beeje)* (29), 1963.   *B) ditto*

1961   Ramrods (1).   *A) Riders In The Sky* (8), 1961.   *B) ditto*

1960   Johnny Ray (1).   *A) I'll Never Fall In Love Again* (26), 1960.   *B) ditto*

1964   Ezz Reco and the Launchers, with Boysie Grant (1).   *A) King of Kings* (44), 1964.   *B) ditto*

1965   Otis Redding (13).   *A) (Sittin' On) The Dock Of The Bay* (3), 1968.   *B) Love Man* (43), 1969

1967   Otis Redding and Carla Thomas (2).   *A) Tramp* (18), 1967.   *B) Knock On Wood* (35), 1967

1964   Jimmy Reed (1).   *A) Shame Shame Shame* (45), 1964.   *B) ditto*

1960   Jim Reeves (22).   *A) Distant Drums* (1), 1966.   *B) But You Love Me Daddy* (15), 1969

1964   Martha Reeves and the Vandellas (7).   *A) Dancing In The Street* (4), 1969 (re-issue).   *B) Nowhere To Run* (42), 1969 (re-issue)

1960   Joan Regan (4).   *A) Happy Anniversary* (29), 1960; *Papa Loves Mama* (29), 1960.   *B) Must Be Santa* (42), 1961

1966   Keith Relf (1).   *A) Mr Zero* (50), 1966.   *B) ditto*

1968   Reparata and the Delrons (1).   *A) Captain Of Your Ship* (13), 1968.   *B) ditto*

1960   Cliff Richard (43).   *A) Please Don't Tease* (1), 1960; *I Love You* (1), 1960; *The Young Ones* (1), 1962; *The Next Time* (1), 1962; *Summer Holiday* (1), 1963; *The Minute You're Gone* (1), 1965; *Congratulations* (1), 1968.   *B) With The Eyes Of A Child* (20), 1969

1965   Righteous Brothers (6).   *A) You've Lost That Loving Feeling* (1), 1965.   *B) Island In The Sun* (36), 1966

1968   Jeannie C Riley (1).   *A) Harper Valley PTA* (12), 1968.   *B) ditto*

1961   Danny Rivers (1).   *A) Can't You Hear My Heart* (36), 1961.   *B) ditto*

1960   Marty Robbins (4).   *A) Devil Woman* (5), 1962.   *B) Ruby Ann* (24), 1963

1967   Malcolm Roberts (3).   *A) May I Have The Next Dream With You* (8), 1968.   *B) Love Is All* (12), 1969

1966   Smokey Robinson and the Miracles (5).   *A) Tracks Of My Tears* (9), 1969.   *B) ditto*

1964   Rockin' Berries (6).   *A) He's In Town* (3), 1964.   *B) The Water Is Over My Head* (43), 1966

1969   Clodagh Rodgers (3).   *A) Come Back And Shake Me* (3), 1969.   *B) Biljo* (22), 1969

1962   Jimmie Rodgers (1).   *A) English Country Garden* (5), 1962.   *B) ditto*

1962   Tommy Roe (6).   *A) Dizzy* (1), 1969.   *B) Heather Honey* (24), 1969

1964   Julie Rogers (3).   *A) The Wedding* (3), 1964.   *B) Hawaiian Wedding Song* (31), 1965

1969   Kenny Rogers (1).   *A) Ruby Don't Take Your Love To Town* (2), 1969.   *B) ditto*

1963   Rolling Stones (15).   *A) It's All Over Now* (1), 1964; *Little Red Rooster* (1), 1964; *The Last Time* (1), 1965; *(I Can't Get No) Satisfaction* (1), 1965; *Get Off My Cloud* (1), 1965; *Paint It Black* (1), 1966; *Jumping Jack Flash* (1), 1968; *Honky Tonk Women* (1), 1969.   *B) Honky Tonk Women* (1), 1969

1969   Max Romeo (1).   *A) Wet Dream* (10), 1969.   *B)*

ditto

1963 Ronettes (4). *A) Be My Baby* (4), 1963. *B) Do I Love You* (35), 1964

1963 Rooftop Singers (1). *A) Walk Right In* (10), 1963. *B) ditto*

1969 Diana Ross and the Supremes, and the Temptations (2). *A) I'm Gonna Make You Love Me* (3), 1969. *B) I Second That Emotion* (18), 1969

1965 Nini Rosso (1). *A) Il Silenzio* (8), 1965. *B) ditto*

1965 Billy Joe Royal (1). *A) Down In The Boondocks* (38), 1965. *B) ditto*

1967 Royal Guardsmen (2). *A) Snoopy vs the Red Baron* (8), 1967. *B) Return Of The Red Baron* (37), 1967

1963 Ruby and the Romantics (1). *A) Our Day Will Come* (38), 1963. *B) ditto*

1966 Jimmy Ruffin (3, plus one re-issue). *A) What Becomes Of The Broken Hearted* (10), 1966. *B) I've Passed This Way Before* (33), 1969 (re-issue)

1968 Barry Ryan (3). *A) Eloise* (2), 1968. *B) Hunt* (34), 1969

1965 Paul and Barry Ryan (8). *A) Don't Bring Me Your Heartaches* (13), 1965. *B) Claire* (47), 1967

1960 Bobby Rydell (6). *A) Wild One* (7), 1960. *B) Forget Him* (13), 1963

1966 Mitch Ryder and the Detroit Wheels (1). *A) Jenny Take A Ride* (33), 1966. *B) ditto*

1966 Staff Sergeant Barry Sadler (1). *A) Ballad Of The Green Berets* (24), 1966. *B) ditto*

1960 Mike Sagar (1). *A) Deep Feeling* (44), 1960. *B) ditto*

1965 Barry St John (1). *A) Come Away Melinda* (47), 1965. *B) ditto*

1966 St Louis Union (1). *A) Girl* (11), 1966. *B) ditto*

1966 Crispian St Peters (3). *A) You Were On My Mind* (2), 1966. *B) Changes* (47), 1966

1963 Kyu Sakamoto (1). *A) Sukiyaki* (6), 1963. *B) ditto*

1967   Sam and Dave (4).   *A) Soul Sister Brown Sugar* (15), 1969.   *B) ditto*

1965   Sam the Sham and the Pharaohs (2).   *A) Wooly Bully* (11), 1965.   *B) Lil' Red Riding Hood* (46), 1966

1966   Mike Sammes Singers (1).   *A) Somewhere My Love* (14), 1967 (re-entry).   *B) ditto*

1960   Dave Sampson (1).   *A) Sweet Dreams* (29), 1960.   *B) ditto*

1963   Chris Sandford (1)   *A) Not Too Little Not Too Much* (17), 1963.   *B) ditto*

1966   Sandpipers   (3).   *A)   Guantanamera*   (7), 1966.   *B) Kumbaya* (39), 1969

1960   Tommy Sands (1).   *A) Old Oaken Bucket* (25), 1960.   *B) ditto*

1960   Santo and Johnny (1).   *A)   Teardrop* (50), 1960.   *B) ditto*

1962   Mike Sarne (4).   *A) Come Outside* (1), 1962.   *B) Code Of Love* (29), 1963

1969   Peter Sarstedt (2).   *A)   Where Do You Go To My Lovely* (1), 1969.   *B) Frozen Orange Juice* (10), 1969

1960   Al Saxon (2).   *A) Blue-Eyed Boy* (39), 1960. *B) There I've Said It Again* (48), 1961

1967   Scaffold (4).   *A) Lily The Pink* (1), 1968.   *B) Gin Gan Goolie* (38), 1969

1960   Jack Scott (2).   *A) What In The World's Come Over You* (11), 1960.   *B) Burning Bridges* (32), 1960

1961   Linda Scott (2).   *A) I've Told Every Little Star* (7), 1961.   *B) Don't Bet Money Honey* (50), 1961

1964   Simon Scott (1).   *A) Move It Baby* (37), 1964. *B) ditto*

1963   Searchers (14).   *A) Sweets For My Sweet* (1), 1963; *Needles and Pins* (1), 1964; *Don't Throw Your Love Away* (1), 1964.   *B) Have You Ever Loved Somebody* (48), 1966

1963   Harry Secombe (1).   *A) This Is My Song* (2), 1967.   *B) ditto*

1961   Neil Sedaka (9).   *A) Happy Birthday Sweet Sixteen* (3), 1961.   *B) Let's Go Steady Again* (42), 1963

1965   Seekers (9).   *A) I'll Never Find Another You* (1),

1965; *The Carnival Is Over* (1), 1965.   B) *Emerald City* (50), 1967

1965   Peter Sellers (1).   A) *A Hard Day's Night* (14), 1965.   B) *ditto*

1960   Peter Sellers and Sophia Loren (2).   A) *Goodness Gracious Me* (4), 1960.   B) *Bangers And Mash* (22), 1961

1961   Semprini (1)   A) *Theme from Exodus* (25), 1961.   B) *ditto*

1960   Shadows (25).   A) *Apache* (1), 1960; *Kon-Tiki* (1), 1961; *Wonderful Land* (1), 1961; *Dance On!* (1), 1962; *Foot.Tapper* (1), 1963.   B) *Maroc 7* (24), 1967

1964   Shangri-Las (1).   A) *Leader Of The Pack* (11), 1965.   B) *ditto*

1961   Del Shannon (14).   A) *Runaway* (1), 1961.   B) *Stranger In Town* (40), 1965

1961   Helen Shapiro (11).   A) *You Don't Know* (1), 1961; *Walkin' Back To Happiness* (1), 1961.   B) *Fever* (38), 1964

1963   Dee Dee Sharp (1).   A) *Do The Bird* (46), 1963.   B) *ditto*

1964   Sandie Shaw (17).   A) *(There's) Always Something There To Remind Me* (1), 1964; *Long Live Love* (1), 1965; *Puppet On A String* (1), 1967.   B) *Think It All Over* (42), 1969

1962   George Shearing (1).   A) *Baubles Bangles and Beads* (49), 1962.   B) *ditto*

1961   Anne Shelton (1).   A) *Sailor* (10), 1961.   B) *ditto*

1963   Tony Sheridan and the Beatles (1).   A) *My Bonnie* (48), 1963).   B) *ditto*

1963   Allan Sherman (1).   A) *Hello Muddah Hello Faddah* (14), 1963.   B) *ditto*

1964   Tony Sheveton (1).   A) *Million Drums* (49), 1964.   B) *ditto*

1961   Shirelles (3).   A) *Will You Love Me Tomorrow* (4), 1961.   B) *Foolish Little Girl* (38), 1963

1961   Troy Shondell (1).   A) *This Time* (22), 1961.   B) *ditto*

1968   Showstoppers (2).   A) *Ain't Nothing But A*

Houseparty (11), 1968.   *B) Eeny Meeny* (33), 1968

1965   Silkie (1).   *A) You've Got To Hide Your Love Away* (28), 1965.   *B) ditto*

1960   Harry Simeone Chorale (1)..   *A) Onward Christian Soldiers* (35), 1960.   *B) ditto*

1966   Simon and Garfunkel (4).   *A) Mrs Robinson* (4), 1968.   *B) The Boxer* (6), 1969

1965   Nina Simone (3).   *A) Ain't Got No-I Got Life/Do What You Gotta Do* (2), 1968.   *B) To Love Somebody* (5), 1969

1960   Frank Sinatra (16).   *A) Strangers In The Night* (1), 1966.   *B) Love's Been Good To Me* (8), 1969

1962   Frank Sinatra and Sammy Davis Jr (1).   *A) Me and My Shadow* (20), 1962.   *B) ditto*

1966   Nancy Sinatra (5).   *A) These Boots Are Made For Walkin'* (1), 1966.   *B) Highway Song* (21), 1969

1967   Nancy Sinatra and Lee Hazelwood (1).   *A) Ladybird* (47), 1967.   *B) ditto*

1967   Nancy Sinatra and Frank Sinatra (1).   *A) Somethin' Stupid* (1), 1967.   *B) ditto*

1963   Singing Nun (Soeur Sourire) (1).   *A) Dominique* (7), 1963.   *B) ditto*

1965   Sir Douglas Quintet (1).   *A) She's About A Mover* (15), 1965.   *B) ditto*

1967   Skatalites (1).   *A) Guns Of Navarone* (36), 1967.   *B) ditto*

1966   Percy Sledge (2).   *A) When A Man Loves A Woman* (4), 1966.   *B) Warm And Tender Love* (34), 1966

1965   P F Sloan (1).   *A) Sins Of The Family* (38), 1965.   *B) ditto*

1968   Sly and the Family Stone (3).   *A) Dance To The Music* (7), 1968.   *B) Everyday People* (36), 1969

1965   Small Faces (12).   *A) All Or Nothing* (1), 1966.   *B) Afterglow Of Your Love* (36), 1969

1966   Jimmy Smith (1).   *A) Got My Mojo Working* (48), 1966.   *B) ditto*

1965   Keely Smith (1).   *A) You're Breaking My Heart* (14), 1965.   *B) ditto*

1968   O C Smith (1).   *A) Son Of Hickory Holler's*

Tramp (2), 1968. *B) ditto*

1967   Whistling Jack Smith (1). *A) I Was Kaiser Bill's Batman* (5), 1967. *B) ditto*

1967   Smoke (1). *A) My Friend Jack* (45), 1967. *B) ditto*

1965   Sonny & Cher (8). *A) I Got You Babe* (1), 1965. *B) The Beat Goes On* (29), 1967

1965   Sorrows (1). *A) Take A Heart* (21), 1965. *B) ditto*

1963   Jimmy Soul (1). *A) If You Wanna Be Happy* (39), 1963. *B) ditto*

1965   Soul Brothers (1). *A) I Keep Ringing My Baby* (42), 1965. *B) ditto*

1964   Sounds Incorporated (2). *A) The Spartans* (30), 1964. *B) Spanish Harlem* (35), 1964

1969   Sounds Nice (1). *A) Love At First Sight (Je T'Aime)* (18), 1969. *B) ditto*

1964   Sounds Orchestral (2). *A) Cast Your Fate To The Wind* (5), 1964. *B) Moonglow* (43), 1965

1969   Joe South (1). *A) Games People Play* (6), 1969. *B) ditto*

1963   Bob B Soxx and the Blue Jeans (1). *A) Zip-A-Dee Doo-Dah* (45), 1963. *B) ditto*

1962   Johnny Spence (1). *A) Theme From Dr Kildare* (15), 1962. *B) ditto*

1963   Don Spencer (1). *A) Fireball* (32), 1963. *B) ditto*

1962   Spotnicks (4). *A) Hava Nagila* (13), 1963. *B) Just Listen To My Heart* (36), 1963

1963   Dusty Springfield (16). *A) You Don't Have To Say You Love Me* (1), 1966. *B) Am I The Same Girl* (43), 1969

1961   Springfields (5). *A) Island Of Dreams* (5), 1962; *Say I Won't Be There* (5), 1963. *B) Come On Home* (31), 1963

1969   Dorothy Squires (1). *A) For Once In My Life* (24), 1969. *B) ditto*

1961   Dorothy Squires and Russ Conway (1). *A) Say It With Flowers* (23), 1961. *B) ditto*

1964 Terry Stafford (1). *A) Suspicion* (31),
1964. *B) ditto*

1960 Staiffi and his Mustafas (1). *A) Mustafa* (43),
1960. *B) ditto*

1966 Edwin Starr (7). *A) Stop Her On Sight (SOS)*
(11), 1968. *B) 25 Miles* (36), 1969

1966 Statler Brothers (1). *A) Flowers On The Wall*
(38), 1966. *B) ditto*

1968 Status Quo (3). *A) Pictures Of Matchstick Men*
(7), 1968. *B) Are You Growing Tired Of My Love* (46),
1969

1960 Tommy Steele (3). *A) What A Mouth* (5),
1960. *B) Writing On The Wall* (30), 1961

1969 Steppenwolf (1). *A) Born To Be Wild* (30),
1969. *B) ditto*

1963 Steve and Eydie (1). *A) I Want To Stay Here* (3),
1963. *B) ditto*

1966 Cat Stevens (5). *A) Matthew & Son* (2), 1967.
B) Kitty (47), 1967

1960 Connie Stevens (1). *A) Sixteen Reasons* (9),
1960. *B) ditto*

1961 Ricky Stevens (1). *A) I Cried For You* (34),
1961. *B) ditto*

1960 Andy Stewart (3). *A) A Scottish Soldier* (19),
1961. *B) Dr Finlay* (43), 1965

1966 Billy Stewart (1). *A) Summertime* (39),
1966. *B) ditto*

1961 Rhet Stoller (1). *A) Chariot* (26), 1961. *B)
ditto*

1962 Danny Storm (1). *A) Honest I Do* (42),
1962. *B) ditto*

1966 Barbra Streisand (1). *A) Second Hand Rose* (14),
1966. *B) ditto*

1961 String-A-Longs (1). *A) Wheels* (8), 1961. *B)
ditto*

1963 Chad Stuart and Jeremy Clyde (1). *A)
Yesterday's Gone* (37), 1963. *B) ditto*

1968 Sun Dragon (1). *A) Green Tambourine* (50),
1968. *B) ditto*

1964 Supremes (18). *A) Baby Love* (1), 1964. *B) Someday We'll Be Together* (13), 1969

1963 Surfaris (1). *A) Wipe Out* (5), 1963. *B) ditto*

1960 Pat Suzuki (1). *A) I Enjoy Being A Girl* (49), 1960. *B) ditto*

1963 Swinging Blue Jeans (6). *A) Hippy Hippy Shake* (2), 1963. *B) Don't Make Me Over* (31), 1966

1967 Symbols (2). *A) Best Part Of Breaking Up* (25), 1968. *B) ditto*

1966 Norma Tanega (1). *A) Walking My Cat Named Dog* (22), 1966. *B) ditto*

1967 Felice Taylor (1). *A) I Feel Love Comin' On* (11), 1967. *B) ditto*

1968 R Dean Taylor (1). *A) Gotta See Jane* (17), 1968. *B) ditto*

1961 Temperance Seven (4). *A) You're Driving Me Crazy*, 1961. *B) Charleston* (22), 1961

1963 Nino Tempo and April Stevens (2). *A) Deep Purple* (17), 1963. *B) Whispering* (20), 1964

1965 Temptations (10). *A) Get Ready* (10), 1969. *B) Cloud Nine* (15), 1969

1965 Them (2). *A) Baby Please Don't Go* (10), 1965. *B) Here Comes The Night* (2), 1965

1969 Jamo Thomas (1). *A) I Spy For The FBI* (44), 1969. *B) ditto*

1961 Sue Thompson (2). *A) Sad Movies* (46), 1961. *B) Paper Tiger* (30), 1965

1963 David Thorne (1). *A) Alley Cat Song* (21), 1963. *B) ditto*

1963 Ken Thorne (1). *A) Theme From The Film The Legion's Last Patrol* (4), 1963. *B) ditto*

1966 Three Good Reasons (1). *A) Nowhere Man* (47), 1966. *B) ditto*

1969 Thunderclap Newman (1). *A) Something In The Air* (1), 1969. *B) ditto*

1960 Johnny Tillotson (6). *A) Poetry In Motion* (1), 1960. *B) Out Of My Mind* (34), 1963

1968 Timebox (1). *A) Beggin'* (38), 1968. *B) ditto*

1961 Tokens (1). *A) The Lion Sleeps Tonight* (11),

1961.   *B) ditto*

1967   Topol (1).   *A) If I Were A Rich Man* (9),
1967.   *B) ditto*

1963   Mel Torme (1).   *A) Coming Home Baby* (13),
1963.   *B) ditto*

1962   Tornados (5).   *A) Telstar* (1), 1962. *B)
Dragonfly* (41), 1963

1965   Toys (2).   *A) A Lover's Concerto* (5), 1965.   *B)
Attack* (36), 1966

1967   Traffic (4).   *A) Hole In My Shoe* (2), 1967.   *B)
No Face, No Name, No Number* (40), 1968

1969   Trash (1).   *(A) Golden Slumbers – Carry That
Weight* (25), 1969.   *B) ditto*

1967   Tremeloes (13).   *A) Silence Is Golden* (1),
1967.   *B) Hello Buddy* (32), 1971

1965   Jackie Trent (3).   *A) Where Are You Now (My
Love)* (1), 1965.   *B) I'll Be There* (38), 1969

1969   Tony Tribe (1).   *A) Red Red Wine* (46),
1969.   *B) ditto*

1966   Troggs (9).   *A) With A Girl Like You* (1),
1966.   *B) Little Girl* (37), 1968

1969   Troubadours Du Roi Baudouin (1).   *A) Sanctus
(Missa Luba)* (28), 1969.   *B) ditto*

1964   Doris Troy (1).   *A) Whatcha Gonna Do About It*
(37), 1964.   *B) ditto*

1966   Truth (1).   *A) Girl* (27), 1966.   *B) ditto*

1964   Tommy Tucker (1).   *A) Hi-Heel Sneakers* (23),
1964.   *B) ditto*

1966   Ike and Tina Turner (3).   *A) River Deep
Mountain High* (3), 1966.   *B) A Love Like Yours* (16),
1966

1967   Turtles (3).   *A) She'd Rather Be With Me* (4),
1967.   *B) Elenore* (7), 1968

1966   Twice As Much (1).   *A) Sittin' On A Fence* (25),
1966.   *B) ditto*

1964   Twinkle (2).   *A) Terry* (4), 1964.   *B) Golden
Lights* (21), 1965

1960   Conway Twitty (2).   *A) C'Est Si Bon* (40),
1961.   *B) ditto*

1963   Tymes (2).   *A) People* (16), 1969.   *B) ditto*

1964   *A) Just A Little Bit* (49), 1964.   *B) ditto*

1964   Unit Four Plus Two (4).   *A) Concrete And Clay* (1), 1965.   *B) Baby Never Say Goodbye* (49), 1966

1966   Phil Upchurch Combo (1).   *A) You Can't Sit Down* (39), 1966.   *B) ditto*

1969   Upsetters (1).   *A) Return of Django/Dollar In The Teeth* (5), 1969.   *B) ditto*

1960   Ricky Valance (1).   *A) Tell Laura I Love Her* (1), 1960.   *B) ditto*

1962   Leroy Van Dyke (2).   *A) Walk On By* (4), 1962.   *B) Big Man In A Big House* (34), 1962

1967   Vanilla Fudge (1).   *A) You Keep Me Hangin' On* (18), 1967.   *B) ditto*

1968   Vanity Fare (3).   *A) Early In The Morning* (3), 1969.   *B) Hitchin' A Ride* (16), 1969

1960   Frankie Vaughan (13).   *A) Tower Of Strength* (1), 1961.   *B) So Tired* (21), 1967

1962   Norman Vaughan (1).   *A) Swinging In The Rain* (34), 1962.   *B) ditto*

1960   Sarah Vaughan (1).   *A) Let's Serenata* (37), 1960.   *B) ditto*

1961   Bobby Vee (10).   *A) Take Good Care Of My Baby* (3), 1961; *The Night Has A Thousand Eyes* (3), 1963.   *B) Bobby Tomorrow* (21), 1963

1961   Velvets (2).   *A) That Lucky Old Sun* (46), 1961.   *B) Tonight (Could Be The Night)* (50), 1961

1960   Ventures (4).   *A) Perifidia* (4), 1960.   *B) Lullaby Of The Leaves* (43), 1961

1962   Vernons Girls (5).   *A) Lover Please* (16), 1962.   *B) Do The Bird* (31), 1963

1960   Gene Vincent (5).   *A) My Heart* (16), 1960.   *B) I'm Going Home* (36), 1961

1962   Bobby Vinton (2).   *A) Roses Are Red* (15), 1962.   *B) There I've Said It Again* (34) , 1963

1960   Viscounts (2).   *A) Short'nin' Bread* (16), 1960.   *B) Who Put The Bomp* (21), 1961

1961   Adam Wade (1).   *A) Take Good Care Of Her* (38), 1961.   *B) ditto*

1965 Waikikis (1). *A) Hawaiian Tattoo* (41), 1965.
B) ditto

1965 Walker Brothers (9). *A) Make It Easy On
Yourself* (1), 1965; *The Sun Ain't Gonna Shine Anymore*
(1), 1966. *B) Walking In The Rain* (26), 1967

1966 Gary Walker (2). *A) You Don't Love Her* (26),
1966; *Twinkle Lee* (26), 1966. *B) Last mentioned*

1967 John Walker (1). *A) Annabella* (24), 1967. *B)
ditto*

1966 Junior Walker and the All Stars (3). *A) (I'm A)
Road Runner* (12), 1969. *B) What Does It Take (To Win
Your Love)* (13), 1969

1967 Scott Walker. *A) (7)*, 1968. *B) Lights Of
Cincinatti* (13), 1969

1960 Jerry Wallace (1). *A) You're Singing Our Love
Song To Somebody Else* (46), 1960. *B) ditto*

1961 Bob Wallis and his Storyville Jazz Band (1). *A)
Come Along Please* (33), 1961. *B) ditto*

1964 Dionne Warwick (7). *A) Do You Know The
Way To San Jose* (8), 1968. *B) ditto*

1961 Dinah Washington (1). *A) September In The
Rain* (35), 1961. *B) ditto*

1966 Geno Washington and the Ram Jam Band
(4). *A) Water* (39), 1966; *Michael* (39), 1967. *B) last
mentioned*

1960 Bert Weedon (6). *A) Apache* (24), 1960. *B)
Mr Guitar* (47), 1961

1960 Frank Weir (1). *A) Caribbean Honeymoon* (42),
1960. *B) ditto*

1963 Houston Wells (1). *A) Only The `Heartaches*
(22), 1963. *B) ditto*

1964 Mary Wells (1). *A) My Guy* (5), 1964.· *B) ditto*

1961 Alex Welsh (1). *A) Tansy* (45), 1961. *B) ditto*

1965 Dodie West (1). *A) Going Out Of My Head* (39),
1965. *B) ditto*

1967 Keith West (2). *A) Excerpt From A Teenage
Opera* (2), 1967. *B) Sam* (38), 1967

David Whitfield (1). *A) I Believe* (49), 1960. *B) ditto*

1969 Roger Whittaker (1). *A) Durham Town (The*

Leavin') (12), 1969. *B) ditto*

1965   The Who (14).   *A) My Generation* (2), 1965; *I'm A Boy* (2), 1966.   *B) Pinball Wizard* (4), 1969

1960   Marty Wilde (8).   *A) Rubber Ball* (9), 1961.   *B) Ever Since You Said Goodbye* (31), 1962

1962   Andy Williams (10).   *A) Can't Get Used To Losing You* (2), 1963; *Almost There* (2), 1965.   *B) Happy Heart* (19), 1969

1961   Danny Williams (7).   *A) Moon River* (1), 1961.   *B) My Own True Love* (45), 1963

1960   Jackie Wilson (3).   *A) (Your Love Keeps Lifting Me) Higher And Higher* (11), 1969.   *B) ditto*

1966   Stevie Wonder (10).   *A) Yester-Me Yester-You Yesterday* (2), 1969.   *B) ditto*

1967   Brenton Wood (1).   *A) Gimme Little Sign* (8), 1967.   *B) ditto*

1960   Mark Wynter (9).   *A) Venus In Blue Jeans* (4), 1962.   *B) Only You* (38), 1964

1963   Miss X (1).   *A) Christine* (37), 1963.   *B) ditto*

1964   Yardbirds (7).   *A) Heart Full Of Soul* (2), 1965.   *B) Happenings Ten Years Time Ago* (43), 1966

1963   Jimmy Young (2).   *A) Miss You* (15), 1963.   *B) Unchained Melody* (43), 1964

1969   Karen Young (1).   *A) Nobody's Child* (6), 1969.   *B) ditto*

1967   Young Idea (1).   *A) With A Little Help From My Friends* (10), 1967.   *B) ditto*

1967   Young Rascals (2).   *A) Groovin'* (8), 1967.   *B) A Girl Like You* (37), 1967

1964   Helmut Zacharias (1).   *A) Tokyo Melody* (1), 1964.   *B) ditto*

1969   Zager and Evans (1).   *A) In The Year 2525* (1), 1969.   *B) ditto*

1961   Tommy Zang (1).   *A) Hey Good Looking* (45), 1961.   *B) ditto*

1965   Zephyrs (1).   *A) She's Lost You* (48), 1965.   *B) ditto*

1964   Zombies (2).   *A) She's Not There* (12), 1964.   *B) Tell Her No* (42), 1965

Chart Analysis

This section looks at the 1960s in terms of its most successful single artists in Britain. First of all the section gives the basic details: who had the most hits in terms of where their records reached in the charts. In brackets 'total' number of chart hits in the 1960s.

Artist/Group Records at

		I	2	3	4/5	6–10	11–20	21–30
1	Cliff Richard (43) UK	7	7	4	3	10	3	5
2	Elvis Presley (42) US	11	4	1	1	2	14	5
3	Roy Orbison (28) US	3	1	2	0	4	6	5
4	The Shadows (25) UK	5	1	1	3	4	6	2
5	Beatles (23) UK	17	3	0	1	0	1	1
5	Adam Faith (23) UK	1	1	0	6	1	5	4
5	Billy Fury (23) UK	0	1	3	2	4	7	3
8	Jim Reeves (22) US	1	0	1	1	3	7	3
9	Everly Brothers (21) US	3	1	0	2	0	5	5
10	Hollies (20) UK	1	3	3	4	4	4	1

This table is determined by the number of hits achieved. All it does, however, is make obvious how the various records performed in chart position. It makes no distinction between the relative merits of chart positions and likely sales. The next table is a better guide to the most successful artists of the Sixties, since it takes the before mentioned data into consideration.

In a given week the average percentage of total singles *sales* claimed, by records in various ranges of the chart, is something like this

Chart position	Percentage of sales*
I	7.5%
2–5	3.75%
6–10	2.25%
11–20	1.6%
21–30	1.0%

*claimed by average record in range

The same data – as previously given – is utilised. And the same artists and groups are used because each has a minimum of 20 hits. Record re-issues and re-releases have not been considered and the total for each artist is only concerned with records that charted for the 'first' time in the decade.

This produces the following success table of the 1960s

	Artist	Percentage score	1	2–5	6–10	11–20	31–30
1	Beatles	145.10	127.50	15.00	00.00	01.60	01.00
2	Cliff Richard	138.10	52.50	52.50	22.50	04.80	05.00
3	Elvis Presley	136.90	82.50	23.50	04.50	22.40	05.00
4	The Shadows	76.85	37.50	11.25	09.00	09.60	05.00
5	Roy Orbison	58.35	32.50	11.25	09.00	09.60	05.00
6	Hollies	56.90	07.50	37.50	04.50	06.40	01.00
7	Billy Fury	51.70	00.00	22.50	09.00	11.20	03.00
8	Everly Brothers	46.75	22.50	11.25	00.00	08.00	05.00
9	Adam Faith	42.25	01.75	26.25	02.25	08.00	04.00
10	Jim Reeves	35.95	07.50	07.50	06.75	11.20	03.00

It is observed that this table places the Beatles above Cliff Richard and is suggested as a pointer to greater sales, although Cliff had more hits and, of course, began his points tally from the beginning of 1960.

A to Z of Radio

This section is mainly concerned with the two great radio happenings of the decade: the advent of 'pirate radio' and the birth of BBC's Radio One.

Britain may be a 'free country' but in the matter of airwaves and their use *control* has been the operative word. The British Broadcasting Corporation, a body created by Royal charter and operating under a licence from the Postmaster General, was the sole body responsible for radio broadcasting when the 1960s began. There *had* been various proposals for the establishing of 'commercial' radio in which stations would be funded through advertising but in the Pilkington Committee Report of 1960–61 there was no support for this, although commercial television had arrived in 1955.

In terms of young people's listening habits, radio was faring badly when the decade dawned. There was an enormous growth in record buying and a corresponding decrease in sheet music sales. Young people liked the 'recorded' sound of their artists and in most cases were not too thrilled by so-called live performance.

Whatever may or may not be the pros and cons of Britain possessing a radio system similiar to that of the United States, where nowadays a major city may have 30 or more stations, there was a definite cry from young people for more 'pop' oriented radio than was being provided by the BBC's Light Programme.

It would be churlish to attack the Light Programme, since its standards were high and many of its programmes excellent. None-the-less it had to cater for a wide age-range, and only at certain times of day and week did it specifically cater for a young generation enjoying the consumer boom and finding its own musical heroes and life-styles. The main outlet for pop radio was Radio Luxembourg and, for those who knew the right times and could pick up its signal, AFN from Frankfurt in Germany.

But discussion on the future of radio in Britain was rudely interrupted on Easter Sunday, 1964, when Radio Caroline arrived and pirate-ship radio was born. The voice of Simon Dee was heard saying, 'Good morning, ladies and gentlemen. This is Radio Caroline broadcasting on 199, your all-day music station.' A splurge of stations followed. All were based on ships. Parliamentarians were appalled for a number of reasons. Some questioned the legality of the affair while others, in true British elitist fashion, saw the youth of Britain being corrupted and educationally stunted by the non-stop pumping out of awful pop music.

British youth adored the whole affair. They heard radio in-tune with the spirit of fast-growing pop culture and they savoured something of the radio drive and energy that American teenagers had known for years. The pirate ships threw up their own DJ heroes with Caroline and very American sounding London leading the audience ratings.

By 1966 ten pirate ships were operating around the British shores but their life blood was fast ebbing. The British Government desired their end, and so there was a Government Bill sponsored by the third Postmaster General to outlaw broadcasting from ships, abandoned wartime forts and flying aircraft! The bill proposed imprisonment and fines for those who had connections with the pirate ships, whether in supplying equipment, advertising or broadcasting, etc.

Ship supporters raised a great hue and cry, and they claimed the support of 25 million people but in democratic Britain this counted for nothing, for Parliament had already decided that this form of broadcasting should cease. And it did. The Marine Offences Act of 1967 formed the (legal) executionary means.

However, there was a slight sop to pop fans, for the Postmaster General had discussed with the BBC the formation of a service that would cater specifically for young people. So it was that Mr Edward Short, the Postmaster General, told Parliament and its loyal subjects in cities, towns and shires that the BBC would begin a new pop station on 30 September, 1967. A little later it was announced that the Light Programme would end and BBC Radio would be known by numbers, One, Two, Three and Four. Radio Two would correspond, in broadcasting nearness, to the old Light Programme and would be for those who liked their music mellower and sweeter. On 4 September, 1967 the Beeb announced its DJs and the list was more than filled and weighted toward popular jocks from the ships.

The first day's programming on 30 September, 1967 was this:

7.00	am	Tony Blackburn
8.32	am	*Junior Choice* with Leslie Crowther
9.55	am	*Crack The Clue* with Duncan Johnson
10.00	am	*Saturday Club* with Keith Skues
12.00	am	Emperor Rosko with *Midday Spin*
1.00	pm	*The Jack Jackson Show*
1.55	pm	A repeat of *Crack The Clue*
2.00	pm	Chris Denning with *Where It's At*
3.00	pm	Pete Murray *Best of the Newly Pressed*
4.00	pm	*Pete Brady Show*
5.32	pm	Wally Whyton with *Country Meets Folk*
6.32	pm	The magazine programme *Scene And Heard* with Johnny Moran
7.30	pm	*News*
7.35	pm	As for Radio 2
10.00	pm	*Pete's People* with Pete Murray
12.00	pm	*Midnight News Room*
12.05	am	Sean Kelly with *Night Ride*
2.00	am	*Close Down* with *Theme One* – the Radio One signature tune

Radio One quickly picked up its critics and fairly scathing comments were heard but there were also approving voices and by the end of the decade it had firmly established itself and collected a huge listening audience.

In 1964 *Manx Radio* was born, operating on 232 metres during daylight and 188 metres at dawn and dusk. The station was situated on Douglas, Isle of Man and proclaimed itself as Britain's first and only legal commercial station.

Radio Luxembourg broadcast on 208 metres medium wave and its English transmissions were heard from 7.30 *pm* to 3 *am* on summer weekdays and 7 *pm* to 3 *am* on Sundays. During winter it broadcast between the hours of 6.30 *pm* and 2 *am*, weekdays and 6 *pm* and 2 *am* Sundays. Luxembourg's English transmissions, to Great Britain and much of Europe, had begun in 1930 with audiences of many millions during the years, and especially in the Sixties before pirate ships and Radio One, although it continued to hold a huge following even when the two forementioned were operating. Luxembourg was helped by Radio One carrying Radio Two during the evening.

Pirate Ships: These ships operated a broadcasting service: Radio Caroline (South); Radio London; Radio Caroline (North); Radio City; England; Essex; Dolfijn; Invicta; Scotland; Sutch; Britain; King; 390; 355; 270; 277; Atlanta (merged with Caroline).

DJs and Programmes (A to Z) follow, including Radio Luxembourg, pirate ships, BBC Light Programme (as DJs later heard on the new network), Radio One (and Two when presenters were heard on both channels) and Manx Radio.

Mike Ahern ran Liverpool's popular The Teen-Beat Club. Born in the famous city, Ahern had a variety of jobs in Britain and Europe. Born 30 September, 1942, Ahern joined Caroline (South) as a DJ. Later he worked for BBC Radio One where, among other things, he shared DJ duties for a revived *Top Gear*, alas though, merely one programme on 8 October, 1967.

David Allan was born August 1940, in Bury. He had theatrical experience before joining the staff of 390 in

August, 1966. He remained there until the beginning of the following year. He joined Anglia Television as a newsreader.

Barry Alldis joined Luxembourg in 1958 and became head of the British Department. He compered the famed *Top Twenty Show* for eight years. By the mid late 1960s Alldis had become a freelance, and presented *Housewives Choice*, *Newly Pressed*, *Swingalong*, *Monday Monday* and guested on *Juke Box Jury* for BBC radio and television. Alldis also worked for the BBC World Service and BFBS. In 1967 he presented *Late Night Extra* and when Lennox left the BBC in 1968 Alldis took over his slot presenting programmes on Thursday and Friday from 10.00 *pm* to midnight.

Don Allen was born in Winnipeg, Manitoba, Canada. Allen worked for Canadian, USA and Mexico stations before Caroline South and then North.

Ted Allebury was born in Manchester but reared in Birmingham. Allebury ran a Sunday night programme *Redsands Rendevous* for pirate ship 390.

Vince Allen was a DJ with Radio Essex and a local boy. He was an executive of the station.

Michael Aspel was working in the BBC newsroom when the Sixties dawned. He presented various television shows, while on BBC Radio he had a summer series *Holiday Spin*. In October 1967 he became the main London presenter for *Family Favourites*. The following year saw him turn freelance, with the BBC 1 TV *Monday Show* following.

The Baron debuted on Radio Luxembourg in 1967 and replaced Stuart Grundy. His show was *Hi Midnight*. In 1967 he made his television debut on *First Timers* (Granada). On 13 July, 1968, he took over the Radio One spot vacated by Jack Jackson.

Alan Black, born Rosyth, Fife, was a DJ with Radio Scotland. He worked in films and television and was involved in the production of *Yellow Submarine*. On 18 July 1968 he made his Radio One debut as summer relief for Dave Cash on *Midday Spin*.

Tony Blackburn became a household name with Radio One but prior to this he was with Radio London. He was one of the main DJs on whose shoulders and DJ-stylising Radio One launched itself upon the nation. He was the first Radio One voice, along with his make-believe but children-loved dog Arnold. Blackburn, with producer Tim Blackmore, was to gain for the network the highest audiences of the day. Initially Blackburn's show ran daily from 7.00 to 8.30 but was later extended. He also – for a time – broadcast on Saturday mornings. Blackburn was also a singer and made several recordings with *So Much Love* and *It's Only Love* charting near the end of the decade.

Paul Beresford broadcast with 390 from its inception. Prior to this he had tried a number of careers.

Chuck Blair. Boston, Massachusetts-born Blair studied at the University of Maryland, the Emerson College of Theatre and Radio Broadcasting, and the Northeast School of Radio and TV Broadcasting. He worked for AFN and then a number of US home-based stations. A man of many languages Blair found himself with Radio England.

Peter Bowman. Born in Carlisle, Bowman worked for Border TV and Radio Scotland before Radio 270. On the pirate ship he had a twice-daily show.

Robin Boyle was born on 20 March, 1925. He worked with the BBC, BFBS and, with the advent of Radio One, his voice was heard on *Night Ride* (Wednesdays) and *Million Dollar Bill*. He was one of radio's best known voices.

Pete Brady. Montreal, 1942-born Brady had his baptism as a DJ with Jamaica Radio. A water-skier of international class, Brady represented both the West Indies and England in the World Water Ski Championships. When he settled in Britain he found work as an assistant film producer until Radio London became operational. In 1965 he toured in Star Scene '65, a package pop tour that included major stars Cilla Black and the Everly Brothers. In December 1965 he joined Luxembourg. He then joined Radio One and was given the Saturday 2.00 to 4.00 *pm* spot during an early change in the first three months of the network's output. But Brady never became a major DJ for the station.

Tony Brandon was born in Portland, Dorset. Brandon was a journalist who had early aspirations of becoming a broadcaster. Thanks to star Acker Bilk, Brandon found himself compering pop package shows. In 1966 he toured the Middle East with the Combined Services Entertainment. The same year he was signed by Luxembourg, and became a popular broadcaster there and through a number of TV shows. Brandon was an early DJ replacement on Radio One when in 1967 he replaced Duncan Johnson on *Midday Spin*.

Paul Burnett was 270 DJ Of the Sixties. He came from County Durham and like so many fine jocks of the decade he gained his basic skills from working with BFBS.

Dave Cash was once a DJ with Radio CJAV, British Columbia. He was London born but had emigrated. When he began broadcasting for Radio London he was an instant success and attracted an enormous audience, especially for his shows with Kenny Everett. Cash hit the Radio One airwaves on 2 October, 1967

Alan Clark. Croydon, Surrey-born Clark joined Radio City in November 1965 and soon established a popular following. He was a sales rep before that.

Edward Cole was born in Highgate, London, in 1939. Cole was qualified in law and public relations but chose to work for 390 in the Autumn of 1965.

Sam Costa, the comedian, began his work days as a junior copywriter in an advertising agency. He formed his own band and then and later he was a popular singer. His comedy days took off during World War Two when he entertained British troops, and later he was in the legendary radio show *Much Binding In The Marsh*.

Costa found himself DJing and proved popular with listeners of all ages. Luxembourg provided a valuable broadcasting base in the Sixties.

Kris Crookall broadcast for Manx Radio, Douglas, Isle Of Man.

Richard Cullingford. The much travelled Cullingford often adorned the BBC airwaves as an interviewer, but he worked as a general DJ for Radio 390. Cullingford's main show for the ship was *The Voice Of Business*.

Jack Curtiss, born 1943, in San Francisco, worked for KMPX in the Golden Gate City, amongst others, before he joined Radio England. Curtiss stood-in at 6ft 6in.

Robbie Dale was born in Littleborough, Lancashire. He served five years in the Army and worked, among other things, as a press agent and sales promotion staff member, voiced-in on Caroline (South) in 1966 and quickly became known as the jock with the 'sexy voice'.

Rick Dane. Cape Town, South African-born Dane broadcast for home country radio stations and compered an assortment of pop artist tours. An actor, he studied at the Webber Douglas Academy, appeared in general and repertory theatre and found himself a post with Caroline (South) as a DJ. Later he compared the late Brian Epstein Sunday Pop concerts at London's Savile theatre. In October 1967 he was co-presenter of *Top Gear* on BBC Radio One and during January 1968 he had the Saturday afternoon *Swingalong* show for a month while, from March, he had a lunchtime spot with *Radio One O'Clock*.

Roger Day was born in Cheltenham. He worked the dance halls of Kent as a DJ, and eventually became one of the best liked pirate-ship DJs, working for Radio England and for Britain Radio as its senior DJ. Day became one of the major pirate DJ pin-ups.

Larry Dean. An American, Dean gained initial radio experience with Albany's WPTR, amongst others. He then came to Britain and worked with Radio England.

Alex Dee was a former drama student who hosted shows on pirate ship 270 after a spell with Radio City.

Simon Dee, alias Carl Henty Dodd, of Canadian birth, was educated in an English public school, and had his first broadcasting experience with BFBS. In 1964 he joined Radio Luxembourg, and outside of radio he achieved major notice for TV shows like *Thank Your Lucky Stars* and *Ready, Steady, Go!* He was later to work with Radio One, and find major TV show outlet with the BBC.

Alan Dell was born in Cape Town, South Africa. He worked in the library of the South African Broadcasting Corporation and within months was broadcasting and compering a popular *Rhythm Club* show. He became senior announcer. In 1953 he came to England and stayed with major shows for Luxembourg in the 1960s.

Chris Denning learnt his radio with BFBS in Nairobi. He joined Radio London in 1966 and soon proved his professionalism. Denning joined the first BBC Radio One line-up and just before Christmas 1967 he took over *Midday Spin* from Kenny Everett. he compered the Saturday afternoon *Where It's At* show and was one of a team who presented another Saturday afternoon show *What's New*. In 1968 he deputised for Tony Blackburn and with a new look to Saturday afternoons he was one of a pool of DJs presenting the 2.00 to 4.00 spot. But, despite being much heard and liked, Denning never became a top-line lasting Radio One jock.

Dave Dennis known, unsurprisingly, as Double D, studied at the Central School of Speech and Drama. He worked for Radio London.

Pat Doody was born in 1938, on 11 November. He had experience with BFBS and early in the life of Radio One compered the Monday late show *Night Ride*. He also provided continuity links.

Pete Drummond. 29 July, 1943-born Drummond from Bangor, North Wales, was educated at Millfield where he met fellow pupil Tony Blackburn. After a period at art school and then a speech and drama school he took various jobs, married and lived in the States, before joining Radio London in September, 1966. He then joined Radio One, spent a month co-compering *Top Gear*, provided summer relief for Friday's *Midday Spin* and, for a while, had his own Saturday afternoon show.

John Dunn was born in Glasgow. He joined the BBC in the previous decade, with work in the Overseas Programmes Operation, before joining the Domestic Services. He worked regularly on the Light Programme and with the emergence of Radio One he was compere for the *Jazz At Night* show that formed output from both Radios One and Two.

Dave Eastwood was heard presenting a 45 minute show

for Radio One during 1969. He was one of a number of possible new Radio One signings who was given airtime in which to show his skills.

Noel Edmonds, born 1948 in Ilford, made trails for the BBC, and then found himself one of a number of prospective DJs given airtime on a 45 minute show on Sunday evenings during 1969. Edmonds was a household name by the time the next decade ended.

Tom Edwards from Norwich was an announcer for Border TV's *Beat On The Border* before joining Radio City in 1965 and becoming its senior DJ. Edwards freelanced for BBC Radio One and compered *Midday Spin* at the beginning of 1968, but was replaced in the Spring by songwriter Barry Mason. Edwards surfaced again briefly but found a more permanent abode as a BBC announcer and newsreader.

Kenny Everett, born in Liverpool, is one of the best-known DJs. He began work in an advertising department of a newspaper but had a great interest in radio, and apparently plagued stations with demonstration tapes. Eventually he was accepted by Radio London. Everett was in the BBC line-up of Radio One's 1967 labelled 'rogues gallery', and compered the Wednesday edition of *Midday Spin* which, at the time, was shared by Radio Two. Everett, really Maurice Cole, was replaced by Chris Dennis shortly before Christmas. In July 1968 he fronted *Foreverett* and the nick-named 'Cuddley Ken' ran from 6.45 *pm* to 7.30 *pm* but the show ended before the end of the year. He later had a much heard Saturday show but, at the beginning of the next decade, he and the Beeb were to part company, though Everett was far from finished as future history shows.

Paddy Feeny was born in Liverpool. He was part of the Beeb's External Services in the previous decade, prior to turning freelance in 1960. He worked in Belfast as a relief television newsreader, was an interviewer for a series built around singer Anne Shelton entitled *Ask Anne* and, back in England in 1962, he presented documentary shows. He shared DJ work with Judith Chalmers for *Records Round The World* on the Light Programme and from October 1967 to February 1968, and again August 1968, he presented *Junior Choice* for Radios One and Two.

Keith Fordyce. Born October 15, 1928, in Lincoln, Fordyce was a law graduate of Cambridge. He joined the BBC and presented sports and music material. He worked for BFBS and Radio Luxembourg, with the latter allowing him to DJ the station's much heard *Top Twenty* programme. In 1958 he became a freelance. Among 1960s shows were his *Pop Inn* for BBC radio and compering *Thank Your Lucky Stars.* In the first Radio One schedules he presented *Saturday Club* which had been presented from 1958 onwards by Brian Matthew in the schedules of the BBC Light Programme.

Alan 'Fluff' Freeman was born 6 July, 1927, in Melbourne, Australia. He studied accountancy and worked for Australia's largest timber company until 1951. He found himself a job as announcer on 7-LA Tasmania, later the all-nighter 3-AK, with 3-KZ following.

When he came to England he found work in TV advertising voice-overs and in 1958 he was relief DJ during the summer for Luxembourg. During the 1960s he had a daily show. In 1968 he was one of a number of jocks who presented the Saturday show from 2 *pm* to 4 *pm* on BBC Radio One, but his Radio One fame came with his dynamic presentation of *Pick Of The Pops* on Sundays from 5.00 to 7.00 *pm*. Freeman became a major TV pop presenter with *Top Of The Pops* heading the list. He was well on his way in the Sixties to becoming one of the all-time great jocks.

Bill Gates. In 1969 BBC Radio One gave a 45 minute programme to prospective new signings. Gates was one.

David Gell. Born 23 August, 1929, in Canada, David Gell was a full-time staff member of CFAC, the top-rated Calgary station. Gell became their foreign correspondent in the early Fifties and in the summer of 1955 he joined Luxembourg as a summer replacement, but with public response so good Gell was asked to stay which he did. During the Sixties he presented a variety of shows for the station and became one of its best-loved broadcasters.

Stuart Grundy was born on 8 November, 1938, in Doncaster. He was a student at the famed RADA institution, London. He joined BFBS and broadcast from Malta, then Tripoli before finding a permanent place with Luxembourg. Later he became a producer with Radio One and – though he occasionally presented – for all intents and purposes his became a DJ talent lost, although from time to time he still introduces Radio One Specials such as the *Motown Story*.

Tony Hall was born on 1 April, but was no fool; far from it. The Avening, Gloucestershire-born DJ told British young people about US black music, as well as compering, on Luxembourg, regular shows for Decca records. He also broadcast at times for both BBC radio and television.

David Hamilton was born in Manchester on 10 September, 1939. He worked with BFBS late Fifties and, at the outset of the Sixties, after a period script writing he became an announcer for ABC Television and Tyne Tees. He guested for other companies. In radio terms he had a whole list of credits including *The Beat Show*, *The Joe Loss Show* and *Midday Spin*. In 1968 he joined Thames Television (London) as an announcer. His best DJ days lay in the future.

Guy Hamilton was a teenager when he joined and broadcast on Radio Essex.

Drew Hamlyn. London DJ Hamlyn was a former actor before deciding to broadcast full-time for Radio Scotland.

Ben Healy. London DJ Healy worked the ballrooms down South before finding a DJ post with Radio Scotland.

Stuart Henry was his real name, but fans called him 'the Hairy Man'. He was a trained actor and worked for Radio Scotland. Henry's dislike of the sea led to the unusual position of him submitting taped shows from land. At the end of the decade Henry worked for Radio One, where he had a number of shows and gradually became one of the most popular station voices.

Paul Hollingdale had an early career broadcasting with BFBS. During 1959 and 1960 he presented *Two Way Family Favourites* as the relief DJ at the Cologne end. In September 1960 he presented the Philips sponsored programme on Luxembourg. For a while he was a director of a British company CNBC which had been established by Radio Veronica. He appeared on BBC-TV's *Juke Box Jury* and then had a radio series *Teenager's Turn*. In 1962 he was a Luxembourg summer relief and he worked for the Dutchy again in 1963 following work with *ABC At Large*, a TV show from Manchester. In 1964 he worked for the BBC, turned freelance a year later and become the first voice heard on Radio Two when the station began in 1967. He became the regular presenter of *Breakfast Special*.

Bob Holness. A former stage actor in South Africa, Holness worked for Granada TV in 1961. As a freelance he presented a variety of Light Programme shows from 1964 onwards, including *Newly Pressed*, *Roundabout* and

Double Spin. He became one of the team presenting *Late Night Extra* Monday to Friday, from October 1967 to February 1968. Toward the end of the decade he appeared on the *South-East* news magazine programme of Radio Four.

Mel Howard. Before he worked with the Big S station (Radio Scotland), Howard had been with Caroline (South). He had already worked elsewhere overseas before this gaining his radio knowledge.

Jack Jackson was regarded in the 1960s as in the previous decade, as the 'guvennor' of British pop radio.

Belvedere, Kent-born Jackson had been a trumpet player with numerous top dance bands prior to compering for the BBC. Jackson took the growth of recorded music in his stride and presented some of the most individual shows ever heard on radio, for both Luxembourg and the BBC. He occupied the Radio One airwaves until July 1968 with a special Saturday show.

David Jacobs was born 19 May, 1926, in London. He joined the Royal Navy on leaving school, worked with BFBS, became chief-announcer with Radio SEAC in Ceylon and broadcast for Radio Luxembourg and for BBC radio and television. His most famous show for radio was the Sunday, *Pick Of The Pops*: and for television, *Juke Box Jury*, of which he was chairman.

Peter James. Born in New Zealand, James was senior DJ with pirate ship 390. He joined them in the ship's second week.

Phil Jay was born in 1940. He worked for BFBS in Cyprus, compered a number of pop package shows and joined Radio City in 1965.

Duncan Johnson had an extensive background in radio and TV before joining Radio London. A Canadian, possessed of a handsome deep voice, Johnson joined Radio One and in early days presented the Tuesday edition of *Midday Spin*. After eight weeks he was replaced by Tony Brandon with his removal attracting media attention. 'Disc Jockey Duncan "too old" at 29,' read the *Mail*'s headline.

Paul Kay was an actor by training, but spent time with the Kenya police and African Broadcasting Service. He worked for BFBS and eventually with Radio London.

Sean Kelly was born in 1932. He joined the BBC in 1964 as an announcer in the Presentation Unit. He was heard regularly on *Night Ride* on Radios One and Two.

Jonathan King. Oxford graduate Jonathan King accumulated pop hits under his, and other, names and at the same time persuaded producers that his was a voice that should be heard on radio. He became one of the most distinctive presenters and commentators on the pop scene, whether it was on radio or television. He was one of the team that presented the Radio One show *Pick Of What's New* and was seen and heard on most pop TV shows.

Andy Kirke was the youngest DJ on board 270. He came from Yorkshire. He broadcast an evening show for the station.

Peter Kneale was a DJ with the Isle of Man station, Manx Radio.

Paul Kramer was a recording engineer for Mercury Films, prior to working for Radio City.

Peter Latham was born 12 December, 1926. He came from Liverpool but was educated in New Zealand where he gained much radio experience with NZBC (New Zealand Broadcasting Corporation) before coming to Britain in 1964 and joining the BBC on contract in June.

Breakfast Special and *Music In The Air* were two of the programmes with which he was associated, before *Night Ride* for Radios One and Two.

Jerry Leighton was senior DJ of Radio Caroline (North). Born in London, Leighton emigrated to Canada with his parents, graduated from the University of British Columbia, and began working for Caroline when moored off Frinton in 1964, and for Radio Atlanta and then Caroline (North).

Mike Lennox was a Canadian from Winnipeg, who achieved a considerable following from his work as a DJ with Radio London. Lennox had considerable broadcasting experience, general film and commercial work, both prior to and following his work with the popular pirate station. Lennox joined the Radio One team, but was never fully utilised. In the first year of the station he was one of the quintet of presenters involved with *Late Night Extra*, a show Radios One and Two shared in the days before their division. Lennox left the Beeb in 1968.

Tom Lodge. Liverpool-born Lodge spent much of his early life in North America. He was a DJ with US, CBS and later with Radio Caroline. In 1968 Lodge compered BBC Radio One's *Radio One O'Clock* produced by Don George.

Stuart Lord was a DJ with Manx Radio during the decade.

Mick Luzvit, known to radio listeners as Mick, was born 24 February, 1944. A singer and musician, he had radio shows in Canada especially for Radio CKY in Winnipeg. Other Canadian stations included the top-rated CHUM and also CHIC and CHWO. He worked for Caroline (North). Also an artist, Mick recorded a debut record *A Long Time Between Lovers* coupled with *Tho' I Still Love You.*

Humphrey Lyttleton, the jazz man, apart from running his own band became a major presenter of jazz on air, through Light Programme days onto Radio One during the Sixties.

Jack McLaughlin was known as Yak MacFisheries to his fans on Radio Scotland. Prior to working for the pirate station he had earned his living from a variety of jobs.

Ian McRae, An Australian, worked for Radio City after previous experience back home for a small country station.

Eric Martin, who was born in 1947, joined pirate ship Radio City immediately he had taken his A levels. He was 19 when he began broadcasting for the station in 1966.

Phil Martin, from Somerset, studied at Bristol University. He broadcast for Britain Radio and also was heard on the airwaves of Radio England.

Barry Mason, part of the successful songwriting team of Reed and Mason, made his radio debut for Radio One on 15 April, 1968, as part of the *Midday Spinners* roster. He was born in Wigan.

Brian Matthew, was born 17 September, 1928, in Coventry. He pre-dated Radio One and pirate days by compering the first two major BBC pop shows for its Light Programme – *Saturday Club* and *Easy Beat*. Matthew, trained as an actor at RADA, had various theatrical commitments before radio work with Radio Netherland Wereldomroep. Matthew made two records in the 1960s – *What's It All About* with Pete Murray and *Goodness Gracious Me* with Maureen Evans. Matthew's Radio One connection came with presenting a long-running *My Top Twelve*.

Tony Meehan. No relation to the Shadows drummer,

Meehan broadcast for Radio Scotland after first being a senior sales executive for the station.

Stevi Merike was one of a number of promising DJs given airtime on a special Radio One show that ran for 45 minutes on Sundays during 1969.

Noel Miller was senior DJ on pirate ship 270. An Australian by birth he was known to his radio listeners as Neddy Noel.

Roger Moffat was born on 25 July, 1927. He worked for Luxembourg and the BBC prior to 1960, with one of his most famous shows *Make Way For Music* ending in that year. He was based in Manchester, which he left for London in 1965, to present *Music Through Midnight*, *Roundabout* and *Night Ride*. In 1968 he became compere of *The Joe Loss Show*. Moffat was one of the all-time great characters of British radio.

Ray Moore was born in Walton, Liverpool. Moore had repertory and TV experience before hitting the BBC airwaves as presenter of *Breakfast Special* in 1968. Moore also broadcast on the BBC's World Service.

Johnny Moran began his radio career in Melbourne, Australia and came to Britain in 1963. He joined Luxembourg as a staff announcer in 1964. In 1966 he was back in Britain where commercials and some filming provided the means to live. In 1967 he found himself freelancing for the Beeb and appeared on *Easy Beat*, *Monday Monday*, *Saturday Club* and *Swingalong*. When Radio One began he became the regular presenter of the magazine show *Scene And Heard*.

Ed Moreno was born in Virginia, USA. He worked for stations in the US, Japan and Hong Kong, and in Germany on the US AFN station. He joined Radio City in August, 1965 and was known as the DJ who played the 'softer' kind of music on the station.

Don Moss from Peterborough, Northants, learnt his radio craft through serving with BFBS. He joined Luxembourg in 1957 and remained a permanent staff member until July 1959. He widened his interests into television and was often seen on *Thank Your Lucky Stars* and *Juke Box Jury* as well as on programmes for an older age-range like *Come Dancing*. Moss continued with his radio work both for Luxembourg and the BBC.

Jim Murphy. Born Texas, USA, Murphy worked for area stations KAML, KIBL, QAKY and KILT. At 6ft 5in. he was one of the tallest of the 1960s jocks. He worked for Radio Caroline (North).

Pete Murray, born 19 September, 1928, in London, was a RADA trained student and at one time seemed to have a promising theatrical career ahead of him. In the previous decade Murray had joined Luxembourg and soon asserted himself as the top DJ in Europe. The Sixties saw his influence grow and outside of having been associated with major television pop shows he continued his Luxembourg associations before finding himself in the first Radio Squad in 1967. As well as being one of the DJs who presented *What's New*, Murray's *Open House* replaced *Family Choice* in 1969.

Pete Myers was born in Venezuela in 1940. he travelled the world and began his DJ career in Ghana. He reached Britain in 1963 and worked for the BBC World Service. For the Light Programme he introduced *Swingalong* and he joined the roster of those presenting *Late Night Extra* for Radios One and Two. Myers compered Monday nights, and from February of 1968 he took over a further evening from Bob Holness.

Anne Nightingale was given a spot on a 1969 45 minute show that gave prospective Radio One jocks the chance to show their prowess. It was not until 1971 that she found herself signed by Radio One, and there then followed considerable success both on radio and television.

Ron O'Quinn from Moultrie, Georgia, broadcast on the local WMGA station when a schoolboy. Later he worked for Georgia's WAAT-ADEL, for WMYR in Fort Myers, WROD Daytona Beach in Florida and Miami's WFUN. He became senior jock with Radio England.

Ray Orchard was born on 25 April, 1931. From Canada, he worked at one time for CJVI in his home area of Victoria, British Columbia. Later he had a job with Radio Nederland based in Hilversum. In the Sixties he broadcast on Luxembourg five nights a week and also compered shows sponsored by EMI. Orchard was known as Ray 'Cream of the Crop' Orchard.

Dick Palmer became senior DJ with Radio Essex and after training and qualifying in engineering he joined the Thames Estuary based station.

John Peel was born on 30 August, 1939. From Heswall, Cheshire, Peel worked for KLIF Dallas in 1964, KOMA in Oklahoma followed this, and then KMEN in San Bernardino. He worked for Radio London in 1967 and joined Radio One in October of the same year. He was a compere of *Top Gear* and was then given Wednesday's *Night Ride*. In 1969 he began a regular Wednesday night hour show from 8.15 to 9.15 *pm*.

Bill Perry. Harrisburg, Pennsylvania-born Perry was educated at a number of American Universities and later broadcast for a handful of radio stations. He joined Radio England in pirate ship days.

Denny Piercy. Born in Reading, Berkshire, Piercy worked with singer Dickie Valentine as a double act. Later he became a top music compere and presented

Parade Of The Pops for the BBC Light Programme.

Tony Prince, born Oldham, 1946, became one of the best known DJs of popular music history. He was once in a Manchester group called The Jasons, had a job in television with TWW (Bristol), appearing on *Discs-A-Go-Go*. He joined Caroline (North) in 1965. Later he was to find fame with Luxembourg. He termed himself 'your Royal ruler'.

Mike Raven began with the BBC and was back with Aunty once pirate ship days were doomed. While a jock with the new sea-based ships, Raven worked with Radio Atlanta – later known as Caroline (South) – Radio King and then 390. He also worked for Luxembourg. Raven's speciality was Rhythm and Blues and it was this speciality that interested Radio One. Raven was photographed in the station's first line-up and initially he had a half-hour show at 7.00 *pm*. In 1968 his show was first doubled in length and then trebled in the Autumn, to 90 minutes. Raven was born in 1924.

David Rider was a studio manager at the BBC between 1963 and 1968 and became involved with many of the top shows. Between 1966 and 1968 he was DJ for a weekly pop show for the European English Service of the BBC. When the new network opened in 1967 he had a three month run presenting *Midday Spin*. In 1968 he became a freelance, with much work for the BBC lying ahead especially in the next decade.

Mark Roman worked for Radio London and was discovered by the station after hearing and seeing him working at Wimbledon Palais. On 'Big L' he presented the 6 *pm* to 9 *pm* show *Roman Empire*. For a while he broadcast the Saturday 2.00 to 4.00 *pm* spot on BBC Radio One. Roman comes from London.

Rosko. Born Michael Pasternak, son of famed film man

Joe Pasternak he worked in commercials, for US Navy radio, Radio Europe and KCVA before eventually signing with Caroline (South). He joined BBC Radio One and soon established himself as one of the zaniest, most exciting DJs ever to grace any pop station or network, with an enormous following from fans and DJs alike.

Norman St John, Australian, broadcast for Radio London. Just prior to this, he had worked as an entertainer.

Jimmy Savile. Leeds-born Savile broadcast a variety of programmes for Luxembourg including *The Teen And Twenty Disc Club* on Wednesdays, and *Guys, Gals and Groups* on Saturdays. He had begun by presenting the *Warner Bros Record Show*. During his Luxembourg period Savile sported long hair – at one time two-tone black and white – wore outlandish clothes to go with his zany actions, ran an £8,000 Rolls, an E-type Jaguar, a three wheel bubble car and a white convertible, had a full-time chauffeur and was reputedly the highest-paid DJ in the land, with estimated earnings of £20,000. Savile regularly topped pop-paper polls and had an hour long TV programme that concentrated on his life. Not surprisingly he was eventually an addition to the Radio One Roster, though not until 2 June, 1968, when he began his long-running *Savile's Travels*. On 29 September he launched into another major show, *Speakeasy*, a mixture of chat with guests and studio audience, plus musical items, something new for radio of the time. Another of his shows was *The Double Top Ten*. Savile was on his way to becoming a British institution.

Roger Scott was a DJ with Radio Essex, who in the next decade and after found considerable DJ fame, even without (surprisingly) finding himself on the national airwaves with Radio One. He was born in North London.

Norman Shaw broadcast with Manx Radio from

Douglas, Isle of Man.

David Sinclair. Motoring enthusiast Sinclair was a DJ with Radio Essex. He was born in 1942.

Keith Skues was born in Timperley, Altrincham in 1939. He worked in insurance before finding himself a radio career with BFBS in Cologne, Nairobi and Aden. He joined Radio London and later BBC Radio One. He presented the important and influential *Saturday Club* that ran for two hours on a Saturday morning and was a continuation of the popular long-running show from Light Programme days. Skues was part of a DJ roster, presenting both *Family Choice* (which had replaced *Housewives Choice*) and *What's New*.

Jerry Smithwick worked for WMTM in Moultrie, US and Gainsville, Georgia's WDUN, before Army service and then joined Radio England. He found notice for his enthusiasm and skill for drag racing.

Bob Spencer worked with Radio City before Radio Scotland, for whom he was the senior DJ.

Bob Stewart was born in Liverpool. He worked in Canada where he attained his famous mid-Atlantic accent He worked for Caroline (North) and with his good looks he became one of the pirate ship's pin-ups.

Ed Stewart worked with Radio Hong Kong, the Government station, Rediffusion before Radio London. He became known as 'Stewpot' and, at the time, for his enormous output in shows. He worked for Radio London from 1965 and joined Radio One when it began in 1967. He soon achieved an enormous audience for *Junior Choice* with TV appearances following, including *Crackerjack* and *Top Of The Pops*. Stewart was born in Devon, 1941.

Dennis Straney, a former Radio City jock, ran the

Dennis 'The Menace' show for 270. He hailed from Australia.

David Symonds. Oxford-born Symonds was an announcer when the call to present pop programmes arrived, and soon he was riding high in the popularity stakes. Prior to his freelance days in 1967, Symonds had presented *Easy Beat* (BBC) on Sunday mornings where he built up a considerable audience. From time to time, he also fronted *Newly Pressed* and *Breakfast Special*. On Radio One he had a daily weekday evening show and made appearances on *Top Of The Pops*.

Leon Tippler was born in Kidderminster in 1943. He worked with Radio City prior to joining 270. Tippler showed exquisite taste with his love for French girl singer Françoise Hardy.

Dave Lee Travis was born in Buxton, near Manchester. He became known as 'DLT' and the 'hairy monster'. Early in his career he ran a one-man hit travelling pop show, toured as support Stateside to fellow Northerners *Herman and the Hermits*, and eventually joined Caroline (South). He joined BBC Radio One and in the station's first year was one of the presenters of *Pick Of What's New*. He soon became, and would remain in the next two decades, one of the station's most popular figures.

Brian Tylney was born on 17 March, 1949. Tylney, from Chigwell, Essex, was once resident DJ at Ilford's Mecca Ballroom. He worked for pirate Britain Radio and also broadcast for Radio England.

Tommy Vance. Oxford-born Vance emigrated to Canada while in his teens and worked for several Canadian and US stations, including KHJ in Los Angeles. He returned to Britain in 1965 and worked as a freelance until landing a post with Luxembourg, then residing in the Duchy. Vance eventually joined Radio One. He was one of the DJ roster utilised for the popular *Top Gear* show and with John Peel became a regular presenter for a short period.

Johnny Walker, from Birmingham, was born in 1945 and educated at Solihull Public School. He became one of the best loved and respected DJs. Walker worked for Britain Radio, Radio England and BBC Radio One. For the latter he began broadcasting in April 1969 with a Saturday show between 2.00 and 3.55 *pm*.

Ken Walton's voice was distinctive and his rapid delivery, with utmost clarity, ensured that he was one of the more noticeable DJs. He was heard on Radio Luxembourg and also carved out a career commentating on wrestling.

Miranda Ward, real name Miranda Kirby, was the first girl reporter for Radio One and was heard on the Saturday evening show presented by Johnny Moran entitled *Scene And Heard*. She left Radio One at the outset of 1968 and became London Correspondent for the American Broadcasting Corporation.

Don Wardell became Luxembourg's senior announcer. He was from Birmingham, born 1940. Prior to Luxembourg he worked with BFBS, with Birmingham Hospital's Broadcasting Network and as an entertainments officer for Fullham Council, London before he became a daily voice from the Duchy.

Bob Wayne was better known as Boom Boom Brannigan and a DJ with Radio England and Britain Radio. He came from the Welsh sounding area of Bryn Mawr in Pennsylvania, USA and Stateside was a DJ for several broadcasting stations.

Mark West broadcast with Radio Essex as a teenager and had his home roots in the county.

Stephen West 1942, Surrey-born West had a variety of jobs, which included working for Decca and in a record shop, before becoming a DJ with 390. He became Head of Library and Planning of Programmes at the station.

Dwight Emerson Whylie. Kingston, Jamaica-born Whylie joined the BBC in July 1965. Previously he had been with Radio Jamaica and the Jamaican Broadcasting Corporation. He became a regular presenter of *Night Ride* on Sundays, on BBC Radios One and Two.

Wally Whyton is the Beeb's folk and country expert, with regular programmes first for the Light Programme and then for Radios One and Two when the new networks began operations from 1967 onwards. Whyton has also broadcast extensively for BFBS and, apart from presenting and reviewing country and folk material, he is a performer in his own right and was once part of minor hit skiffle group The Vipers.

Tony Windsor became one of the best known and loved of the pirate DJs. Known as T 'The Knees' Windsor, he was recognised by the way he said 'Hello', a word mannerism later adopted by Tony Blackburn. He was an Australian with a 'gravel sounding' voice and a style that was unique amidst the verbalising of DJs who adopted an American twang. Windsor was senior DJ with Radio London and, sadly, various personal problems contributed to his never achieving the national fame he ought to have found with, say, Radio One.

Terry Wogan hailed from Dublin, and for Radio Eirean covered most topics and was most things from documentary presenter to pop DJ. In the Sixties he introduced BBC programmes *Roundabout*, *Midday Spin* and inevitably *Housewives Choice*. In 1967 and 1968 he flew to Britain each Wednesday and became one of the team which presented the nightly *Late Night Extra*. He holidayreliefed for Jimmy Young and, in 1969, he was given a regular spot in a time slot vacated by Dave Cash. He was a major star in the making and while Young sponsored the art of cooking Wogan became associated from 1969 with the slogan *Fight The Flab*, as his show included a daily exercise for those who thought they could benefit.

Bruce Wyndham was born in Hove, Sussex. Wyndham was one of a legendary team of BBC announcers and presenters, with his first broadcasting work for Overseas Service. During the previous decade he compered many of the Light Programme's best-loved entertainment shows and this continued into the Sixties. He was associated in latter times with shows like *Music Through Midnight*, *Breakfast Special* and *Night Ride*.

Jimmy Young was from Cinderford, Gloucestershire whose early radio openings were due to his skill as a singer, and he eventually achieved major chart success. He had four Top 10 hits and between 1953 and 1957 ten charting records. Young's DJ work began in 1960 when he presented *Housewives Choice* for a fortnight and soon he was heard on both the BBC and Luxembourg. When Radio One began, Young was prominent in the early schedules which saw Radio One and Two combine for certain periods during the day. He came on the air at 9.55 and cultivated a series of catchphrases including 'MMMMFs' (translated as 'many millions of mid-morning friends'), conducted phone-interviews with listeners, gave out cookery recipes that spawned four high selling books, sang songs and played popular music. Young remained associated with Radio One until One and Two parted company in 1973.

Hal Yorke spent a brief period with the BBC before enlisting with pirate ship 270 as studio manager. He was born in Yorkshire and like many jocks of the time he was over 6ft tall.

Television Pop

Although the television pop output of the 1960s in the UK was limited when compared with that of the Seventies, and meagre when contrasted with the present decade (especially since the advent of Channel Four) there were a number of influential programmes.

Juke Box Jury was one. The show had a chairperson in David Jacobs, and a number of panellists. Jacobs was one of Britain's foremost disc-jockeys. Producer Bill Cotton Jr, said, 'He has a superb knowledge of his job. He never exceeds what he is required to do, and on the other hand he never falls short. He's always there doing the right thing at the right time.' Cotton also said that on *Juke Box Jury* Jacob's style was a veritable 'Rock of Gibraltar'. It was a view shared by BBC radio producer Derek Chinnery (now Controller of Radio One) who called it his 'unflappability'.

The panellists comprised DJs, pop stars and people from the world of entertainment. A reasonable snatch of a new release was played and the team asked to comment on whether the record would be a 'hit' or 'miss'. From time to time an artist whose record was played and commented upon would be present and hidden from the panel. When the critics had done their piece the artist appeared and met either the panel's pleasure or embarrassment.

The show was screened early Saturday evenings and drew a large audience. The show was far more successful for Jacob than one he chaired in the Fifties, for in 1954 BBC TV came up with a panel game series *Music, Music, Music*, which failed on its first showing.

JBJ was first seen on 1 June, 1959 but obviously became established in the Sixties. The first panel comprised Susan Stranks, Gary Miller, Pete Murray and Alma Cogan. Murray became a regular as did DJ Alan Freeman, Bunny Lewis and Eric Syke. Teenagers were few and far between on the show though Jacobs at the time said the best personality teenager they had featured was 16-year-old Jane Asher. *JBJ* was a show for all the family.

The Fifties had seen *6.5 Special* and, between June 1958 and May 1959, the extremely popular half-hour show *Oh Boy!* Jack Good, the producer, has said, 'Oh Boy! was the only rock 'n' roll show there was. Radio hated rock 'n' roll until Brian Matthew (*Saturday Club* – BBC Light Programme) came along and fiddled with it a bit. So we had a tremendous impact.'

And there were other pop shows – mostly short-lived and of little lasting significance – during the late 1950s and early 1960s, but between 1963 and 1966 there was a major pop show, *Ready Steady Go*. It focused on the hits of the day, presented the stars, and widened out into dealing with general clothing fashion for teens and young twenties, hairstyles, and shoes. It even utilised current youth jargon and invented its own terms that soon became common parlance.

Ready Steady Go was presented by the urbane, smart, articulate, genial Keith Fordyce and given 'street' level creedence by employing the captivating Cathy McGowan. The show caught the Mod era of youth beginning to realise its own importance, if only to comprehend that it need not be taken, bought and sold by the ever-rolling, ever enlarging pop consumer industry. The groups themselves were making 'their' music and not being pale copies of American pop heroes. Some would say the show wasn't about music, but that music was the major ingredient in a show that reflected a life-style some teenagers lived and others fancied from afar.

The idea for *Ready Steady Go* came from a BBC programme *Pop Inn*. Elkan Allen, head of Rediffusion's Light Entertainment was discussing the BBC radio show with someone at the 1963 Montreaux Festival. He thought it would be the basis of a really good television show. Rediffusion went ahead, and originally the show was a series of film clips linked together by pop music. Later the clips were discarded, the music stayed and teenage life permeated the proceedings with 19-year-old Cathy telling of lacy stockings, thick chunky-heeled shoes and corduroy, Anello and Davide boots, epaulettes and double-breasted jackets and caps, as well as the fortunes and foibles of pop stars. Cathy once told her audience, 'I've been to Paris and we've overtaken them. They always used to be ahead of us in fashions – now we're the leaders. This country's young people are much more fashion-conscious than elsewhere in Europe.'

For teenagers the show was compulsory viewing. It was not found interesting by many adults, whereas the same cannot be said of a current show like *Top Of The Pops* which has something for everyone in the family.

Top Of The Pops was the 'big' show as far as BBC output was concerned, at least in aiming for a mass audience when utilising pop charts and artists with hits. The central core of the programme – to reflect the best-selling singles – has remained sacrosanct. The setting and the people have changed with the times but outside of a few experiments, like having an album spot with an artist performing several numbers, it is still a show born in the 1960s that has outgrown teenage years.

The only other TV pop show that retains some memory for people is *Thank Your Lucky Stars*.

But there were musical shows. The standard format here being a known singer with a show based around his or her singing, with guests; or else a comedian who had on a hit artist or two to perform their latest release. At the outset of the decade the major, 'singer programme' for showcasing major US names rarely seen here was *The Perry Como Show – Music Hall*. Como's US show ran for ten years, met a schedule of 33 shows a year, and had a viewing audience of 15 countries outside of the States. The BBC began screening it in 1958 and co-inciding with its showing came a mighty boost in Como's disc sales.

It represented one of the first instances of television exposure boosting an artist's career. Como presented the expected MOR singers whose roots lay in the 1950s and further back, but he also presented teen favourites such as Connie Francis, Frankie Avalon, Fabian, Bobby Rydell, the Everly Brothers and Paul Anka.

In 1966 the BBC bought from the States a television series based around the day-to-day adventures of a created pop group The Monkees. The four Monkees were Micky Dolenz (21), David Jones (20), Mike Nesmith (22) and Peter Tork (22). They were described as, 'harmless, happy, hopeful, humorous, home-made to an expensive "Do-it-Yourself-Group-Kit".' Stateside the show received enormous promotional push but Derek Taylor told leading teen magazine *Rave* in late 1966, 'I don't recall any TV series reaping so substantial and haphazard a harvest of contempt before anyone had seen it, heard the music, read the script or evaluated the personnel. We were all in there, at the mass preview, muttering curses, fingers crossed for failure. Lo and behold, It succeeded!'

While British fans waited for the Stones to make a film, or the Beatles their third, *The Monkees* programme arrived on the last Saturday of 1966. The show lasted half-an-hour. Jones, an Englishman from Manchester, flew over to generate media interest and told of how, with their films, The Monkees had achieved an enormous following Stateside.

'After the fourth Monkees film we'd really worked out a comedy style and had confidence. We were used to working with each other and were able to do weird things. During the series we get involved in some crazy adventures – capturing bank robbers, getting mixed up with the Mafia. Anything goes. Sort of Marx Brothers approach.'

And with the action there came the songs and The Monkees enjoyed a run of British chart success.

Record Mirror's critic David Griffiths thought if the first show was typical – then it seemed a trifle old-fashioned, as though Hollywood had caught up with Goon humour and the sort of 'TV commercial' techniques used by Dick Lester in his Beatles pictures.

The Monkees became necessary television food for thousands of British teenagers, who also bought myriads of accompanying Monkees pop paraphernalia that came from a variety of sources.

In the 1960s these were 'the' TV pop shows:

1 *Thank Your Lucky Stars* (ITV).
2 *Ready, Steady, Go!* Miming ceased in 1965, Cathy McGowan became the main presenter. Keith Fordyce and Michael Aldred faded.
3 *Top of the Pops* (BBC). This began the first week of 1964.
4 *The Monkees* (BBC).
5 *Juke Box Jury* (BBC).

Other less remembered shows included.

Five O'Clock Rendevous (originally, *Tuesday Rendevous*). 1963.
A Swinging' Time 1963. With Rolf Harris, music being one ingredient.
Gadzooks! It's All Happening, became *Gadzooks! It's The In Crowd, became just plain Gadzooks!*
Stramash! 1965. An attempt to capture pop à la Glasgow.
A Whole Scene Going. 1966. Incorporated various elements of teen culture.
How It Is. Presented by Tony Palmer.
Good Evening. With Jonathan King, a chat show.
Dee Time. With Simon Dee, chat show, musical personalities.
Colour Me Pop. A BBC show which reflected the heavier element seeping into the music scene. 1968.
Lucky Stars. A Southern TV programme, aimed at the family, which made a point of saying that long-haired artists would not be booked.

Other shows include *Anarchy & Soul*, *New Release*, *Pop The Question*, *Five O'Clock Club*, *Magpie*, *Sound & Picture City*.

A to Z of Books

This A to Z concerns itself with rock and pop music books which have been published (in most cases) in the UK. Where the book is only obtainable in the US special mention is made, although it should be noted that specialist book shops in major cities often stock American publications. It's an almost impossible task to keep track of each and every publication, since many are issued by small book concerns and never find their way into main retail outlets, as they often have localised distribution and sale. However, it is hoped this list contains most publications that concern themselves with the Sixties decade. In some instances notes are given after the title but these should be taken at most as a rough guide. It should be noted that some books listed were published in the Sixties and these may no longer be available from shops, so try the library.

Alex, Peter, *Who's Who In Pop Radio*, Four Square Books, London, 1966. Interesting pirate ship guide.

Barnes, Richard, *The Who: Maximum R&B*, Eel Pie, London, 1982. Visual history of the great group.

Beide, Goldie, *Beatles A to Z*. Eyre Methuen, London, 1981.

Belz, Carl, *Story of Rock*, Oxford University Press, Oxford, 1972. This traces the various progressions in rock music during the Sixties.

Boris, Duane, Grail, *The Rolling Stones: Paroles Et Images*, Editions Glenat, 1976. Lyrics and pictures.

Carr, Roy, *The Rolling Stones: An Illustrated Record*, New English Library, London, 1977. More fine stuff from Carr.

Carr, Roy and Farren, Mick, *Elvis. The Complete Illustrated Record*, Eel Pie, London, 1982.

Carr, Roy and Tyler, Tony, *The Beatles: An Illustrated Record*, New English Library, London, 1981. Great book.

Castleman, Harry Podrazik, *The Beatles Again?*, Ann

Arbor, Pierian, 1977.

Charone, Barbara, *Keith Richard*. Futura, London, 1979. Gripping stuff.

Christgau, Robert, *Any Old Way You Choose It*, Penguin, London, 1973. It runs into the Seventies and only commences with the Sixties from 1967.

Cohn, Nik, *Pop From The Beginning*, Weidenfeld and Nicolson, London, 1969.

Davies, Hunter, *The Beatles: The Authorised Biography*, Panther, London, 1979.

Dellar, Fred, *NME Guide To Rock Cinema*, Hamlyn, London, 1981. Sixties only part of masterful Dellar coverage.

DiLello, Richard, *The Longest Cocktail Party*, Charisma, London, 1972.

Doncaster, Pat and Jasper, Tony, *Cliff*, Sidgwick and Jackson, London, 1981. Includes extensive facturama.

Eisen, Jonathan (editor), *Age Of Rock: Sounds Of The American Cultural Revolution*, Random House, New York, 1969.

Frame, Pete, *Rock Family Trees*, Omnibus, London, 1980. Traces many current figures back to their roots in 1960s and even beyond. Marvellous.

Gillet, Charlie, *Making Tracks*, Panther, St Albans, 1975. Tells the story of Atlantic Records.

Gillet, Charlie (edited), *Rock File*, various Volumes, New English Library, London, others Panther, London. If you ever wondered where the idea for the indispensable volume series *The Guinness Hit Singles* came from then here it is. Also some good essays that include reflections on Sixties decade.

Gillet, Charlie, *Sound of the City: The Rise of Rock And Roll*, Souvenir Press, London, 1971. Some say this or *Mystery Train* by Greil Marcus is the best rock book, certainly authoritative study of rock music's development.

Gray, Michael, *Song And Dance Man*, Abacus, London, 1973. Careful balanced portrait of Dylan the lyricist.

Hardy, Phil and Laing, Dave (editors), *Encyclopedia of Rock Volume 2*, Panther, St Albans, 1976. The Sixties

A to Z of artists, also volumes on Fifties and Seventies.

Harry, Bill, *Merseybeat: The Beginnings of the Beatles*, Omnibus, London, 1977.

Harry, Bill, *Beatles: Who's Who*, Aurum, London, 1984.

Harry, Bill, *The Book Of Lennon*, Aurum, London, 1984.

Harry, Bill, *Paperback Writers: The Beatles Bibliography*, Virgin, London, 1984.

Harry, Bill, *Beatlemania: The Beatles On Screen*, Virgin, 1984.

Harry, Bill, *The Book Of Beatle Lists*, Blandford Press, Poole, 1984.

Hoare, Ian (edited), *The Soul Book*, Eyre Methuen, London, 1975.

Hopkins, Jerry, Marshall Jim, Wolfman Baron, *Festival*, Collier, New York, 1970.

Hopkins, Jerry and Sugerman, Danny, *No One Here Gets Out Alive*, Plexus, London, 1980. Biography of Jim Morrison, huge US seller but hardly so in UK.

Jasper, Tony (edited), *The Top 20, The British Record Charts 1955–1983*, Blandford Press, Poole, 1984. Slight change of title from previous volumes that were published by Futura and Macdonald and Jane.

Jasper, Tony, *Johnny* W H Allen, London, 1983, Mathis in Sixties with extensive facturama.

Jasper, Tony, *The Rolling Stones*, Bounty books, London, 1984. Revised version of 1976-published volume by Octopus.

Jasper, Tony, *Silver Cliff*, Sidgwick and Jackson, London, 1983. Cliff Richard, year by year through decade. See also *Cliff* under Doncaster but joint authorship with Jasper.

Jasper, Tony and Savile, Jimmy, *Nostalgia Book Of Hit Singles*, Muller, London, 1982.

Jasper, Tony, *Rock Mastermind*, Blandford Press, Poole, 1983. Extensive and testing 'quizzes' on Sixties music world and other decades.

Jenkinson, Philip and Warner, Alan, *Celluloid Rock*, Lorrimer, 1974. Only partly concerned with the Sixties. Recommended.

Laing, Dave, *Sounds of Our Time*, Sheed and Ward,

London, 1969. Laing traces late 1960s rock.

Leaf, David, *The Beach Boys And The Californian Myth*, Grosset and Dunlap, New York, 1979.

Lichter, Paul, *Elvis: The Boy Who Dared To Rock*, Sphere, London, 1980.

Logan, Nick and Woffiden, Bob (editors), *Illustrated New Musical Express Encyclopedia Of Rock*, London, 1977. Fine guide of music scene that of course goes before and after Sixties.

McGregor, Craig (edited), *Bob Dylan: A Retrospect*, Picador, London, 1975. Abridged from the 1972-published edition by William Morrow, USA.

Marchbank, Pete, *Illustrated Rock Almanac*, Paddington Press, London, 1977. Paddington Press no longer exist.

Marcus, Greil, *Mystery Train*, Omnibus, London, 1978. Images of America as seen in rock 'n' roll with scope extending beyond the Sixties.

Marks, J, *Mick Jagger*, Studio Vista, London, 1971.

May, Chris and Phillips Tim, *British Beat*, Socion, London, no date given.

Mellers, Wilfred, *Twilight of the Gods: The Beatles In Retrospect*, Faber, London, 1976.

Millar, Bill, *The Drifters*, Studio Vista, London, 1971.

Miller, Jim (editor), *Rolling Stone Illustrated History of Rock 'n' Roll*, Pan, London, 1981.

Miller, William Robert, *The Christian Encounters the World of Pop And Jazz*, Concordia, St Louis, USA, 1965. Only available Stateside.

Morse, David, *Motown*, Studio Vista, London, 1971.

Norman, Philip, *Shout! The True Story of the Beatles*, Elm Tree Books, London, 1981.

Norman, Philip, *The Stones*, Elm Tree Books, London, 1984.

Palmer, Tony, *All You Need Is Love*, Futura, London 1977. Only partially concerned with the Sixties decade.

Preiss, Bryon, *Beach Boys: The Authorised Biography*, Ballentine, New York, 1979. US published.

Rice, Tim, and others, *The Guiness Book Of British Hit Albums*, Guinness, London, 1983. Covers artists and their hit singles of the decade but only in same tables as other decades from the Fifties.

Rogan, John, *Timeless Flight: The Definitive Biography of the Byrds*, Scorpion Publications, London, 1980.

Roxon, Lilian (edited), *Rock Encyclopedia*, Angus and Robertson, London, 1980. Some people make this their favourite guide to US scene, note date here is deceptive for book material ends in early Seventies.

Sanford, Jeremy and Red, Ron, *Tomorrow's People*, Jerome, London/New York, 1974. British festival-itis.

Scaduto, Antony, *Bob Dylan*, Abacus, London, 1972. My personal favourite on Dylan and much better than the writer's book on the Stones.

Scaduto, Antony, *Mick Jagger*, Mayflower, St Albans, 1975.

Skues, Keith, *Radio Onederland: The Story of Radio One*, Landmark, Lavenham, 1968. Excellent guide to Radio in the Sixties until end of 1967.

Somma, Robert (edited), *No One Waved Goodbye*, Charisma, London, 1973. Various known writers give the casualty report on rock and roll with Brian Jones and Brian Epstein from the Sixties.

Spitz, Robert Stephen, *Barefoot In Babylon: The Creation Of The Woodstock Music Festival 1969*, Viking, 1979.

Taylor, Derek, *As Time Goes By*, Abacus, London, 1974. Beatle press agent with lovingly and amusingly narrated memories.

Torgoff, Martin, *The Complete Elvis*, Sidgwick and Jackson, London, 1982.

Turner, Steve and Davis, John, *Decade of the Who: An Authorised History In Music, Paintings, Words and Photographs*, Elm Tree Books, London, 1977.

Wallraf, Rainer and Plehn, Heinz, *Elvis Presley: An Illustrated Biography*, Omnibus, London, 1979.

Whitburn, Joel, *The Billboard Book of US Top 40 Hits*, Guinness, Enfield, 1983. US version (UK published) with slightly different lay-out to UK Guinness; invaluable.

Williams, Richard, *The Sound of Phil Spector: Out Of His Head*, Abacus, London, 1972.

Films of the Decade

Pop films came out with a great rush during the first half of the Sixties, with not a great deal to interest the serious film buff but plenty for the artist's fans. Generally speaking these films were a vehicle for the artist or group to sing some songs that appeared on an album with everyone making some money. In some cases 'making money' seemed the most obvious intent. The second half of the decade suggested 'pop' films could have some substance and be of general interest to the filmgoer. This is an A to Z of films from the 1960s. More detailed knowledge can be obtained from the two books mentioned under the *Media* section of the Book listing.

Although this listing is long it does not include all 1960s films. For instance, those with unknown music-writers or stars are left out.

Adventures of the Son of Exploding Sausage (David Korr) 1969. A vehicle for the humour of Viv Stanshall and the Bonzos.

Alice's Resturant (Arthur Penn) 1969. The film is based on Arlo's epic song of the same title. Pete Seeger appears.

American Music – From Folk To Jazz And Pop (Stephen Fleishman) 1969. As it says, interesting footage.

Amougies Music Power (Jérome Lapérousaz and Jean Noël Roy) 1969. Whole pile of popular rock figures make an appearance in this French derived film and they include Pretty Things, Zappa, Chicago, Nice, Beefheart and Soft Machine.

Angels from Hell (Bruce Kessler) 1968. Music in the film comes from Peanut Butter Conspiracy.

Banjoman (Richard G Abrhamson and Michael C Varhol) 1977. This was intended as a tribute to legendary Earl Scruggs of banjo fame.

A bevy of folk and folk-rock people sing a song or two including Joan Baez, The Byrds, Jack Elliott and Bobby McGee. But little can be said that is praise.

Beach Ball USA (Lennie Weinrib) 1964. Fun people provide the background music for college fun jinks. The Walker Brothers, Jerry Lee Lewis, Supremes, Righteous Brothers and The Four Seasons are amongst those seen and heard.

Beach Blanket Bingo (William Asher) 1965. US teen pop rage Frankie Avalon stars and sings.

Beach Party (William Asher) 1963. Surf tunes and little else save for pictures of how lucky West Coast Americans are – provided they're rich.

Beat Girl (Wild for Kicks) (Edmond T Grenville) 1960. For pop fans it was a 'must' to see Adam Faith, while others could dwell on the beauty of Shirley Ann Field. Film buffs would not be there.

Be Glad For The Song Has No Ending (Peter Neal) 1969. A rather liked film about one of the most interesting musical outfits of the decade, The Incredible String Band.

The Big TNT Show (Larry Peerce) 1966. As the title suggests a great many things happen, and certainly the film presents a mass of stars, mainly of pop and folk-rock.

Bikini Beach (William Asher) 1964. More Avalon, more girls and beaches.

Blue Hawaii (Norman Taurog) 1961. Visual heaven for Elvis fans and mildly interesting for others.

Buddy Knox At The 100 Club. (Charlie Gillet) 1969. A fifteen minute mini-featurette on Knox from writer and record company man Gillet.

Bye Bye Birdie (George Sidney) 1963. US teen knock-out Bobby Rydell in an acceptable film.

California Holiday (Norman Taurog) 1966. More Presley and not one of his best, I would have thought.

Catalina Caper (Lee Sholem) 1967. Mary Wells sings the title song and along the way there's Little Richard and the Cascades.

Catch Us If You Can (Having A Wild Weekend) (John Boorman) 1965. Basically a means of letting us see the Dave Clark Five and hearing them. The sub-title is enough to make you doubt. Oddly enough it's not too bad.

Chappaqua (Conrad Rooks) 1967. Fugs and Shankar give the music and the theme centres on the trials, stresses and pointlessness of heroin addiction.

Charlie Is My Darling (Peter Whitehead) 1965. It has a certain genre of its own – the first film footage of The Rolling Stones.

Charro (Charles Marquis Warren) 1969. Elvis and Elvis and Elvis, and not one people remember.

Clambake (Arthur Nadel) 1967. Looking up and casting one's eye around the film world makes me aware of how many films Elvis made and how many of those, like this, we never recall. But Elvis die-hards think differently, presumably.

Climb Up The Wall (Michael Winner) 1960. The film centres around Jack Jackson, the top-notch DJ before his time. Several early pop faces sing, including Mike Preston, Craig Douglas and a lady often seen with Cliff, Cherry Wainer.

C'Mon Let's Live A Little (David Butler) 1967. US teen heart-throb Bobby Vee sings and there's also Jackie De Shannon.

College Confidential (Albert Zugsmith) 1960. Conway Twitty provides some of the music.

The Committee (Peter Sykes) 1968. Pink Floyd provide the soundtrack and there's an appearance by late 1960s cult people, The Crazy World Of Arthur Brown. The film stars Paul Jones.

Cream Last Concert (Tony Palmer) 1969. The famous concert of July 1969, enjoyable but oh for more music and less chat.

Crystal Voyager (George Greenough) 1974. Pink Floyd contribute *Echoes*.

Cuckoo Patrol (Duncan Wood) 1965. the title is enough and align that with Freddie and the Dreamers and you can smell something is wrong.

Dateline Diamonds (Jeremy Summers) 1965. Small Faces appear in concert, Kiki Dee, Everett, and The Chantells are around but no-one really remembers the film too well.
A Degree Of Murder (Mord und Totschlag) (Volker Schondorff) 1966. Brian Jones wrote the score.
Disk-O-Tek Holiday (not known) 1966. Chiffons, Freddie Cannon and The Vagrants sing along the way.
Don't Knock The Twist (Oscar Rudolph) 1962. This followed *Twist Around The Clock* and naturally Chubby is on hand, so too are Gene Chandler and others.
Don't Look Back (D A Pennebaker) 1965. Frequently shown, it follows Dylan's tour of England, 1965. Joan Baez is around, so also Donovan.
Double Trouble (Norman Taurog) 1967. More of Elvis.

Easy Rider (Dennis Hopper) 1969. Late 1960s atmosphere beautifully captured, always loved this, with a soundtrack of star names to accompany the visuals.
Everyday's A Holiday (Seaside Swingers) (James Hill) 1965. Built around John Leyton, one-time heart throb.
Experience (Peter Neal) 1969. Anything on Hendrix is a must and this is fairly interesting.

Ferry Cross The Mersey (Jeremy Summers) 1965. Gerry and assortment of Merseyside singers vocalise.
Festival (Murray Lerner) 1967. 1963–66 Newport Folk Festival memories, with many famous people singing, including Dylan, Judy Collins, Baez, etc.
Finders Keepers (Sidney Hayers) 1966. Cliff and The Shadows in action.
Flaming Star (Don Siegel) 1960. An Elvis triumph.
Frankie And Johnny (Fred de Cordova) 1966. Elvis again.
Fugs (Edward English) 1966. It features cultist Fugs.

G I Blues (Norman Taurog) 1960. That man Elvis again, in an OK movie.
Gather No Moss (Steve Binder) 1964. Big names of the

early 1960s in concert including Chuck Berry, Supremes, Lesley Gore.

Get Yourself A College Girl (The Swingin' Set) (Sidney Miller) 1964. Lots of music from lotsa people, including Animals, Dave Clark Five, Freddie Bell.

The Ghost Goes Gear (Hugh Chadwick) 1966. Few Takers for a film that has Spencer Davis Group.

The Girl Can't Help It (Frank Tashlin) 1965. Bevy of pop stars to sing and Jayne Mansfield to look at.

Girls! Girls! Girls! (Norman Taurog) 1962. Elvis with a bag of songs and pretty girls.

Girl Happy (Boris Sagal) 1965. Another of Elvis's films.

Cirl On A Motorcycle (Naked Under Leather) (Jack Cardiff) 1968. With Marianne in early full bloom little else is remembered.

The Girls On The Beach (William Witney) 1965. Crickets, Lesley Gore, Beatles and others provide music.

Gonks Go Beat (Robert Hartford-Davis) 1965. Lulu and the Nashville Teens provide some of the music.

Good Times (William Friedkin) 1966. Sonny and Cher centred movie.

The Graduate (Mike Nichols) 1967. Simon and Garfunkel contribute music for very watchable film.

Harum Scarum (Gene Nelson) 1965. Yes, Elvis, again.

Head (Bob Rafelson) 1968. The Monkees are featured.

Help (Richard Lester) 1965. Beatles and humour and very watchable.

Here We Go Round The Mulberry Bush (Clive Donner) 1967. Spencer Davis Group provide the soundtrack music.

Hey Let's Twist (Greg Garrison) 1960. Joey Dee and the Starlighters provide vocal excitement.

Hold On! (Arthur Lubin) 1966. Many songs and visual action built around Herman's Hermits.

Hootenanny Hoot (Gene Nelson) 1963. Country people with pop overtones play for us including Mr Cash.

How To Stuff A Wild Bikini (William Asher) 1965. Brian Wilson spotted but not with Beach Boys.

I'm an Elephant, Madam (Peter Zadek) 1968. Velvet Underground provide the music.

Invocation Of My Demon Brother (Kenneth Anger) 1969. Shots of the Stones in concert but most of it an occult jamboree.

It Happened At The World's Fair (Norman Taurog) 1963. And again, Elvis.

It's All happening (The Dream Maker) (Don Sharp) 1962. Tommy Steele in major role and among songsters Paul and Barry Ryan.

It's All Over Town (Douglas Hickox) 1964. Hmm, early Dusty Springfield seen, plus other pop acts like Frankie Vaughan.

It's Trad, Dad! (Ring A Ding Rhythm) (Richard Lester) 1962. Helen Shapiro gets star credits with Craig Douglas, seemingly endless stream of songs from well known artists of the time.

I've Gotta Horse (Kenneth Hulme) 1965. Billy Fury stars and sings, and some would rather forget this.

Just For Fun (Gordon Fleming) 1963. Mark Wynter gets a top credit and a huge crowd of US and UK teen pop idols sing so happily and like the Tornadoes, just play.

Just For You (Douglas Hickox) 1964. The Merseybeats, Millie, Peter and Gordon, Band of Angels, among those seen and a-singing; seems rather an excuse to show groups.

Kissin' Cousins (Gene Nelson) 1964. No wonder Elvis couldn't make it to the UK – he was always making films.

Last Summer Won't Happen (Peter Gessner) 1969. Procol Harum and Country Joe supply the music.

The Legend Of Bo Diddley (Gary Sherman, Peter Weiner) 1966. No need to say who this is about.

Live A Little, Love A Little (Norman Taurog) 1968. It stars an Elvis Presley.

The Lively Set (Jack Arnold) 1964. US college kids and pop music.

Living It Up (Sing And Swing). Gene Vincent is one of those who sings, as are The Outlaws.

The Lone Ranger (Richard Stanley) 1968. A short prize-winning film with music from Pete Townshend.

Lonely Boy (Wolf Koenig) 1962. Centres solidly on Paul Anka, songs and music.

Love And Kisses (Ozzie Nelson) 1965. Rick Nelson takes the credits and Dad Produces.

Midnight Cowboy (John Schlesinger) 1969. The film with *Everybody's Talkin* and other music.

Mix Me A Person (Leslie Norman) 1962. Stars Adam Faith. He sings the title theme.

Mondo Daytona (Weekend Rebellion) (Frank Willard) 1968. Another 'brave' US title that promises. Here you get the life-style of holidaying students. The Tams, Billy Joe Royal, The Swinging Medallions head the music roster.

Monterey Pop (D A Pennabaker) 1969. Great visuals, great songs, lovely. Many famous names.

More (Barbet Schroeder) 1969. Floyd provide some of the music.

Muscle Beach Party (William Asher) 1964. Frankie Avalon is in the credits, Little Stevie Wonder is around, lots of ordinary songs.

Nothing But A Man (Michael Roemer) 1963. Motown goodies sing the soundtrack and include Mary Wells, Stevie, Miracles, Martha and the Vandellas.

One Plus One (Sympathy for the Devil) Jean-Luc Goddard) 1969. Must for Stones fans, most certainly.

Otley (Dick Clement) 1968. Amusing film with music from people like The Herd and Don Partridge.

Out Of Sight (Lennie Weinrib) 1966. The Turtles provide the interest for music fans, seen and heard.

Paradise – Hawaiian Style (Michael Moore) 1966. More and more Elvis. Fans would say, 'Why ask for anything else?' *Performance* (Nicolas Roeg and Donald Cammell) 1968. Jagger's film of the decade, James Fox is around in fine style. Jagger sings, so does Randy Newman, Merry Clayton and Buffy Saint-Marie.

Petulia (Richard Lester) 1968. US West Coast and capturing mid-1960s innocence. Music from Big Brother and the Holding Company plus Grateful Dead.

Play It Cool (Michael Winner) 1962. Billy Fury is in the main credits list. Songs from others as well including Fenton alias Alvin Stardust, Helen Shapiro and Jimmy Crawford.

Pop Down (Fred Marshall) 1968. Late Sixties British pop culture, Brian Augur and Julie Driscoll amongst the music people.

Pop Gear (Go-Go Mania) (Frederick Goode) 1965. Loads of chart pop people of the time run through their hits with Jimmy Savile playing the introductions.

Privilege (Peter Watkins) 1967. Paul Jones stars and sings in a film that keeps cropping up.

Psych-Out (Richard Rush) 1968. Late 1960s in San Francisco and Haight Ashbury, some psychedelic groups of the time provide music and visual colour.

Quiet Days In Clichy (Jens Jorgen Thorsen) 1969. Country Joe provides some of the songs.

Revolution (Jack O'Connell) 1969. Another film about Haight Ashbury, hippy temple territory, of late Sixties, lots of the psychedelic heroes of music-land play.

Roustabout (John Rich) 1964. Elvis Presley is in this film and many, many others.

Run With The Wind (Lindsay Shonteff) 1966. Nashville Teens and brief famed Hedgehoppers Anonymous in the music credits.

The Savage Seven (Richard Rush) 1969. The Cream provide a few songs for this biker war gang drama.

Scorpio Rising (Kenneth Anger) 1963. Shortish film packed with pop stars like Little Peggy March, Ricky

Nelson, The Crystals, and The Surfaris.
Ski Party (Alan Raftkin) 1965. An all-time 'thrill' title –
music comes from such divergent heroes as James Brown
and Lesley Gore.
Speedway (Norman Taurog) 1968. And this stars Elvis
Presley.
Stay Away Joe (Peter Tewsbury) 1968. Elvis is in the
credits.
Summer Holiday (Peter Yates) 1963. Cliff, The Shadows
in a pleasant romp on screen and record.
Swingin' Set (Frank Gilpin) 1964. A trio of DJs present
British hit groups from this period and they include the
Four Pennies and Millie.
A Swingin' Summer (Robert Sparr) 1965. Gary Lewis
and the Righteous Brothers sing.

Teenage Millionaire (Lawrence Doheny) 1961. A great
wad of US pop stars of the early Sixties and some who
could look back sing for their party food. The late Jackie
Wilson is one of them.
Tickle Me (Norman Taurog) 1965. This has Elvis
Presley.
Tonite Let's All Make Love In London (Peter Whitehead)
1967. Flower-power 'love' is intended, lots of UK
vaguely pscyhedelic outfits play and there's Floyd, Small
Faces, Burdon, Chris Farlowe.
To Sir, With Love (James Clavell) 1967. General cinema
film, music and songs from Lulu, The Mindbenders.
The Trip (Roger Corman) 1967. Electric Flag provide the
musical background.
Twist Around The Clock (Oscar Rudolph) 1961. Chubby
and friends show us the Twist and sing about it.
Two A Penny (James Collier) 1967. Stars Cliff Richard
acting and singing.
Two Tickets To Paris (Greg Garrison) 1962. And again
it's Joey Dee plus friends of the Twist early Sixties cult.

UK Swings Again (Frank Gilpin) 1964. How do they
think of these titles? Same DJ trio as for *Swinging UK*

present another current UK pop pockage.

Up The Junction (Peter Collinson) 1967. Major film of the time, Manfred Mann provide main music.

Up Tight (Jules Dassin) 1968. Booker T and the MGs dish out very good music.

Velvet Underground And Nico (Andy Warhol) 1966. Title tells the facts, obvious must for their fans.

Viva Las Vegas (George Sidney) 1964. More Elvis.

Voices (Richard Mordaunt) 1968. The Stones pop in from time to time.

What A Crazy World (Michael Carreras) 1963. Joe Brown gets the main notice but Marty Wilde and Susan Maughan also in the credits.

What's Good For The Goose (Menahem Golan) 1969. Pretty Things serve up the musical flavouring.

What's Happening (Albert and David Maysles) 1967. A good insight into how pop stars often have to face dumb interviewers and are supposed to remain sane. Beatles star.

What's Up, Tiger Lily? (Woody Allen, Senkichi Taniguohi) 1966. The Lovin' Spoonful push their film inexperience aside and write the songs.

When The Boys Meet The Girls (Alvin Ganzer) 1965. Various pop artists like Herman's Hermits and Connie Francis sing.

Where The Boys Are (Henry Levin) 1960. Neil Sedaka shoulders the title song and some others.

Wild In The Country (Philip Dunne) 1961. Every alphabetical letter seems to have an Elvis film and this is the one for W.

Wild In The Streets (Barry Shear) 1968. Mann-Weil songs and sung by no-one in particular for British audiences.

Wild On The Beach (Maury Dexter) 1965. Sandy Nelson and Sonny and Cher are the known names amongst others unlikely to find recognition this side of the Atlantic.

Wonderful Life (Sydney J Furie) 1964. Fun for fans, Cliff, The Shadows and others.

Wonderwall (Joe Massot) 1968. George Harrison provided the score.

The World's Greatest Sinner (Timothy Carey) 1962. Zappa is responsible for the music score.

Yellow Submarine (George Dunning) 1969. Under-rated animated feature utilising les Beatles, the latter sing and George Martin is on the music credits.

You Are What You Eat (Barry Feinstein) 1968. Lots of late Sixties groovy groups including Harpers Bizarre.

The Young Ones (Sidney J Furie) 1961. Lots of fresh sounding tunes, Cliff and The Shadows do us proud.

The Swingers (Maury Dexter) 1963. Lots of songs and Gene McDaniels steals the music credits.

You're A Big Boy Now (Francis Ford Coppola) 1967. Sebastian and the Lovin' Spoonful provide songs and performance.

There is no Presley film under Y and Z!

Top People

Any selection of important people and groups from whatever decade or period chosen is open to disagreement, and even more so when the number described is relatively small. After all, it took editors Phil Hardy and Dave Laing of the excellent 1976-published *The Encyclopedia Of Rock, Volume 2*, all of 369 pages to tell of the groups and artists of the 1960s!

However, it would be a sad omission from this volume if some attempt was not made to at least fill in the details of the decade's key people and their groups even if such coverage cannot compete with the overall guide found in the book by Hardy and Laing.

I have taken as a base *Record Mirror's* A to Z guide of the decade's top people as published in January 1970 but I have also utilised my own knowledge and considered other sources.

Joan Baez. Dylan was called the King of folk and his Queen was Joan Baez, with whom he lived for a time. She had a marvellous untrained pure voice and with it went looks that only deserve superlatives. Early in her career she sang traditional folk; some would say she never really 'felt' the music, but others disagree. She joined Dylan in his adoption of electric guitar, recorded many of his songs and took the best from elsewhere. She aligned her music with political and social concerns of the time, supported non-violent peace measures and doubtless antagonised right-wing American political camps. She had occasional single hits but her main forté was in albums and in live performances.

The Beach Boys were one of America's 'greats' of the decade, and also popular in the UK. Their material was written against the backcloth of West Coast America and reflected the affluence of American youth. Four and five part harmonies, use of falsetto and a pushing beat characterised much of their early music. Later they reflected a growth in recording techniques with *Pet Sounds* their major album in this field. The sheer magic of many songs enabled them to cross cultural barriers, although many British fans doubtless fantasised a life-style they hardly knew – surfing, hod-rodding, high school hops, large, gas consuming cars, brown-skinned girls and general fast living.

Beatles. The group of the decade, of all pop times. At first the Quarrymen, then Silver Beatles, finally the name by which everyone knows them. The final line-up was Paul McCartney, John Lennon, George Harrison and Ringo Starr. Starr was the last to join. After being turned down by various companies they signed with EMI and were produced by in-house whizz-kid George Martin. They charted first, somewhat tentatively, with *Love Me Do* in November of 1962. During the decade they became superstars in the States (from 1964) and in the rest of the world. They were awarded the MBE. They made films, founded their own label and cultural clearing house, Apple.

After an initial start, of recording other people's songs, they became their own hit-writing outfit with the compositions of Lennon-McCartney predominating. Other artists recorded Beatle numbers. Whatever they did someone copied, whether in hairstyle, clothes, or spiritual search. By the decade's end tensions bit hard and their demise was a sad but foregone conclusion.

James Brown was Soul Brother No. 1 Stateside. In Britain the R&B fraternity treated him as a great, but in general terms outside of less than a handful of hit records Brown never made great impact: although he had – and the situation remained unchanged in the Seventies – little worry about selling-out a tour.

Chubby Checker, alias a rather uninspiring Ernest Evans, Was the King of the Twist, a dance form which was more popular Stateside than in Britain where new dances take their time to become accepted.

It's said that Checker sold 15 million records by 1965 and he spearheaded Stateside a major release industry in twist music (see section – *Musics of the Decade*).

Ray Coleman edited *Melody Maker*, the music paper that covered pop, jazz, folk, classical and was prima donna when it came to classified ads for 'musicians wanted'. The paper took the music scene seriously and was highly regarded for its extensive coverage.

Cream was the *crème de la crème* of rock outfits, a short-lived but highly successful marriage between guitarist Eric Clapton, drummer Ginger Baker and bass and harmonica player Jack Bruce. Cream helped give rise to the term 'supergroup', which was popular toward the last part of the decade when, in a time of serious musicianship, many 'stars' joined together to create what always seemed 'the' line-up, with none to really last, save for the likes of Led Zeppelin.

Bob Dylan, alias Robert Allen Zimmerman, was a one-time English student at the University of Minnesota whose lyrics and tunes were some of the most original and compelling of the decade.

At first he was part of a new folk movement and became its king, but he assumed a wider mantle once he took up the electric guitar and joined the general rock fraternity. Many musics other than rock permeated even his later material (as exemplified in albums like *John Wesley Harding* and *Nashville Skyline*) and he was heard and followed with almost guru reverence by students worldwide. To many people his song *Like A Rolling Stone* caught the mood of American youth that had during the 1960s known the Berlin Blockade, Cuba and the Vietnam War. Many of Dylan's songs were taken and made hits by people as varied as Manfred Mann and Jimi Hendrix.

Brian Epstein managed the Beatles and was involved with other popular Liverpool bands of the early mid 1960s. Although with little knowledge and experience of the music business he managed to implant British music consciousness amongst music lovers worldwide. Sadly he died before the decade ended (for further details see under *Obituary Notices*).

Georgie Fame was in reality Clive Powell. One of the decade's main blues popularisers, he was the man who married jazz and pop. The latter was clearly shown when he toured as support to Count Basie, lent musical backing to Annie Ross and was much applauded by Blossom Dearie, the American songstress.

Michael Fish was clothing designer to the stars and reached his public exhibitionist peak (or was it Jagger's?) when the Stones lead singer appeared in London's Hyde Park sporting a mini-skirt, in 1969. His dressing of the pop heroes filtered into both general buying consciousness and wants, and he was in-part responsible for the colourful splendour of psychedelia from 1967 onwards.

Aretha Franklin was born in 1942. From a gospel-based family, she became known as the 'Queen of Soul' and, from a beginning that saw her sing alongside many future stars in her father's Detroit Baptist Church, she assumed a status that was solely due to the power and rhythm of her voice. She was a legendary name of the decade.

Jack Good. The late 1950s and early 1960s saw a crop of pop TV shows that were produced by Good and owed much to his enthusiasm and drive for doing something different, rather than merely projecting a public relations show for the record industry. Among his show credits were *6.5 Special*, *Oh Boy*, *Shindig* and *Shazam*.

Andy Gray was editor of the *New Musical Express* and under his editorship the *NME* reached, for then, the enormous circulation figure of 300,000 plus. The paper had a huge impact and fully covered and fed off the British explosion from 1963 onwards. In the 1960s, and subsequent decades, it was 'the' paper for music news under the excellent news editorship of Derek Johnson.

The Hollies. Manchester's Hollies never achieved anywhere near the wild acclaim that greeted the Beatles, yet in their less noisy fashion the group had hit after hit that only bears comparison in total with the Liverpool foursome. For the most part they were a singles band. One of their most famous members was Graham Nash who left in 1967 and eventually found himself part of the renowned Crosby, Stills and Nash, a trio later made into a foursome with the addition of Neil Young.

Howard and Blaikley. Ken Howard and Alan Blaikley enjoyed chart success from the mid-1960s onwards with groups like The Honeycombs, the constant hit outfit Dave Dee, Dozy, Beaky, Mick and Tich and eventually The Herd. They wrote 17 Top 20 singles.

Dick James sang the TV theme *Robin Hood* in 1955, a session produced by later legendary Beatles producer George Martin. When Epstein brought the Beatles to EMI, Martin suggested their music should be published by James who had set up DJM. The publishing house became one of the world's most successful with Elton John a later signing toward the end of the decade.

Peter Jones was writer and eventual editor for *Record Mirror*. *RM* never achieved the high sales its flair and coverage deserved. It was first with the Beatles and Stones, first with colour and giving wide chart coverage. In 1969 the paper was acquired by US music publishing giant Billboard. Later it was bought by Spotlight Publications.

Kinks. The nucleus of this London-based band formed around the two Davies brothers Ray and Dave. During the Sixties they produced a stream of top-rate singles, with the period from 1966 onwards seeing them develop into a clever satirical outfit. The Kinks, in-common with other major bands, utlised the popular 'concept album' – in their case it was (*The Kinks Are*) *The Village Green Preservation Society* in 1968, with *Arthur* (*Or The Decline And Fall Of The British Empire*) a year later.

Alexis Korner has been termed a 'seminal influence' on British R&B. Apart from possessing considerable knowledge of trad jazz, skiffle, blues and soul, Korner was a good guitarist and, throughout this decade and the next, gathered round him numerous musicians who were to become major figures in the rock world. Sadly he died on New Year's Day 1984.

Gordon Mills was manager of Engelbert Humperdinck and Tom Jones, with both artists scoring hit after hit and translating easily into the lucrative American club and cabaret scene.

Mickie Most may have been an artist and achieved one lowly hit in the Sixties but here he is remembered for his production successes with the likes of The Animals, Donovan, Brenda Lee, Lulu, Herman's Hermits and Jeff Beck. Even though greater success lay ahead in the 1970s, he is undoubtedly one of Britain's best-known producers of the Sixties decade. He formed his own company RAK in 1969.

Monkees. Individually the four Monkees hardly deserve the generalised description of top people of the decade nor, come to that, the group itself in so far as others had as many or more hits. But the Monkees qualify on the basis that they fulfilled the dream of most record business people that a successful group can be created. The members were chosen to form The Monkees and so star in a television comedy series that spawned hit pop songs. During 1966 and 1967 The Monkees had innumerable hits both sides of the Atlantic.

Larry Parnes was one of music's backroom boys, better known to those in the music business than the general record-buying public. He managed Tommy Steele and in his growing empire roster of the 1960s were the likes of Billy Fury, Marty Wilde and the unlucky Duffy Power who deserved more success than he found.

John Peel was the jock who made 'underground' music known and appreciated by thousands. He was the champion of progressive music and more than most implanted the fact – sometimes forgotten by radio programmers – that there is a world beyond the Top 50 singles. Peel was of retiring nature and seemed genuinely puzzled by his popularity.

Les Perrin. In music public relation circles Perrin was the 'guvernor', with Sinatra and The Rolling Stones among his clients. Tough and fair Perrin always had a word and time for anyone, and he was the master of stunt and gimmick that invariably helped spread the right message from his client.

Elvis Presley was the undisputed 'King' of rock 'n' roll in the previous decade and during the 1960s his stature and popularity grew, although he had become more of an all-round entertainer than an out-and-out rocker by the time the decade closed. He made countless films, rarely appeared in public and, other than being in 'no-man's land' at Scotland's Prescott Airport, he failed to visit Britain, the only stain upon his magnificient career. During the decade he was a $60 a month GI, stationed for a time with the American forces in Europe.

His record sales, whether singles, EPs or albums, were enormous and in Britain his chart assertiveness was only threatened by Cliff Richard in the singles stakes.

Rave appeared monthly and was the 'class' glossy. It began in the early 1960s and in many respects was the printed version of *Ready Steady Go* with its mix of music and pop culture. It had a number of editors, including Don Wedge, Pat Lamborne, Terry Hornett, Bill Williamson, Colin Bostock Smith and, at the end, Betty Hale. Surprisingly for a 72 page plus magazine it carried only one staff writer in Maureen O'Grady, and relied on freelance contributions to supplement the excellent material of Ms O'Grady.

Rave utilised colour and in overall concept pushed itself as the essential guide for anyone who wanted to get the most out of life. It boldly proclaimed, 'We're what's happening! Are you?.'

Cliff Richard. Late 1950s hero Cliff Richard maintained and enlarged his appreciation empire during the 1960s and he vied with Presley for the most hit singles. He made countless media appearances, starred in films with his backing group The Shadows (also stars in their own right), in pantomime and cabaret, and toured frequently. He became a world star, though he only made minimal impact in the all-important American market. In 1966 he announced his conversion to Christianity and after a period when it seemed he might forsake show-business for the business of teaching religious knowledge he became both pop and religious star and in the latter context was a frequent speaker and attender at religious rallies and conventions.

Jean Shrimpton. Vivacious and glamorous, the 'face' and 'legs' of a decade that saw music and fashion intertwined, Jean Shrimpton was photographed by David Bailey. She helped popularise the mini-skirt, a garment that seemed synonymous with the decade's so-called 'freedom'. She appeared in the pop-film *Privilege*.

Simon and Garfunkel. Retrospective looks often suggest that Simon and Garfunkel were the coffee-table purveyors of songs about vague social injustices and the hazy world of personal relationships. Yet they captured the mood and spirit of the times, from a perspective that seemed to lack either the drug involvement of other commentators or closeness to the somewhat artificial world that music-biz purveyors erect. Undoubtedly in their music they lacked much of the anger and general aggression that came with other groups and artists of the late 1960s, but then theirs was a gentler, subtler world that, in the end, may have helped to shape attitudes as much as the extravagances of a Lennon.

Phil Spector helped provide one of the all-time classic pop songs of the 1950s or any decade with *To Know Him Is To Love Him* as part of The Teddy Bears. He became renowned in the 1960s for establishing his own record sound and giving vinyl flesh through a host of artists that included Darlene Love, The Crystals, Ronettes, Ike and Tina Turner (the all-time classic *River Deep, Mountain High*), The Righteous Brothers, Bob B Soxx and the Blue Jeans, and most of these – and others – were gathered together on the unexpected *Christmas Gift For You* album (1963), later renamed *Phil Spector's Christmas Album*.

Jimmy Savile, the flamboyant jock from Leeds was one of the few DJs who made national acceptance without the patronage of the BBC's pop services. His hair colour, the extravagances of his sartorial style the gimmicks and overall concept of, 'If you're going to do something, then do it larger than life', endeared him to many. During the decade he did much for charity, and sponsored the concept that music people should and could help the less fortunate.

Derek Taylor was the antithesis of the bumptious arrogant press man. Originally with the *News Chronicle* and *Daily Express* he joined the Beatles as their press officer, an unenviable task, which involved placating virtually every media person in the world who desired their ounce of Beatle flesh. Taylor was involved with the Monterey Pop Festival and, from 1968, he worked for the Beatle, Apple company.

Robin Scott was the all-powerful head of Radio One when it began its transmissions in 1967. He had a chequered past history in both radio and television, with considerable overseas experience. Scott was also responsible for Radio Two with his official title that of 'Controller of Radio One and Two'.

Twiggy suprised many in 1976 with her vocals but in the Sixties she was the schoolgirl discovery of Justin de Villenueve who, with her extra thin looks, became *the* model to rival Jean Shrimpton, part of pop culture lore and a mixer amongst the pop hierarchy.

Andy Warhol was the New York artist who implanted his designs and fantasies in much of pop-land, whether it was visual design and concept of album covers and stage backcloths or, later, film with *Chelsea Girls* and *Lonesome Cowboys* being two of his efforts. He was much associated with the so-called 'tacky' side of New York, US East-Coast music and in particular the Velvet Underground (Lou Reed) and Nico.

The Who. The combination of Pete Townshend, Roger Daltrey, Keith Moon and John Entwistle produced one of the great groups of this decade (and the next). Initially the band became darlings of the Mod movement, the stars of influential *Ready Steady Go*, the purveyors of golden classic pop moments that often covered unusual sexual themes (in terms of general pop output). They produced several album blockbusters that included *Tommy* and *The Who Sell Out*. They were an exciting live act with Townshend as the lead vocalist and writer of most songs.

Those Forgotten?

Each pop decade has a long list of people who come and go, tipped for stardom and recipients of music press coverage, DJ airplay and record company advertisements: and yet somehow the promise never materialises. This section reminds us of artists who, sadly, fall under this description, who perhaps still recall those days, maybe even still gig. Here is my list, in no particular order.

Haytocks Rockhouse made radio and TV debuts in January, 1966.

Studio Six came from Glasgow, had a disc entitled *When I See My Baby*.

The Gnomes Of Zurich were CBS group with releases in 1966.

The Koobas received publicity for reviving the 1930s hit song of Gracie Fields, *Sally*. They toured with the Beatles.

Normie Rowe was an artist with a huge Australian seller *Ooh La La* that meant little here in-spite of Polydor push.

Judith Powell was tipped for instant stardom. *Greener Days* was the record which it was thought might give her the break. She was a former student of Nottingham Art College.

Loot came from Trogg country, Andover. *Baby Come Closer* was their single. They were discovered by Larry Page.

Carol Friday was eight years old at the time of issuing *I Look Around Me*. She filmed *Half A Sixpence* with Tommy Steele.

The Mirage recorded for Philips and came from Much Haddam, Herrfordshire, with one member Clive Sarstedt, brother of Eden Kane.

Purple Gang were Stockport College of Art students who recorded for the new Transatlantic label Big T. They had disc called *Granny Takes A Trip*.

Flies, a London based outfit, took part in the 14 hour Technicolour Dream event at Alexandra Palace.

Barbara Ruskin. On *Juke Box Jury* they said her *Euston Station* single would be a hit. She had been involved with music since the age of 7.

Danielle was blonde schoolgirl from Willesden Green, London. She recorded *Oh Mama* (Philips), a song associated with late 1940s hero Rudy Vallee.

Lionel Morton was with the Four Pennies but went solo and recorded Leiber Stoller song *What To Do With Laurie*. He married Julie Foster, star of Alfie, *Half A Sixpence*, etc. The solo career did not blossom.

Episode Six recorded *Morning Dew* for Pye in 1965, and had issued Hollies song *Put Yourself In My Place* as debut disc.

Lomax Alliance hailed from New York and were discovered by Beatle manager Brian Epstein. They included Wallasey man and ex-Undertaker Jackie Lomax who later recorded in his own right for Apple.

The Cardinals broke the world record by playing non-stop for five days at London's Scene Club. They signed with EMI.

The New Breed had an average age of 17, with one Briton and two cockney-speaking Greeks. *Friends and Lovers Forever* was their debut disc.

The Frugal Sound recorded Beatle number *Norwegian Wood.* Girl in group was Rosalind Rankin. The guys were Mike Brown and Brian Stein.

Deke Arlon appeared regularly as actor on TV series *Crossroads.* He recorded for Columbia, discs included *Hard Times For Young Lovers.*

Peter Bs Looners were a foursome, whose debut disc *If You Wanna Be Happy* (Columbia), included ex-Them organist Peter Bardens, Peter Green from Mayall's Bluesbreakers, drummer Mick Fleetwood of Bo Street Runners, and bass man Dave Ambrose who had been with Tony Colton's Big Boss Band. With these names (admittedly famous later) what went wrong?

Thursday's Children Have Far To Go was the name of Barry and Lynette Husband. They began by recording Sonny Bono's *Just You*, followed by *Crawfish* from the Presley movie *King Creole.*

Jimmy Wilson came from Belfast, recorded *See That Girl* for Decca. Spent time in the Merchant Navy.

Gullivers People were four guys and two girls. *Splendour In The Grass* was their debut single for Parlophone, a song penned by prolific US singer-songwriter Jackie de Shannon.

The Truth. Long before the 1980's Truth there was a duo which comprised former hairdressers Frank and Steve. They tried for the charts with a Ray Davies composition *I Go To Sleep*. They came from North London and were seen as typical mods, certainly clothes conscious.

Karol Keyes. Blonde Karol wore a large photographic slide that pictured each member of the Rolling Stones. Among her singles was *A Fool In Love* for Columbia.

Carrolls were a foursome on Polydor with *Surrender Your Love* as their first disc. They came from Liverpool and were managed by Len Wady.

The Amboy Dukes, a seven piece outfit, recorded for Polydor and played R&B with some blue-beat. *Turn Back To Me* was their first release. They had nothing to do with US band of Ted Nugent!

Gene Latter came from Shirley Bassey territory – Tiger Bay, Cardiff. He recorded *A Little Piece Of Leather* for CBS in 1967.

Anni Anderson. Extremely good looking she recorded her debut disc *Ma Vie* for Mercury. She sang in various languages.

Carri Chase, a former member of the Royal Ballet Company, debuted with *Magic Music Box* for RCA at the age of 19 (September, 1967).

Cuppa T. Two guys Terry Widlake and Viv Lythgoe penned a song *Miss Pinkerton* and had it issued on the Deram label.

Smoke, a foursome from Yorkshire were managed by Chris Blackwell. Their record *My Friend Jack* was issued by EMI.

The Dead Sea Fruit. This fivesome once called themselves Some Sloane Squares with a first record *Kensington High Street* for Camp records.

Rosanella sang with Bob Millers Band. Her first record on Pye was *I Only Dream Of You* which was penned by the late Alma Cogan.

Quik recorded *Love Is A Beautiful Thing* on Deram but DJ reaction meant flipping their record and concentrating on *Crumble*, a pacey instrumental.

Lynn Holland recorded *One Man In My Life* for Polydor in May, 1967. One of the men involved with its production was Dave Dee.

Dane Hunter was discovered by Ruby Murray and husband Bernie Burgess. Dane, a 24-year-old, was singing with the Apex Group in Northampton, at the time. He recorded *Evergreen Tree* in February 1965.

Rick And Sandy had their first disc *Half As Much* issued by Mercury. Both were 20 in February 1965. Their past experience had included night club work in St Tropez.

Gitte was an 18-year-old girl from Denmark, with a father who was a singer by the name Otto Haenning. She once recorded a duet with Laurie London and with Oscar Pettiford, *It Might As Well Be Spring*.

Spencer's Washboard King were styled in the mould of a 1920s outfit and had the dubious honour of getting no airplay for their alluringly titled disc *Masculine Women, Feminine Men! Which Is The Rooster? Which is the Hen?* for Polydor.

Gillian Hills almost appeared in a Roger Vadim film when she was 14. Her first British record release was *Look At Them* and landed her a part with Adam Faith in *Beat Girl*.

Mick Softly intended a life as a Jesuit Priest but instead travelled, and recorded for Immediate. On his TV dates his gimmick was to wear a monk's habit.

Carol Elvin wished to be known as a 'tomboy' in her press interviews and not as 'sweet and demure'. For Columbia she had a debut disc *'Cos I Know* coupled with *C'Mon Over*.

Denny Laine and the Diplomats made their debut on BBC's *Midlands At Six*. Denny played lead guitar and the line-up was musically as the Beatles. They formed in 1962. (Laine went on to the Moody Blues and later to Paul McCartney's Wings.)

Hat and Tie. The group was one person, Pat Campbell Lyons, who said he owned 200 hats and 200 ties. His record was *Finding It Rough* for President.

Musics of the Decade

Every musical decade has particular musics that typify the period. The 1960s had a number. This section lists the artists and people involved in: 1 Twist, 2 Surf Music, 3 R&B, Soul, 4 Tamla Motown, 5 Beatle Music, 6 Folk-Rock, and 7 Psychedelic Music.

Obviously Motown could be described as soul music, but its own identity and strength make it worthy of separate classification.

1 TWIST

Some titles are obvious, others less so and in many of the latter's cases they've been titles adopted by the twist dancers and made theirs. Here in random order:

Singles
Chubby Checker – *The Twist*
Chubby Checker – *Let's Twist Again*
US Bonds – *Dear Lady Twist*
Bill Black – *Twist Her*
Bert Weedon – *Twist Me Pretty Baby*
Eric Delaney – *Washboard Blues Twist*
Danny and the Juniors – *Twistin' All Night Long*
Billy Vaughan – *Everybody's Twisting Down In Mexico*
Bill Haley – *Spanish Twist*
The Champs – *Tequila Twist*
Brian Poole – *Twist Little Sister*
King Curtis – *Soul Twist*
Jimmy Soul – *Twistin' Matilda*
Danny Peppermint – *Peppermint Twist*
Joey Dee – *Peppermint Twist*
Elvis Presley – *Rock-A-Hula-Baby*
Frankie Vaughan – *Don't Stop, Twist*
Jerry Lee Lewis – *I've Been Twistin'*
Steve Lawrence – *The Lady Wants To Twist*

US Bonds – *Twist, Twist Senora*
Emile Ford – *Doin' The Twist*
Joe Loss – *Twisting The Mood*
Chubby Checker – *Slow Twistin'*
Frank Sinatra – *Everbody's Twistin'*
Bobby Rydell – *Teach me To Twist*
Goodtimers – *It's Twisting Time*
Johnny Morisette – *Met Me At The Twistin' Place*
Pet Clarke – *Ya Ya Twist*
Bobby Rydell – *Dancin' Party*
Dovells – *Bristol Twistin' Annie*
Viscounts – *Mama's Doin' The Twist*
Streamliners – *Everybody's Doin' The Twist*
Donnie Brooks – *Oh, You Beautiful Doll*
Susan Maughan – *Mamma Do The Twist*
Susan Maughan – *Baby Doll Twist*
Ernie Maresca – *Shout, Shout*
Ernie Maresca – *Mary Jane*
Curtis Lee – *A Night At Daddy Gee's*
Dion – *The Wanderer*
Frankie Vaughan – *I'm Gonna Clip Your Wings*
Dion – *Little Diane*
Vernon Girls – *Lover Please*
Vernon Girls – *You Know What I Mean*
Cliff Richard – *It'll Be Me*
Cliff Richard – *Do You Want To Dance*
Bobby Darin – *If A Man Answers*
Freddy Cannon – *Palisades Park*
B Bumble – *Nut Rocker*
Dee Bee Sharp – *Mashed Potato Time*
Gene Vincent – *Be-Bop-A-Lula* (not the original)
Jimmy Dean – *Little Black Book*

Albums
Joey Dee – *Doin' The Twist*
Bill Black – *Hey Let's Twist*
The Chipmunks – *The Alvin Twist*
Chubby Checker – *Let's Twist Again*
Chubby Checker – *Twist-A-Long With Chubby*

Duane Eddy – *Twistin' and Twangin'*
Fats Domino – *Twistin' The Stomp*
Cyril Stapleton – *Come Twistin'*
Connie Francis – *Do The Twist*
Chuck Marshall – *Twist To The Songs Everybody Knows*
Fats and the Chessmen – *Let's Twist*
Oliver and the Twisters – *Look Who's Twistin'*
Sam Cooke – *Twistin' The Night Away*
Rabin Band – *Twistin' The Trad*
Fats and the Chessmen – *Let's Twist*

Films included *Twist Around The Clock*, *Don't Knock The Twist* with the twist featuring in films such as *Band Of Thieves*, *Play It Cool* and *It's Trad Dad*.

2 SURF MUSIC

Surf music was hardly a major British preoccupation, not suprising, when you consider that the British teenager neither knew the monetary wealth and materialism of his US West-Coast counterpart nor the joy and splendour of gorgeous white-sanded beaches and rolling surf heading toward land. But the overall 'image' penetrated, as typified mainly in the Beach Boys, and the US West-Coast sound made some in-roads into British record buying consciousness.

The listing of records here is American based, and were Top 40 national chart entries.

BEACH BOYS
Surfin' Safari (Capitol) 1962
Surfin' USA (Capitol) 1963
Shut Down (Capitol) 1963
Surfer Girl (Capitol) 1963
Little Deuce Coupe (Capitol) 1963
Be True To Your School (Capitol) 1963
In My Room (Capitol) 1963
Fun, Fun, Fun (Capitol) 1964
I Get Around (Capitol) 1964
Don't Worry Baby (Capitol) 1964

When I Grow Up (To Be A Man) (Capitol) 1964
Dance, Dance, Dance (Capitol) 1964
Do You Wanna Dance (Capitol) 1964
Help Me, Rhonda (Capitol) 1964 (UK: 27, 1965)
California Girls (Capitol) 1965 (UK: 26, 1965)
The Little Girl I Once Knew (Capitol) 1965
Barbara Ann (Capitol) 1966 (UK: 3, 1966)
Sloop B John (Capitol) 1966 (UK: 2, 1966)
God Only Knows (Capitol) 1966 (UK: 2, 1966)
Good Vibrations (Capitol) 1966 (UK: 1, 1966)

Albums: *All Summer Long/California Girls: Dance Dance Dance/Fun Fun Fun: Endless Summer: Little Deuce Coupe: Surfer Girl. Surfin' USA.*

CHANTAYS
Pipeline (Dot) 1963. (UK: 16, 1963 London)

JAN & DEAN
Surf City (Liberty) 1963 (UK: 26, 1963)
Honolulu Lulu (Liberty) 1963
Drag City (Liberty) 1963
Dead Man's Curve (Liberty) 1964
The New Girl In School (Liberty) 1964
The Little Old Lady (From Pasadena) (Liberty) 1964
Ride The Wild Surf (Liberty) 1964
Sidewalk Surfin' (Liberty) 1964
You Really Know How To Hurt A Guy (Liberty) 1965
I Found A Girl (Liberty) 1965
Popsicle (Liberty) 1965

Albums: *Legendary Masters* (Liberty): *Gotta Take That Last Ride* (Liberty): both were compilations.

An earlier record *Baby Talk* (Dore) 1959 had made people aware of the vocal stylisation that became very much part of Surf music: a mix of falsetto and doo-wop.

JACK NITZSCHE
The Lonely Surfer (Reprise) 1963

RIP CHORDS
Hey Little Cobra (Columbia) 1964
Three Window Coupe (Columbia) 1964

RONNY AND THE DAYTONAS
GTO (Mala) 1964
Sandy (Mala) 1966

SUFARIS
Wipe Out (Dot) 1963, with re-entry 1966 in US charts.
(UK: 5, 1963 London)

Other well-known 'surfin' records of the time included Bruce and Terry with *Custom Machine*, *Summer Means Fun*, also *Hot Rod USA*. Del-Tones with *Surf Beat*. Disc were produced by hundreds of other groups with names like Fantastic Baggys, Four Speeds, The Rogues, Superstocks, Challengers, Astronauts, Routers, Sandals, Hondells, Hod Rodders, Trashmen, Ghouls (with the rather macabre *Dracula's Deuce!*), Super Stocks, Rod and the Cobras, Scramblers, Jerry Cole and Spacemen, Calvin Cool and Surf Knobs, Blasters, Tokens, Fireballs, Dave Myers and Surftones, Kicks, Bel-Aires, Beach Girls, etc. US labels releasing Surf music included Liberty, Aden, Vault, Lucky Token, Aertaun, Downey, VJ, GNP, Capitol, Crown, Imperial, Dot, Mala and Dunhill, etc.

But few of these records were issued in the UK, though they were assiduously collected by cult followers.

Outside of the Beach Boys the only UK charting acts have been noted next to their US credit.

3   R&B, SOUL

Record Mirror was very much to the fore in making people aware of R&B from the mid-1960s onwards, especially once they began a regular chart from July 1965 onwards. The first R&B chart listed 20 records and was headed by the Four Tops with *I Can't Help Myself*.

Among R&B best-sellers were:

1965

Donnie Elbert – *A Little Piece Of Leather* (Sue)
Solomon Burke – *Maggie's Farm* (Atlantic)
Anglos – *Incense* (Fontana)
Gene Chandler – *Nothing Can Stop Me* (Stateside)
Elmore James – *Dust My Blues* (Sue)
Inez and Charlie Fox – *My Momma Told Me* (London)
Impressions – *Woman's Got Soul* (HMV)
Alvin Robinson – *Down Home Girl* (Red Bird)
Ike and Tina Turner – *Please, Please, Please* (Sue)
Junior Walker – *Boomerang* (Motown)
James Brown – *Night Train* (Sue)
Marvelettes – *I'll Keep Holding On* (Motown)
Booker T and the MGs – *Boot-Leg* (Atlantic)
Doris Troy – *Heartaches* (Atlantic)
Brenda Holloway – *Operator* (Motown)
Drifters – *Follow Me* (Atlantic)
Fred Hughes – Ooh Wee Baby I Love You (Fontana)
Little Milton – *Who's Cheating Who* (Chess)
Billy Stewart – *Sittin' In The Park* (Chess)
Astors – *Candy* (Atlantic)
Little Joe Cook – *Stormy Monday Blues* (Sue)
Sam The Sham – *Ju Ju Hand* (MGM)

Irma Thomas – *I'm Gonna Cry Till My Tears Run Dry* (Liberty)
Temptations – *Since I Lost My Baby* (Motown)
Carla Thomas – *I've Got No Time To Lose* (Atlantic)
Jackie Wilson – *No Pity In The Naked City* (Coral)
Martha and the Vandellas – *You've Been In Love Too Long* (Motown)
Barbara Lewis – *Make Me Your Baby* (Atlantic)
Joe Tex – *I Want To Do Everything For You* (Atlantic)
Arthur Prysock – *It's Too Late Baby, Too Late* (CBS)
Impressions – *Amen* (HMV)
Bobby Bland – *Here's The Man* (Vocation)
Castaways – *Liar Liar* (London)
Jackie Wilson – *I Believe I'll Fall In Love* (London)
Patti La Belle and the Bluebells – *All or Nothing* (Atlantic)
Miracles – *My Girl Has Gone* (Motown)

Brook Benton – *Mother Nature, Father Time* (RCA)
Madeleine Bell – *What The World Needs Now Is Love* (Philips)
Charlie Rich – *Mohair Sam* (Philips)
Bo Diddley – *Let The Kids Dance* (Chess)
Bessie Banks – *Go Now* (Red Bird)
Professor Longhair – *Baby Let Me Hold Your Hand* (Sue)

1966
Bob and Earl – *Harlem Shuffle* (Sue)
Fontella Bass – *Recovery* (Chess`
Roy Head – *Apple Of My Eye* (Vocalion)
Gloria Jones – *Heartbeat* (Capitol)
Drifters – *We Gotta Sing* (Atlantic)
Toys – *Attack* (Stateside)
Packers – *Hole In The Wall* (Pye)
Bobby Freeman – *The Duck* (Pye)
Ben E King – *Goodnight My Love* (Atlantic)
Jackie Lee – *The Duck* (Fontana)
Don Covay – *Mercy Mercy* (Atlantic)
Mary Wells – *Dear Lover* (Atlantic)
Wilson Pickett – *634–5789* (Atlantic)
Deon Jackson – *Love Makes The World Go Round* (Atlantic)
Carla Thomas – *Comfort Me* (Atlantic)
Lee Dorsey – *Get Out Of My Life Woman* (Stateside)
Darrow Fletcher – *The Pain Gets A Little Deeper* (London)
Irma Thomas – *Take A Look* (Liberty)
Markeys – *Philly Dog* (Atlantic)
James Brown – *The New Breed* (Philips)
Garnet Mimms – *I'll Take Good Care Of You* (United Artists)
Little Mac and the Boss Sounds – *In The Midnight Hour* (Atlantic)
Jimmy Smith – *Got My Mojo Working* (Verve)
Phil Upchurch Combo – *You Can't Sit Down* (Sue)
Edwin Starr – *Stop Her On Sight* (Polydor)
Sharpees – *Tired Of Being Lonely* (Stateside)

Little Richard – *Holy Mackerel* (Stateside)
Sam and Dave – *Hold On I'm Coming* (Atlantic)
Billy Preston – *Billy's Bag* (Sue)
18 Capitols – *Cool Jerk* (Atlantic)
Jamo Thomas – *I Spy For The FBI* (Polydor)
OV Wright – *Gone for Good* (Vocation)
Esther Phillips – *When A Man Loves A Woman* (Atlantic)
Bobby Moore – *Searching For My Love* (Chess)
Otis Redding – *My Lover's Prayer* (Atlantic)
Ike and Tina Turner – *Tell Her I'm Not Home* (Warner)
Wilson Pickett – *Ninety-Nine And A Half (Won't Do)*
(Atlantic)
Rex Garvin and the Mighty Cravers – *Sock It To 'Em JB*
(Atlantic)
Otis Redding – *I Can't Turn You Loose* (Atlantic)
Homer Banks – *A Lot Of Love* (Stateside Soul Supply)
Roscoe Robinson – *That's Enough* (Pye International)
Lorraine Ellison – *Stay With Me* (Warner)
Willie Mitchell – *Mercy* (London)
Prince Harold – *Forget About Me* (Mercury)
BB King – *Don't Answer The Door* (HMV Pop)
JJ Barnes – *Day Tripper* (Polydor)
Booker T and the MGs – *Jingle Bells* (Atlantic)

1967
Lorraine Ellison – *Stay With Me* (Warner)
Knight Bros – *That'll Get It* (Chess)
Homer Banks – *60 Minutes Of Your Love* (Liberty)
Olympics – *Baby Do The Philly Dog* (Fontana)
Percy Sledge – *It Tears Me Up* (Atlantic)
Howard Tate – *Look At Granny Run Run* (Verve)
William Bell – *Never Like This Before* (Atlantic)
Aaron Neville – *Tell It Like It Is* (Stateside)
Ben E King – *What Is Soul* (Atlantic)
Sam and Dave – *You Got Me Hummin'* (Atlantic)
Jimmy Ruffin – *I've Passed This Way Before* (Motown)
Velvelettes – *He Was Really Sayin' Something* (Motown)
Felice Taylor – *It May Be Winter Outside* (President)
Eddie Floyd – *Raise Your Hand* (Stax)

Lowell Fulsom – *Tramp* (Fontana)
Albert King – *Crosscut Saw* (Atlantic)
Cannonball Adderly – *Mercy, Mercy Mercy* (Capitol)
Prince Buster – *Al Capone* (Blue Beat)
James Carr – *The Dark End Of The Street* (Stateside)
Mattie Moultrie – *That's How Strong My Love Is* (CBS)
Sam and Dave – *Smooth Me* (Stax)
Aretha Franklin – *I Never Loved A Man (The Way I Love You)* (Atlantic)
Booker T and the MGs – *Hip Hug Her* (Stax)
Percy Sledge – *Out Of Left Field* (Atlantic)
Toussaint McCall – *Nothing Takes The Place Of You* (Pye)
Mable John – *Same Time, Same Place* (Stax)
Sam and Bill – *I Feel Like Crying* (Brunswick)
Eddie Floyd – *Things Get Better* (Stax)
Rufus Thomas – *Greasy Spoon* (Stax)
Soul Bros – *Some Kind Of Wonderful* (Atlantic)
Willie Tee – *Thank You John* (Atlantic)
Oscar Toney – *For Your Precious Love* (Stateside)
Otis Redding and Carla Thomas – *Tramp* (Stax)
Soul Agents – *Rock Steady* (Crystal)
Booker T and the MGs – *Slim Jenkins' Place* (Stax)
Martha and the Vandellas – *Love Bug Leave My Heart Alone* (Motown)
Sam and Dave – *Soul Man* (Stax)
King Curtis – *Memphis Soul Stew* (Atlantic)
Wilson Pickett – *Funky Broadway* (Atlantic)
Esquires – *Get It Up* (Stateside)
Temptations – *You're My Everything* (Motown)
Norman Fraser – *First Cut Is The Deepest* (Coxone)
Felice Taylor – *I Feel Love Coming On* (President)
Jackie Wilson – *Higher and Higher* (Coral)
Moses and Joshua Dillard – *My Elusive Dreams* (Stateside)
Erma Franklin – *Piece Of My Heart* (London)

1968
Clarence Carter – *Thread The Needle* (Atlantic)
Sam and Dave – *I Thank You* (Atlantic)

Albert King – *Cold Feet* (Stax)
Inez and Charlie Fox – *(1-2-3-4-5-6-7) Count The Days* (Direction)
Etta James – *Tell Mama* (Chess)
James Carr – *Man Needs A Woman* (Bell)
John Roberts – *Sockin' 1-2-3-4* (Sue)
Clarence Carter – *Looking For A Fox* (Atlantic)
Etta James – *Security* (Chess)
Willie Mitchell – *Soul Seranade* (London)
Arthur Conley – *Funky Street* (Atlantic)
Ike and Tina Turner – *So Fine* (London)
Bessie Banks – *Go Now* (Soul City)
Percy Sledge – *Take Time To Know Her* (Atlantic)
William Bell – *Tribute To A King* (Stax)
Maurice and Mac – *You Left The Water Running* (Chess)
Mowhawks – *The Champ* (Pama)
Homer Banks – *Sixty Minutes Of Your Love* (Minit)
Wilson Pickett – *She's Looking Good* (Atlantic)
Erma Franklin – *Open Up Your Soul* (London)
Sam and Dave – *You Don't Know What You Mean To Me* (Atlantic)
Cliff Nobles – *The Horse* (Direction)
Pigmeat Markham – *Here Comes The Judge* (Chess)
Arthur Conley – *People Sure Act Funny* (Atlantic)
The Maximum Breed – *Cupid* (Fab)
Shorty Long – *Here Comes The Judge* (Motown)
Otis Redding – *Hard To Handle/Amen* (Atlantic)
Fantastic Johnny C – *Hitch It To The Horse* (London)
The Soul Clan – *Soul Meeting* (Atlantic)
Wilson Pickett – *I'm A Midnight Mover* (Atlantic)
Valentinos – *It's All Over Now* (Soul City)
Bill Black's Combo – *Turn On Your Lovelight* (London)
Willie Mitchell – *Prayer Meeting* (London)
Jimmy James and the Vagabonds – *Red Red Wine* (Pye)
Ernie K Doe – *Dancing Man* (Action)
Doris Troy – *I'll Do Anything* (Toast)
Wilmer and the Dukes – *Give Me One More Chance* (Action)

Sly and the Family Stone – *M'Lady* (Direction)
Bandwagon – *Breaking Down The Walls Of Silence*
(Direction)
Otis Redding – *Champagne and Wine* (Stax)
Bobby Williams – *Baby I Need Your Love* (Action)
Otis Redding – *Papa's Got A Brand New Bag* (Atlantic)
James Brown – *Say It Loud (I'm Black and I'm Proud)*
(Polydor)

1969
Thelma Houston – *Jumpin' Jack Flash* (Stateside)
Mark-Kays – *Black* (Stax)
William Bell – *Happy* (Stax)
Percy Sledge – *Come Softly To Me* (Atlantic)
Sam and Dave – *Soul Sister Brown Sugar* (Atlantic)
Leon Hayward – *Mellow Moonlight* (MCA)
Wilson Pickett – *Mini Skirt Mini* (Atlantic)
The Checkmates – *Love Is All I Have To Give* (A&M)
The Cats – *Swan Lake* (BAF)
Billy Butler – *The Right Track* (Soul City)
Jnr Walker and the All Stars – *Shotgun/Road Runner*
(Motown)
James Carr – *Freedom Train* (B&C)
The Anglos – *Incense* (Island)
James and Bobby Purify – *Let Love Come Between Us*
(Bell)
Dionne Warwick – *People Got To Be Free* (Pye)
Bob and Earl – *Harlem Shuffle* (Motown)
Z Z Hill – *Make Me Yours* (Action)
Sam and Dave – *You Don't Know What I Know* (Atlantic)
Tony Clark – *The Entertainer* (Chess)
Barbara Acklin – *Am I The Same Girl* (MCA)
Donnie Elbert – *Without You* (DM)
Dells – *Love Is Blue* (Chess)
Checkmates Ltd with Sonny Charles – *Black Pearl* (AFM)
William Bell – *Everyday Will Be A Holiday* (Atlantic)
Shirley and the Shirelles – *Look What You've Done To Me
Heart* (Bell)
Otis Redding – *A Lover's Question* (Atlantic)

Aretha Franklin – *The Weight* (Atlantic)
Nina Simone – *Revolution* (RCA)
David Ruffin – *My Whole World Ended* (Motown)
The Three Caps – *Cool Jerk* (Atlantic)
Clarence Carter – *Snatching It Back* (Atlantic)
Otis Redding – *Free Me* (Atlantic)
Edwin Hawkins Singers – *Ain't Like Him* (Buddah)
Percy Sledge – *Kind Woman* (Atlantic)
Isley Brothers – *I Turned You On* (Major Minor)
Eddie Floyd – *Don't Tell Your Mama* (Stax)
Arthur Conley – *Star Review* (Atco)

R&B/Soul chart singles in British pop listings included:
P P Arnold – *First Cut Is The Deepest* (Immediate)
Bar-Kays – *Soul Finger* (33, 1967) (Stax)
Fontella Bass – *Rescue Me* (11, 1965) (Chess)
William Bell – *Tribute To A King* (31, 1968) (Stax)
James Brown – *Papas Got A Brand New Bag* (25, 1965)
(London): *I Got You* (29, 1966) (Pye): *It's A Man's Man's
Man's World* (13, 1966) (Pye)
Gene Chandler – *Nothing Can Stop Me* (41, 1968) (Soul
City)
Dells – *I Can Sing A Rainbow/Love Is Blue* (15, 1969)
(Chess)
Drifters – *Baby What I Mean* (49, 1967) (Atlantic)
Equals* – *I Get So Excited* (44, 1968) (President): *Baby
Come Back* (1, 1968) (President): Laurel and Hardy (35,
1968) (President): *Softly Softly* (48, 1968) (President):
Michael And The Slipper Tree (24, 1969) (President):
Viva Bobby Joe (6, 1969) (President): *Rub A Dub Dub* (34,
1969) (President)
Eddie Floyd – *Knock On Wood* (19, 1967) (Atlantic):
Raise Your Hand (42, 1967) (Stax): *Things Get Better* (31,
1967) (Stax)
Four Tops – (*see under* Motown)
Inez and Charlie Foxx – *Mockingbird* (United Artists)
Aretha Franklin – *Respect* (10, 1967) (Atlantic): *Baby
I Love You* (39, 1967) (Atlantic): *Chain Of Fools/
Satisfaction* (37, 1967) (Atlantic): *Since You've Been*

Gone (47, 1968) (Atlantic): *Think* (26, 1968) (Atlantic): *I Say A Little Prayer* (4, 1968) (Atlantic)

Otis Redding – *My Girl* (11, 1965) (Atlantic): *Satisfaction* (33, 1965) (Atlantic): *My Lover's Prayer* (37, 1966) (Atlantic): *I Can't Turn You Loose* (29, 1966) (Atlantic): *Fa Fa Fa Fa Fa (Sad Song)* (23, 1966) (Atlantic): *Try A Little Tenderness* (46, 1967) (Atlantic): *Day Tripper* (48, 1967) (Atlantic): *Let Me Come On Home* (43, 1967) (Stax): *Shake* (28, 1967) (Stax): *My Girl* (36, 1968) (Stax) re-issue: *(Sittin' On) The Dock of the Bay* (3, 1968) (Stax): *Happy Song* (24, 1968) (Stax): *Hard To Handle* (15, 1968) (Atlantic): *Love Man* (43, 1969) (Atco)

Otis Redding and Carla Thomas – *Tramp* (18, 1967) (Stax): *Knock On Wood* (35, 1967) (Stax)

Martha Reeves and the Vandellas *(see under* Motown)

Smokey Robinson and the Miracles *(see under* Motown)

Diana Ross and the Supremes *(see under* Motown)

Roy C – *Shotgun Wedding* (6, 1966) (Island)

Jimmy Ruffin *(see under* Motown)

Sam and Dave – *Soothe Me* (48, 1967) (Stax): *Soul Man* (24, 1967) (Stax): *I Thank You* (34, 1968) (Stax): *Soul Sister Brown Sugar* (15, 1969) (Stax)

Sam The Sham and the Pharaohs – *Wooly Bully* (11, 1965) (MGM): *Lil' Red Riding Hood* (46, 1966) (MGM)

Showstoppers – *Ain't Nothing But A Houseparty* (11, 1968) (Beacon): *Eeny Meeny* (33, 1968) (MGM)

Marvin Gaye *(see under* Motown)

Marvin Gaye and Tammi Terrell *(see under* Motown)

Marvin Gaye and Mary Wells *(see under* Motown)

Marvin Gaye and Kim Weston *(see under* Motown)

Happenings – *I Got Rhythm* (28, 1967) (Stateside): *My Mammy* (34, 1967) (Pye/B T Puppy)

Edwin Hawkins Singers – *Oh Happy Day* (2, 1969) (Buddah)

Jimi Hendrix* – *Hey Joe* (6, 1967) (Polydor): *Purple Haze* (3, 1967) (Track): *All Along The Watchtower* (5, 1968) (Track)

Isley Brothers *(see under* Motown)

Jimmy James and the Vagabonds – *Red Red Wine* (36,

1968) (Pye)

Gladys Knight and the Pips (*see under* Motown)

Marvelettes (*see under* Motown)

Willie Mitchell – *Soul Serenade* (43, 1968) (London)

Robert Parker – *Barefootin'* (24, 1966) (Island)

Wilson Pickett – *In The Midnight Hour* (12, 1965) (Atlantic): *Don't Fight It* (29, 1965) (Atlantic): *634–5689* (36, 1965) (Atlantic): *Land Of A Thousand Dances* (22, 1966) (Atlantic): *Mustang Sally* (28, 1966) (Atlantic): *Funky Broadway* (43, 1967) (Atlantic): *In The Midnight Hour* (38, 1968) (Atlantic) re-issue: *Hey Jude* (16, 1969) (Atlantic)

Percy Sledge – *When A Man Loves A Woman* (4, 1966) (Atlantic): *Warm and Tender Love* (34, 1966) (Atlantic)

Sly and the Family Stone – *Dance To The Music* (7, 1968) (Direction): *M'Lady* (32, 1968) (Direction): *Everyday People* (36, 1969) (Direction)

O C Smith – *Son Of Hickory Holler's Tramp* (2, 1968) (CBS)

Edwin Starr – *Stop Her On Sight (SOS)* (35, 1966) (Polydor): *Headline News* (39, 1966) (Polydor): *Stop Her On Sight (SOS)/Headline News* (11, 1968) (Polydor) re-issue: *see also* Motown

Supremes (*see under* Motown)

Felice Taylor – *I Feel Love Comin' On* (11, 1967) (President)

R Dean Taylor (*see under* Motown)

Temptations (*see under* Motown)

Toys – *A Lover's Concerto* (5, 1965) (Stateside): *Attack* (36, 1966) (Stateside)

Ike and Tina Turner – *River Deep Mountain High* (3, 1966) (London): *Tell Her I'm Not Coming Home* (48, 1966) (London): *A Love Like Yours* (16, 1966) (London): *River Deep Mountain High* (33, 1969) (London) re-issue

Upsetters* – *Return Of Django/Dollar In The Teeth* (5,

---

* these records may not be accepted by some people as R&B but whatever the pros and cons they were listed at the appropriate period in the British R&B chart.

1969) (Upsetter)
Vanilla Fudge* – *You Keep Me Hangin' On* (18, 1967)
(Atlantic)
Geno Washington and the Ram Jam Band – *Water* (39,
1966) (Piccadilly): *Hi Hi Hazel* (45, 1966) (Piccadilly):
Que Sera Sera (43, 1966) (Piccadilly): *Michael* (39, 1967)
(Piccadilly)
Jackie Wilson – *(Your Love Keeps Lifting Me) Higher
And Higher* (11, 1969) (MCA)
Stevie Wonder (*see under* Motown)

4   TAMLA MOTOWN
This section traces the Sixties chart fortunes of one of the
most famous black music labels in record history.

At the outset of the Sixties, Motown distributed its
product on the London American label with seven singles
issued between May 1959 and March 1961. In June 1961
Motown moved to Philips and its product appeared on
Fontana. Between November 1961 and March 1962 there
were four releases.

Motown then moved to Oriole but without success.
Eventually Motown was released by EMI on Stateside
and then on its own Motown label with *Heatwave* from
Martha and the Vandellas the first release in 1963.

The following were Motown chart hits in Britain's Top
50.

FOUR TOPS
I Can't Help Myself (23, 1965) TMG 515
It's The Same Old Song (34, 1965) TMG 528
Loving You Is Sweeter Than Ever (21, 1966) TMG 568
Reach Out I'll Be There (1, 1966) TMG 579
Standing In The Shadows (6, 1967) TMG 589
Bernadette (8, 1967) TMG 601
Seven Rooms Of Gloom (12, 1967) TMG 612
You Keep Running Away (26, 1967) TMG 623
Walk Away Renee (3, 1967) TMG 634
If I Were A Carpenter (7, 1968) TMG 647

Yesterday's Dreams (23, 1968) TMG 665
I'm In A Different World (27, 1968) TMG 675
What Is A Man? (16, 1969) TMG 698
Do What You Gotta Do (11, 1969) TMG 710

MARVELETTES
When You're Young And In Love (13, 1967) TMG 609

MARVIN GAYE
How Sweet It Is (49, 1964) Stateside SS 360
Little Darlin' (50, 1966) TMG 574
I Heard It Through The Grapevine (1, 1969) TMG 686
Too Busy Thinking 'Bout My Baby (5, 1969) TMG 705

MARVIN GAYE AND TAMMI TERRELL
If I Could Build My Whole World (41, 1968) TMG 635
Ain't Nothin' Like The Real Thing (34, 1968) TMG 655
You're All I Need To Get By (19, 1968) TMG 668
You Ain't Livin' Till You're Lovin' (21, 1969) TMG 681
Good Lovin' Ain't Easy To Come By (26, 1969) TMG 697
Onion Song (9, 1969) TMG 715

MARVIN GAYE AND MARY WELLS
Once Upon A Time (50, 1964) Stateside SS 316

MARVIN GAYE AND KIM WESTON
It Takes Two (16, 1967) TMG 590

ISLEY BROTHERS
Twist And Shout (42, 1963) Stateside SS 112
This Old Heart Of Mine (47, 1966) TMG 555
I Guess I'll Always Love You (45, 1966) TMG 572
Behind A Painted Smile (5, 1969) TMG 693
Put Yourself In My Place (13, 1969) TMG 708

GLADYS KNIGHT AND THE PIPS
Take Me In Your Arms And Love Me (13, 1967) TMG 604

I Heard It Through The Grapevine (47, 1967) TMG 629

MARTHA REEVES AND THE VANDELLAS
Dancing In The Street (28, 1964) Stateside SS 345
Nowhere To Run (26, 1965) TMG 502
I'm Ready For Love (29, 1966) TMG 582
Jimmy Mack (21, 1967) TMG 599
Honey Chile (30, 1968) TMG 636
Dancing In The Street (4, 1969) TMG 684 (re-issue on Motown)
Nowhere To Run (42, 1969) TMG 694 (re-issue, new number)

SMOKEY ROBINSON AND THE MIRACLES
Going To A Go-Go (44, 1966) TMG 547
(Come Round Here) I'm The One You Need (45, 1966) TMG 584
I Second That Emotion (27, 1967) TMG 631
If You Can Want (50, 1968) TMG 648
Tracks Of My Tears (9, 1969) TMG 696

DIANA ROSS AND THE SUPREMES, AND THE TEMPTATIONS
I'm Gonna Make You Love Me (3, 1969) TMG 685
I Second That Emotion (18, 1969) TMG 709

JIMMY RUFFIN
What Becomes Of The Broken Hearted (10, 1966) TMG 577
I've Passed This Way Before (29, 1967) TMG 593
Gonna Give Her All The Love I've Got (26, 1967) TMG 603
I've Passed This Way Before (33, 1969) TMG 703 re-issue, new number.

SUPREMES
Where Did Our Love Go (3, 1964) Stateside SS 327
Baby Love (1, 1964) Stateside SS 350
Come See About Me (27, 1965) Stateside SS 376

Stop In The Name Of Love (7, 1965) TMG 501
Back In My Arms Again (40, 1965) TMG 516
I Hear A Symphony (39, 1965) TMG 575
You Can't Hurry Love (3, 1966) TMG 575
You Keep Me Hangin' On (8, 1966) TMG 585
Love Is Here And Now You're Gone (17, 1967) TMG 597
The Happening (6, 1967) TMG 607
Reflections (5, 1967) TMG 616
In And Out Of Love (13, 1967) TMG 632
Forever Came Today (28, 1968) TMG 650
Some Things You Never Get Used To (34, 1968) TMG 662
Love Child (15, 1968) TMG 677
I'm Living In Shame (14, 1969) TMG 695
No Matter What Sign You Are (37, 1969) TMG 704
We'll Be Together (13, 1969) TMG 721

R DEAN TAYLOR
Gotta See Jane (17, 1968) TMG 656

TEMPTATIONS
My Girl (43, 1965) Stateside SS 395
It's Growing (45, 1965) TMG 504
Ain't Too Proud To Beg (21, 1966) TMG 565
Beauty Is Only Skin Deep (18, 1966) TMG 578
(I Know) I'm Losing You (19, 1966) TMG 587
You're My Everything (26, 1967) TMG 620
I Wish It Would Rain (45, 1968) TMG 641
I Could Never Love Another (47, 1968) TMG 658
Get Ready (10, 1969) TMG 688
Cloud Nine (15, 1969) TMG 707

JUNIOR WALKER
How Sweet It Is (22, 1966) TMG 571
(I'm A) Road Runner (12, 1969) TMG 691
What Does It Take (To Win Your Love) TMG 712

MARY WELLS
My Guy (5, 1964) Stateside SS 288

(LITTLE) STEVIE WONDER
Uptight (14, 1966) TMG 545
Blowin' In The Wind (36, 1966) TMG 570
A Place In The Sun (20, 1967) TMG 588
I Was Made To Love Her (5, 1967) TMG 613
I'm Wondering (22, 1967) TMG 626
Shoo Be Doo Be Doo Da Day (46, 1968) TMG 653
For Once In My Life (3, 1968) TMG 679
I Don't Know Why (14, 1969) TMG 690
My Cherie Amour (4, 1969) TMG 690
Yester-Me Yester-You Yesterday (2, 1969) TMG 717

5 BEATLE MUSIC

During the 1960s a large number of Beatle compositions were covered by other artists and never released by the foursome as singles. In some instances songs were offered or written especially for the artist. The list given here makes no distinction between US and UK release:

Cilla Black – *Love Of The Loved* (1966)
Applejacks – *Like Dreamers Do* (1964)
E-Types – *Love Of The Loved* (1966)
The Foppees – *Love Of The Loved* (1966)
Cilla Black – *Step Inside Love* (1968): – *It's For You* (1964)
Chad and Jeremy – *It's For You* (1964)
Black Dyke Mills Band – *Thingumybob* (1969)
Three Dog Night – *Thingumybob* (1969)
The Rolling Stones – *I Wanna Be Your Man* (1963)
Ray Columbus and the Invaders – *I Wanna Be Your Man* (1964)
Peter & Gordon – *A World Without Love* (1964)
Bobby Rydell – *A World Without Love* (1964)
Fourmost – *I'm In Love* (1964)
New Breed – *I'm In Love* (1964)
P J Proby – *That Means A Lot* (1965)
Peter and Gordon – *Nobody I Know* (1964)
Peter and Gordon – *I Don't Want To See You Again* (1964)

Billy J Kramer – *Bad To Me* (1963)
Fourmost – *Hello Little Girl* (1963)
Mike Shannon and the Strangers – *One And One Is Two* (1964)
Mary Hopkin – *Goodbye* (1969)
Billy J Kramer – *I'll Keep You Satisfied* (1964)
Tommy Quickly – *Tip Of My Tongue* (1963)

Some of the above songs, along with others were taken and without copying the album original they became Top 20 single hits for these artists (songs in alphabetical order):

Billy J Kramer – *Bad To Me* (1, 1963) US 9
Cream – *Badge* (18, 1969) song by George Harrison
Billy J Kramer – *Do You Want To Know A Secret?* (2, 1963)
Billy J Kramer – *From A Window* (10, 1964)
St Louis Union – *Girl* (11, 1966)
Mary Hopkin – *Goodbye* (2, 1969)
Cliff Bennett and the Rebel Rousers – *Got To Get You Into My Life* (6, 1966)
Peter Sellers – *A Hard Day's Night* (14, 1966)
Fourmost – *Hello Little Girl* (9, 1963)
Wilson Pickett – *Hey Jude* (16, 1969)
Hollies – *If I Needed Someone* (20, 1966) George Harrison composition
Billy J Kramer – *I'll Keep You Satisfied* (4, 1963)
Fourmost – *I'm In Love* (17, 1964)
Cilla Black – *It's For You* (7, 1964)
Rolling Stones – *I Wanna Be Your Man* (12, 1963)
Applejacks – *Like Dreamers Do* (20, 1964)
David and Jonathan – *Michelle* (11, 1966)
Peter and Gordon – *Nobody I Know* (10, 1964)
Marmalade – *Ob-La-Di Ob-La-Da* (1, 1968)
Bedrocks – *Ob-La-Di Ob-La-Da* (20, 1969)
Cilla Black – *Step Inside Love* (8, 1968)
Young Idea – *With A Little Help From My Friends* (10, 1967)
Peter and Gordon – *World Without Love* (1, 1964)
Matt Monroe – *Yesterday* (8, 1965)

The Beatles themselves recorded songs from outside sources: these were:

Act Naturally (Buck Owens, 1963) found on *Help; Yesterday And Today* (Ringo on lead vocal).

Ain't She Sweet (Paul Ash and his Orchestra, 1927) *The Beatles First: The Early Years: In The Beginning*. It was issued as a single by Polydor and the recording stems from the period the Beatles backed Tony Sheridan. 1964 released (John on lead vocal).

Anna (Go To Him) (Arthur Alexander, 1962). *Please Please Me: Introducing The Beatles: The Early Beatles* (John on lead vocal).

Baby It's You (Shirelles, 1961). *Please Please Me: Introducing the Beatles: The Early Beatles*. Issued 1963 (lead vocals by John).

Boys (Shirelles, 1961). *Please Please Me! Introducing The Beatles: The Early Beatles: Rock and Roll Music: The Beatles At Hollywood Bowl*. Issued 1963 (lead vocalist is Ringo).

Chains (The Cookies, 1962). *Please Please Me: Introducing The Beatles: The Early Beatles*. First released 1962 (lead singer is George).

Devil In Her Heart (The Donays, 1962). *With The Beatles: The Beatles Second Album*. First released 1963 (lead vocals by George).

Dizzy Miss Lizzie (Larry Williams, 1958). *Beatles VI: Help!: Live Peace In Toronto: Rock and Roll Music: The Beatles At Hollywood Bowl*. First released 1965 (lead vocalist is John).

Everybody's Trying To Be My Baby (Carl Perkins, 1958). *Beatles For Sale: Beatles '65: Rock And Roll Music: The Beatles Live At The Star Club*. First issued 1964 (lead singer is George).

Honey Don't (Carl Perkins, 1956). *Beatles For Sale: Beatles '65*. First released 1964 (lead singer is Ringo).

Kansas City (Little Willie Littlesfield, 1952). *Beatles For Sale: Beatles VI: The Beatles Live At The Star Club: Rock And Roll Music*. First released 1964 (lead vocals by Paul).

Long Tall Sally (Little Richard, 1956). *The Beatles Second*

Album: The Beatles Live At The Star Club: The Beatles Rock And Roll Music: The Beatles At The Hollywood Bowl: The Beatles Rarities. First issued 1964 (lead singer is Paul).

Matchbox (Carl Perkins, 1958). *Something New: Rock And Roll Music: The Beatles Live At The Star Club: The Beatles Rarities.* First issued 1964 (lead singer is Ringo).

Mr Moonlight (Dr Feelgood and the Interns, 1962). *Beatles For Sale: Beatles '65: The Beatles Live At The Star Club.* First released 1965 (lead singer is John).

Money (That's What I Want). (Barret Strong, 1959). *With the Beatles: The Beatles Second Album: Live Peace In Toronto: Rock And Roll Music.* First released 1963 (lead singer is John).

Please Mr Postman (Marvelettes, 1961). *With the Beatles: The Beatles Second Album.* First released 1963 (lead singer: John).

Rock And Roll Music (Chuck Berry, 1957). *Beatles for Sale: Beatles '65: Rock And Roll Music.* First released 1964 (lead singer: John).

Roll Over Beethoven (Chuck Berry, 1956). *With The Beatles: The Beatles Second Album: Rock And Roll Music: The Beatles At Hollywood Bowl: The Beatles Live At The Star Club.* First released 1963 (lead singer is George).

Slow Down (Larry Williams, 1958). *Something New: Rock And Roll Music: The Beatles: Rarities.* First released 1964 (lead singer: John).

A Taste Of Honey (Bobby Scott and Combo, 1960). *Please Please Me: Introducing The Beatles: The Early Beatles: The Beatles Live At The Star Club.* First released 1963 (lead singer is Paul).

Till There Was You (Robert Preston and Barbara Cook, 1958). *With The Beatles: Meet The Beatles: The Beatles Live At The Star Club.* First released 1963 (lead singer: Paul).

Twist and Shout (Isley Brothers, 1962). *Please Please Me: Introducing The Beatles: The Early Beatles: Rock and Roll Music: The Beatles Live At The Star Club: The Beatles Live At The Hollywood Bowl.* First released 1963 (vocals by John).

Words Of Love (Buddy Holly, 1957). *Beatles for Sale: Beatles VI: Love Songs*. Released first in 1964 (vocals by John and Paul).

You Really Got A Hold On Me (The Miracles, 1962). *With The Beatles: Beatles Second Album*. First issued 1963. (sung on the *Let It Be* soundtrack, vocals by John).

6 FOLK-ROCK

These records charted in the singles listings for the decade:

Joan Baez – *We Shall Overcome* (26, 1965) (Fontana): *There But For Fortune* (8, 1965) (Fontana): *It's All Over Now Baby Blue* (22, 1965) (Fontana): *Farewell Angelina* (35, 1965) (Fontana): *Pack Up Your Sorrows* (50, 1966) (Fontana)

Brothers Four – *Greenfields* (40, 1960) (Philips)

Byrds – *Mr Tambourine Man* (1, 1965) (CBS): *All I Really Want To Do* (4, 1965) (CBS): *Turn! Turn! Turn!* (4, 1965) (CBS): *the Byrds had other hits, but these seem more in the domain of electric rock*

Ian Campbell Folk Group – *The Times They Are A-Changin'* (42, 1965) (Transatlantic)

Countrymen – *I Know Where I'm Going* (45, 1962) (Piccadilly)

Adge Cutler and the Wurzels – *Drink Up Thy Zider* (45, 1967) (Columbia)

Dubliners – *Seven Drunken Nights* (7, 1967) (Major Minor): *Black Velvet Band* (15, 1967) (Major Minor): *Never Wed An Old Man* (43, 1967) (Major Minor)

Judith Durham – *Olive Tree* (33, 1967) (Columbia)

Bob Dylan – *Times They Are-A-Changin'* (9, 1965) (CBS): other Dylan hits seem more reflective of electric rock

Highwaymen – *Michael* (1, 1961) (HMV): *Gyspy Rover* (41, 1961) (HMV)

Burt Ives – *A Little Bitty Tear* (9, 1962) (Brunswick): *Funny Way Of Laughin'* (29, 1962) (Brunswick)

Lettermen – *They Way You Look Tonight* (36, 1961) (Capitol)

Trini Lopez – *If I Had A Hammer* (4, 1963) (Reprise): *Kansas City* (35, 1963) (Reprise): *I'm Coming Home Cindy* (28, 1966) (Reprise): *Gonna Get Along Without Ya Now* (41, 1967) (Reprise)

Frankie McBride – *Five Little Fingers* (19, 1967) (Emerald)

Miki and Griff – *Rockin' Alone* (44, 1960) (Pye): *Little Bitty Tear* (16, 1962) (Pye): *I Wanna Stay Here* (23, 1963) (Pye)

Nina and Frederick – *Listen to the Ocean* (46, 1960) (Columbia): *Little Donkey* (3, 1960) (Columbia): *Longtime Boy* (43, 1961) (Columbia): *Sucu Sucu* (23, 1961) (Columbia)

Pentangle – *Light Flight* (43, 1970) (Big T)

Peter Paul and Mary – *Blowing In The Wind* (13, 1963) (Warner): *Tell It On The Mountain* (33, 1964) (Warner): *The Times They Are A-Changin'* (44, 1964) (Warner)

Jeannie C Riley – *Harper Valley PTA* (12, 1968) (Polydor)

Jimmie Rodgers – *English Country Garden* (5, 1962) (Columbia)

Sandpipers – *Guantanamera* (7, 1966) (Pye): *Quando M'Innamoro (A Man Without Love)* (33, 1968) (A&M): *Kumbaya* (39, 1969) (A&M)

Andy Stewart – *Donald Where's Your Troosers* (37, 1960) (Top Rank): *A Scottish Soldier* (19, 1961) (Top Rank): *The Battle's O'er* (28, 1961) (Top Rank): *Dr Finlay* (43, 1965) (HMV)

Obviously there can be debate over the inclusion of several artists listed. But recording 'single hits' hides the considerable popularity of many artists whose main selling point was either in the clubs and concerts, on folk radio and TV shows or more so, in albums. Pete Seeger, Phil Ochs, Joan Baez, Tom Paxton, Judy Collins, the early Dylan, Kingston Trio, Odetta, Weavers, Buffy Saint Marie, Julie Felix and Donovan were among the many artists whose sales were high.

7 PSYCHEDELIC MUSIC

The States spawned a seemingly endless list of psychedelic bands, with most of them emanating from the US West Coast. Ralph Gleason in his excellent *The Jefferson Airplane and The San Francisco Sound* (US: Ballentine) lists an amazing collection of Bay Area bands, some of them were temporary, bands that blew up after first rehearsals as well as a number who, because they bedded down West, became honorary San Francisco bands – The Youngbloods (from New York), the Sir Douglas Quintet (from Texas), Linn County (from Chicago), Seatrain and Everything Is Everything (from New York).

Among Gleason's roster came A Cid Symphony, Amplified OHM, Angels Own Social Grace & Deliverance Band, Asmadius, Birth, Bitter Seeds, Black Shit Puppy Farm, Blue Cheer★, The Charlatans★, Cleanliness and Godliness Skiffle Band, Country Joe and the Fish★, Creedence Clearwater Revival★, Daisy Overkill, Deepwater Toad, Earth Mother★, The Electric Flag★, Evergreen Tangerine, Family Cow, Flamin' Groovies★, Flying Circus, Frosted Suede, G String Quartet, Gossamer Kyte, The Grateful Dead★, The Great Society★, Harpers Bizarre★, Hmmm, Dr Humbeads's New Tranquility String Band and Medicine Show, Immaculate Contraption, It's A Beautiful Day★, Jefferson Airplane★, Joy of Cooking★, Land of Milk and Honey, Little Miss Cornshucks and the Loose Troupe, Mama Clover and the Rising Spirit, Lee Michaels★, Buddy Miles Express★, Steve Miller Band★, Mother Earth★, Mysore Suggoundhi Dhoop Factory, New Breed★, The Only Alternative And His Other Possibilities, Pacific Gas & Electric★, Pipe Joint Compound, Quicksilver Messenger Service★, Recurring Love Habit, Savage Resurrection,Seatrain, Sir Douglas Quintet★, Slippery Gulch Band, Sly and the Family Stone★, Sopwoth Camel★, Steppenwolf★, Summerfall Winterspring, 39 Homer Lane, Tongue And Groove, Universal Parking Lot, Vejtables, Peter Wheat and the Bread Men, Wild Honey, You, The Youngbloods★.

And there were others. Those carrying★ became known beyond the Bay Area and within it were heroes.

Dave Marsh and Kevin Stein in their *The Book of Rock Lists* (Dell – USA Sidgwick – UK) name their psychedelic Top 40 – most of their list I would choose, perhaps shuffle the order slightly and produce this: their positions in brackets

1 Iron Butterfly – *In-A-Gadda-Da-Vida*   (13)
2 The Beatles – *A Day In The Life*   (5)
3 Doors – *The End*   (7)
4 Doors – *Break On Through*   (2)
5 Beatles – *Lucy In The Sky With Diamonds*   (17)
6 Jimi Hendrix – *Are You Experienced*   (1)
7 Jefferson Airplane – *White Rabbit*   (37)
8 Who – *I Can See For Miles*   (10)
9 The Byrds – *Eight Miles High*   (6)
10 Jimi Hendrix – *Room Full Of Mirrors*   (24)
11 Buffalo Springfield – *Expecting To Fly*   (–)
12 Jefferson Airplane – *Streetmasse*   (–)
13 Jefferson Airplane – *Somebody To Love*   (29)
14 Jimi Hendrix Experience – *Purple Haze*   (22)
15 Spirit – *I Got A Line On You*   (11)
16 Grateful Dead – *Dark Star*   (4)
17 Pink Floyd – *See Emily Play*   (26)
18 Jefferson Airplane – *Crown Of Creation*   (3)
19 The Strawberry Alarm Clock – *Incense and Peppermints*   (14)
20 The Electric Prunes – *I Had Too Much To Dream (Last Night)*   (12)
21 Eric Burdon and the Animals – *A Girl Named Sandoz*   (8)
22 Jimi Hendrix Experience – *Third Stone From The Sun*   (–)
23 HP Lovecraft – *At The Mountains Of Madness*   (–)
24 Doors – *When The Music's Over*   (36)
25 Love – *Revelation*   (23)
26 Beatles – *Strawberry Fields Forever*   (31)
27 Beatles – *Magical Mystery Tour*   (EP) (18)
28 Grateful Dead – *St Stephen*   (25)
29 The Amboy Dukes – *Journey To The Centre Of Your*

Mind   (16)

30 The Who – *Tommy*   (LP)
31 Cream – *Strange Brew*   (30)
32 Rolling Stones – *2000 Light Years From Home*   (35)
33 Rolling Stones – *She's A Rainbow*   (27)
34 Vanilla Fudge – *You Keep Me Hangin' On*   (38)
35 The Temptations – *Psychedelic Shack*   (20)
36 Count Five – *Psychotic Reaction*   (21)
37 Love – *You Set The Scene*   (39)
38 Beatles – *She Said She Said*   (28)
39 13th Floor Elevator – *You're Gonna Miss Me*   (40)
40 The Chambers Brothers – *Time Has Come Today*
    (33)

Figures in parenthesis refer to positions in *The Book of Rock Lists*.

Britain produced few psychedelic sounds of worth, and there were equally few groups, with the Beatles, Stones, Eric Burdon, Who, Cream, Floyd, stealing the honours and also with a track like *Itchycoo Park*, the Small Faces.

A glance through the releases of 1967 and 1968 suggest these groups and records – in release or review order – might qualify (as well as fitting into a 'flower-powers image') though in many instances it was more a case of looking for a commercial sound and image. (*indicates US Chart.) Records have been chosen if they were marketed with psychedelic, 'underground' overtones or, in some cases, because the records were adopted by flower-people (or whatever term you care to use!). A number of 'blues' oriented bands and artists have been included, for this particular musical idiom seeped into the general 'underground' consciousness of the time.

It's not always been easy to remember whether certain records were psychedelic based and, in some instances, whether the artist/group was British, American or something else. This long list is not intended as an exhaustive table. It is confined to material issued in Britain.

January Releases
The Misunderstood – *I Can Take You to The Sun* (Fontana), one group member came from South Shields
Leaves – *Hey Joe* (Mira, US)
Jim Hendrix* – *Hey Joe/Stone Free* (Polydor)

February Releases
Electric Prunes* – *I Had Too Much To Dream (Last Night)* (Reprise)

March Releases
Pink Floyd – *Arnold Layne/Candy And A Currant Bun* (Columbia)
Jimi Hendrix Experience* – *Purple Haze/51st Anniversary* (Track)

April Releases
The Move – *I Can Hear The Grass Grow* (Deram)
The Apostolic Intervention – *(Tell Me) Have You Ever Seen Me* (Immediate)
The Electric Prunes* – *Get Me To The World On Time* (Reprise)

May Releases
Julian Covey and the Machine – *A Little Bit Hurts* (Island)
Jimi Hendrix Experience* – *The Wind Cries Mary* (Track)
Procol Harum – *Whiter Shade Of Pale* (Deram)
Jimi Hendrix Experience* – *Are You Experienced*, LP (Track)
Jefferson Airplane* – *Somebody To Love* (RCA)
Beatles – *Sgt Pepper's Lonely Hearts Club Band*, LP (Parlophone)
Traffic – *Paper Sun* (Island)

June Releases
The Cream – *Strange Brew* (Reaction)

Pink Floyd – *See Emily Play* (Columbia)
The Fifth Estate★ – *Ding Dong! The Witch Is Dead* (Stateside)
Scott McKenzie★ – *San Francisco What's The Difference* (CBS)
Mamas and Papas – *Mamas and Papas Deliver* (RCA)

July Releases
Nirvana – *Tiny Goddess* (Island)
John's Children – *Come and Play With Me In The Garden* (Track)
Peanut Butter Conspiracy★ – *It's A Happening Thing* (CBS)

August Releases
The Young Rascals★ – *A Girl Like You* (Atlantic)
The Electric Prunes – *The Great Banana Hoax* (Reprise)
The Vanilla Fudge★ – *You Keep Me Hanging On* (Atlantic)
The Flowerpot Men – *Let's Go To San Francisco* (Deram)
West Coast Consortium – *Some Other Someday* (Pye)
The Doors★ – *Light My Fire/The Crystal Ship* (Elektra)
Small Faces – *Itchycoo Park* (Immediate)
The Fifth Dimension★ – *Up-Up And Away* (Liberty)
Moby Grape★ – *Hey Grandma* (CBS)
The Sunshine Company – *Happy* (Liberty)
Eric Burdon – *Good Times* (MGM)
Rolling Stones – *We Love You/Dandelion* (Decca)
Jimi Hendrix★ – *Burning Of The Midnight Lamp* (Track)
Traffic – *Hole In My Shoe* (Island)

September Releases
Pink Floyd – *The Piper At The Gates Of Dawn*, LP (Columbia)
Kaleidoscope – *Flight From Asmiya* (Fontana)
Jefferson Airplane★ – *Surrealistic Pillow* (RCA)
The Marmalade – *I See The Rain* (CBS)
David Garrick – *Don't Go Out Into The Rain, Sugar*, LP (Pye)

Paul Revere And The Raiders – *I Had A Dream* (CBS)
The Turtles – *You Know What I Mean/Rugs Of Woods And Flowers* (London)
The Crazy World Of Arthur Brown – *Devil's Grip/Give Him A Flower* (Track)
The Herd – *From The Underworld* (Fontana)
The Amboy Dukes★ – *High Life In Whitley Wood* (Polydor)
Tomorrow – *Revolution* (Parlophone)
The Fairytale – *Lovely People* (Decca)
Fleur-De-Lys – *I Can See The Light* (Polydor)
The Incredible String Band – *The 5000 Spirits or The Layers Of Onions* (Elektra)
Jefferson Airplane★ – *White Rabbit* (RCA)
Procol Harum – *Homburg* (Regal Zonophone)

October Releases
Every Mother's Son★ – *Every Mother's Son*, LP (MGM)
Vanilla Fudge★ – *Eleanor Rigby* (Atlantic)
The Barron Knights – *Here Comes The Bees* (Columbia), a take-off of flower people
John's Children – *Go-Go Girl* (Track)
Nirvana – *Pentecost Hotel* (Island)
Who – *I Can See For Miles* (Track)
Blossom Toes – *Look At Me* (Marmalade)
The Troggs – *Love Is All Around/When Will The Rain Come (Page One)*, included because even the Troggs picked up the mood of the times
Eric Burdon – *San Franciscan Nights/Gratefully Dead* (MGM)
The Timebox – *Don't Make Promises* (Deram)
Julie Felix – *Flowers* LP (Fontana): *The Magic Of The Playground* (Fontana), although American she settled here
Simon Dupree and the Big Sound – *Kits* (Parlophone)
Kippington Lodge – *Shy Boy* (Parlophone)
The Left Banke – *Desiree* (Philips)
The Seeds★ – *Future*, LP (Vocation)

November Releases
The Nice – *The Thoughts of Enerlist Davjack* (Immediate)
Tim Buckley★ – *Morning Glory* (Elektra)
The Flowerpot Men – *A Walk In The Sky* (Deram)
The Moody Blues – *Nights In White Satin* (Deram)
Strawberry Alarm Clock★ – *Incense and Peppermints* (Pye)
Felius Andromeda – *Meditations* (Decca)
Country Joe and the Fish★ – *Electric Music For The Mind and Body* (Fontana)
The Moody Blues – *Days Of Future Passed*, LP (Deram)
Pink Floyd – *Apples and Oranges/Paint Box* (Columbia)
Buffalo Springfield★ – *Rock 'n' Roll Woman* (Atlantic)
Beatles – *I Am The Walrus* (Parlophone), main side was *Hello, Goodbye*
Tim Buckley★ – *Goodbye & Hello* (Elektra)
The Herd – *Paradise Lost* (Fontana)
The Subway – *The Tickle* (Regal Zonophone)
Jefferson Airplane – *The Ballad Of You And Me And Pooneil* (RCA)
Tintern Abbev – *Beeside* (Deram)
Moby Grape★ – *Moby Grape*, LP (CBS)
Eric Burdon and the Animals – *Winds of Change*, LP (MGM)
Country Joe and the Fish★ – *Not So Sweet Martha* (Fontana)
The Lovin' Spoonful★ – *She Is Still A Mystery* (Kama Sutra)

December Releases
Beatles – *Magical Mystery Tour*, LP (Parlophone)
Kaleidoscope – *Tangerine Dream* (Fontana)
Traffic – *Here We Go Round The Mulberry Bush* (Island)
Doors – *Love Me Two Times/Moonlight Drive* (Elektra)
Stone Poneys – *Different Drum* (Capitol)
The Electric Prunes – *Long Day's Flight* (Reprise)
Traffic – *Mr Fantasy* (Island)
Beatles – *Magical Mystery Tour*, EP (Parlophone)

Rolling Stones – *Their Satanic Majesties Request* (Decca)
Nirvana – *The Story Of Simon Simopath*, LP (Island)
Art – *Supernatural Fairy Tales*, LP (Island)
The State Of Micky and Tommy – *Frisco Bay* (Mercury)
The Sand Pebbles – *Love Power* (Track)
Mamas and Papas★ – *Glad To Be Unhappy* (RCA)
Pregnant Insomnia – *Wallpaper* (Direction)

1968

January Releases
Maharishi Mahesh Yogi – *Love – The Untapped Source Of Power That Lies Within You*, LP (Liberty)
The Loot – *Don't Turn Around* (CBS)
The Rose Garden★ – *Next Train To London* (Atlantic)
Love – *Alone Again Or* (Elektra)
Spooky Tooth – *Sunshine Help Me* (Island)
The Who – *The Who Sell Out*, LP (Track)
Grapefruit – *Dear Delilah* (RCA)
The Creation – *How Does It Feel To Feel* (Polydor)
The Move – *Fire Brigade* (Regal Zonophone)

February Releases
Eric Burdon – *Sky Pilot* (MGM)
Van Morrison – *Blowin' Your Mind* (London)
HP Lovecraft★ – *HP Lovecraft*, LP (Philips)
Captain Beefheart And His Magic Band★ – *Safe As Milk* (Pye)
Classics IV★ – *Spooky* (Liberty)
Traffic – *No Face, No Name And No Number* (Island)

March Releases
The Strawberry Alarm Clock★ – *Incense and Peppermints*, LP (Polydor)
Leonard Cohen – *The Songs of Leonard Cohen (CBS)*
Blossom Toes – *I'll Be Your Baby Tonight* (Marmalade)
Simon Dupree and The Big Sound – *For Whom The Bell Tolls* (Parlophone)
Judy Collins★ – *Wildflowers*, LP (Elektra)

The Butterfield Blues Band★ – *The Resurrection of Pigboy Crabshaw*, LP (Elektra)
The Electric Prunes★ – *Mass In F Minor* (Reprise)
The Turtles – *Sound Asleep* (London)
Blue Cheer★ – *Summertime Blues* (Philips)
Beatles – *The Inner Light* (Parlophone), main side was *Lady Madonna*
Country Joe and the Fish★ – *I Feel Like I'm Fixin' To Die*, LP (Fontana)
Dr Marigold's Prescription – *My Old Man's Groovy* (Pye)
The Incredible String Band – *Painting Box* (Elektra)
The Berkeley Kits – *Hang Up City* (Polydor)

April Releases
Jefferson Airplane – *After Bathing At Baxters* (RCA)
Nirvana – *Rainbow Chaser* (Island)
The Incredible String Band – *The Hangman's Beautiful Daughter*, LP (Elektra)
The Jimi Hendrix Experience – *Smash Hits*, LP (Polydor)
Clear Light★ – *Night Sounds Loud* (Elektra)
Pink Floyd – *It Would Be So Nice* (Columbia)
Lovin' Spoonful★ – *Everything Playing*, LP (Kama Sutra)

May Releases
Donovan – *A Gift From A Flower To A Garden*, LP (Pye)
Rainbow Follies – *Sallies Forth* (Parlophone)
Genesis – *A Winter's Tale* (Jonjo)
Eric Burdon and the Animals – *Monterey* (MGM)
Donovan – *Hurdy Gurdy Man* (Pye)
Hearts and Flowers★ – *She Sang Hymns Out Of Tune* (Capitol)

June Releases
Rotary Connection – *Rotary Connection* (Chess)
Eric Burdon and the Animals – *The Twain Shall Meet*, LP (MGM) Ultimate Spinach – *Ultimate Spinach* (MGM)
Velvet Underground★ – *White Light/White Heat* (Verve)

Canned Heat – *On The Road Again* (Liberty)
The Lemon Pipers★ – *Jelly Jungle* (Pye)
Mothers Of Invention – *We're Only In It For The Money* (Verve)
Eclection – *Nevertheless* (Elektra)
Arthur Brown – *The Crazy World Of Arthur Brown*, LP (Track)
The Moody Blues – *Voices In The Sky* (Deram)

July Releases
Doors – *The Unknown Soldier* (Elektra), flip of *We Could Be So Good Together*
Nirvana – *Girl In The Park* (Island)
The Electric Flag★ – *A Long Time Comin'*, LP (CBS)
Blue Cheer★ – *Vincebus Eruptum*, LP (Mercury)
Tyrannosaurus Rex – *My People Were Fair And Had Sky In Their Hair* (Regal Zonophone)
Joni Mitchell – *Joni Mitchell*, LP (Reprise), Canadian
Various★ – *The Rock Machine Turns You On*, LP (CBS)
Moody Blues – *In Search Of The Lost Chord*, LP (Deram)
Spanky and Our Gang – *Like To Get To Know You* (Mercury)
Chicken Shack – *40 Blue Fingers Freshly Packed*, LP (Blue Horizon)

August Releases
Pink Floyd – *A Saucerful Of Secrets*, LP (Columbia)
The West Coast Experimental Band★ – *A Child's Guide To Good And Evil*, LP (Reprise)
The United States Double Quarter★ – *Life Is Groovy* (BT Puppy)
The Savage Resurrection★ – *The Savage Resurrection*, LP (Mercury)
The Evergreen Blues★ – *7 Do Eleven*, LP (Mercury)
World Of Oz – *King Croesus* (Deram)
The Perishers – *How Does It Feel* (Fontana)
The Peppermint Rainbow★ – *Walking In Different Circles* (MCA)
Ten Years After – *Undead*, LP (Deram)

Laura Nyro* – *Eli And The Thirteenth Confession*, LP
(CBS)
Tyrannosaurus Rex – *One Inch Rock* (Regal Zonophone)
The Rascals* – *People Got To Be Free* (Atlantic)
The Yellow Balloon – *Stained Glass Window* (Stateside)
Butterscotch Caboose – *Melinda* (Bell)
Cream – *Wheels Of Fire*, LP (Polydor)
The Beatles – *Hey Jude/Revolution* (Apple)
Fleetwood Mac – *Mr Wonderful*, LP (Blue Horizon)
Earth Opera* – *Earth Opera*, LP (Elektra)
Big Pink* – *The Weight*, LP (Capitol)

September Releases
Jefferson Airplane* – *I You Feel Like China Breaking*
(RCA)
Kaleidoscope – *Jenny Artichock*, LP (Fontana)
The Steve Miller Band* – *The Steve Miller Band*, LP
(Capitol)
Doors* – *Waiting For The Sun*, LP (Elektra)
Simon Dupree and the Big Sound – *Thinking About My
Life* (Parlophone)
The Grateful Dead* – *Anthem Of The Sun*, LP (Warner)
Deep Purple – *Shades Of*, LP (Parlophone)
Procession* – *Every American Citizen* (Mercury)
Harper's Bizarre* – *The Secret Life Of*, LP (Warner)

October Releases
Big Brother and the Holding Company* – *Piece Of My
Heart* (CBS)
The Grateful Dead* – *Born Cross-Eyed* (Warner)
The Who – *Magic Bus* (Track)
Colours – *Love Heals* (Dot)
Jimi Hendrix Experience* – All Along The Watchtower
(Track)
The Chambers Brothers* – *Time Has Come Today*
(Direction)
Doors* – Light My Fire/Crystal Ship (Elektra)
The United States Of America* – *The Garden Of Earthly
Delights* (CBS)

Ravi Shanker – *At The Monterey International Pop Festival* (Columbia)
Joe Cocker – *With A Little Help From My Friends* (Regal Zonophone)
The Web – *Fully Interlocking*, LP (Deram)
The Nazz★ – *Open My Eyes* (SGC): *Nazz*, LP (SGC)
Steve Miller★ – *Living In The USA* (Capitol)
Buffalo Springfield★ – *Again*, LP (Atlantic)
Moody Blues – *Ride My See Saw* (Deram)
Blue Cheer★ – *Outside, Inside*, LP (Philips)

November Releases

The Cowsills★ – *Captain Sad And His Ship Of Fools* (MGM)
The Fugs★ – *Crystal Liaison*, LP (Transatlantic)
Steppenwolf★ – *Magic Carpet Ride*, LP (Stateside)
The Crazy World Of Arthur Brown – *Nightmare* (Track)
The Deviants – *You've Got To Hold On* (Stable)
The Nice – *Ars Longa Vita Brevis*, LP (Immediate)
The Beatles – *The Beatles* (white album), LP (Apple)
Simon and Garfunkel★ – *Wednesday Morning 3 am*, LP (CBS)
Omega – *Red Star*, LP (Decca)
Aphrodites Child – *Rain And Tears* (Mercury)
Ten Years After – *Hear Me Calling/I'm Going Home* (Deram)
Rolling Stones – *Beggars Banquet*, LP (Decca)
The Move – *Blackberry Way* (Regal Zonophone)
Canned Heat – *Going Up The Country* (Liberty)
Jeff Beck – *Truth*, LP (Columbia)
Kiki Dee – *Now The Flowers Cry* (Fontana)

December Releases

Pink Floyd – *Point Me To The Sky* (Columbia)
Galt Macdermot★ – *Hare Krishna* (Verve)
Grapefruit★ – *Someday Soon* (Dunhill)
Donovan – *Atlantis* (Pye)
Country Joe and the Fish★ – *Together*, LP (Fontana)
James Taylor★ – *James Taylor*, LP (Apple)

Steppenwolf* – *The Second*, LP (Dunhill)

John Mayall's Bare Wires – *And Now From Laurel Canyon* (Decca)

Blossom Dearie – *Hey John* (Fontana), tribute to John Lennon

The Cream – *Live At The Filmore*, LP (Polydor)

Rhubarb Rhubarb – *Rainmaker* (President)

The Tea Company* – *Come And Have Some Tea With Me*, LP (Mercury)

Stars Whose Records Missed

This is a random list of records that missed the chart. The records come from known names of the decade (or previous decade) or, in some instances, from people yet to make a significant impact upon the record world.

Carol Deene had *When He Wants A Woman* (CBS) as her return to the record scene in 1968 after a car crash. A powerful ballad.

Bachelors issued *If Ever I Would Leave You* (Decca) as reviewers said – the Bachelors go on and on – but 1967 was the year of their final hit, and this well reviewed disc meant nothing.

Denny Laine on *Too Much In Love* (Deram), Laine – ex-other bands, and Moody Blues especially – want Latin and semi-classical but missed. 1968

Kiki Dee tried with *Can't Take My Eyes Off You* (Fontana) but Andy Williams had already charted with his Stateside hit version before this was released. The talented lady said she loved the song and the charts could stand two versions. It was not so. The year was 1968.

Petula Clark sang *Don't Give Up* (Pye) which seemed an apt title for Petula: three hits in 1967, including the chart-topper *This Is My Song* could not save her from an icy response in 1968. Another ominous title *Kiss Me Goodbye* charted at 50 in March, but this one didn't chart at any time.

Graham Bonney tried *Thank You Baby* (Columbia). One-hit, *Supergirl*, Graham had a Bruce Johnston song and production but to no avail. 1967.

The Mindbenders issued *We'll Talk About It* (Fontana). Life wasn't quite at an end, for the four week charting *The Letter* (1967) was yet to come, but this March record of the same year could do little, even with its commercial air.

Billy Fury sang *Suzanne In The Mirror* (Parlophone) and the reviewers said it was a tremendous song, and an equally tremendous performance, but it failed to regain chart momentum for Billy whose last hit before this September, 1967 hit, was August of the previous year with *Give Me Your Word*.

Susan Maughan had three hits 1962–63 but the lady's releases continued into 1964 and here in 1965 with, *Make Him Mine* (Philips) a catchy disc. No joy came from the record buyers.

Kathy Kirby issued *The Way Of Love* (Decca). Her last chart hit was in March of 1965 and this follow-up to *I Belong* fizzled and so did the others that followed. The critics highly commended it.

Small Faces followed their first UK chart hit *Whatcha Gonna Do About It*, with *I've Got Mine* (Decca). It built excitingly and seemed a certain follow-up hit, alas it was not so. 1965.

David Essex had already been knocking at chart's door for some time, and the general opinion suggested he might have a minor breakthrough with *That Takes Me Back* (Decca), but the efforts of Essex and manager Bowman were not chart rewarded until 1973. Year of this was 1969.

Roger Miller had hits in 1965 and 1969, with 1966 merely seeing a carry-over of *England Swings*. *Husbands And Wives* (Philips) in 1966 a rather gentle countryish number had novelty but sold little.

Percy Sledge had *Heart Of A Child* on Atlantic. *When A Man Loves A Woman* and *Warm & Tender Love* had already given him two hits in 1966 but there was no hat trick for this rather lack-lustre song, even if Percy worked hard vocally to resurrect something.

Frank Ifield's 1965 was a mixed affair. There were two minor hits, *Paradise* (26) and *No One Will Ever Know* (25), with the first coming in August. But *I'm So Lonesome* (Columbia) issued in March meant little.

Rolf Harris tried with *Iko, Iko* (Columbia). Its catchy repetitive title line suggested a minor hit but Harris had no hit between 1963 and 1969. This was a May release, 1965.

Murray Head: *Alberta* (Columbia). *Superstar*-famed Head – with records galore for a number of companies – has only had Seventies success (and that for one week) with the theme song of the Lloyd-Webber musical. But he's been trying for some time. This was May 1965.

Petula Clark had just one 1963 hit with *Casanova* (39). *Valentino* (Pye), follow-up, failed to show.

Tommy Roe was just off a top five success with *The Folk Singer*, but *Kiss And Run* (HMV), a catchy ballad, could not continue his momentum, although his September single *Everybody* would give him another 1963 hit.

Pat Boone sang *Memory Mountain* (London/Dot). Boone lasted into 1963 thanks to *The Main Attraction*. His UK chart career was fading. Previously *Meditation* had flopped, this tuneful affair went the same way, even though reviewers thought it would put him back into the charts.

Connie Francis issued *Follow The Boys* (MGM) in

1963. Her last chart hit *I'm Gonna Be Warm This Winter* had only a one week chart run but no-one imagined that it would take until 1965 before she hit the Top 30 once more. This was a film title cut and most expected some kind of chart showing in 1963.

The Drifters sang on *Stranger On The Shore* (London), a vocal version from the States of the tune Acker charted to the top, but it meant little. The Drifters did have a minor hit the same year (1962) with *When My Little Girl Is Smiling*.

The Allisons were Eurovision entrants of 1961 with *Are You Sure* charting at number two. *Words* went to 34 but even February-1962 *Lessons In Love* reaching 30 could not give the necessary push for Sweet And Lovely (Fontana), a soulful piano, excited chorus and energetic vocal number of 1962.

Jackie Lynton issued *All Of Me* (Pye). Indeed talented Mr Lynton was trying for fame in 1962 but it didn't come with this or any other single.

Cloda Rodgers sang *Believe Me I'm No Fool* (Decca) in 1962. She was seen as a rival of Helen Shapiro but this weakish number was to do little. (Later called Clodagh)

Dave Berry and the Sponge. With *Huma Luma* (Decca), Berry was still trying in April 1969 for a follow-up hit to his last, *Mama* (5, 1966), but this Carterter-Stephens number for all the reviewer's praise did little.

Doors *Touch Me* (Elektra). A rather lukewarm press for the US group and a tarnished image doubtless contributed to a no-hit 1969 for the famed Stateside group, the previous year they had a Top 20 hit with *Hello I Love You*.

Stevie Wonder had *Nothing's Too Good For My Baby*

(Motown) sandwiched between his first UK hit *Uptight* from February 1966 onward and mid-August chart entry of Dylan's, *Blowin' In The Wind*, but it didn't do anything.

Overlanders tried with *Go Where You Wanna Go* (Pye). *Michelle* had given them an early 1966 number one, but for all the beat this one fizzled out.

Dave Clark Five had *Nineteen Days* from Columbia, but 1966 was bad year for the DC5. They had one week in May for *Look Before You Leap* and nothing for this.

Tony Orlando sang *Shirley* (Columbia). *Bless You* was a hit in 1961 (5), but this soft gentle affair was hardly the one to restore his fortunes. It would be 1971 and then with Dawn before he became chart-bound.

Gene Pitney had a minor, and second, hit with *Town Without Pity* in 1962, but *Mecca* (United Artists) was not to improve things for him, though at the end of 1963 he was to begin charting strong with *24 Hours From Tulsa*.

Chris Farlowe sang the Jagger-Richard song *Yesterday's Papers* (Immediate) with production by Jagger, and despite being sandwiched between minor hits *My Way Of Givin' In* and *Moanin'* in 1967, it missed entirely.

The Dubliners failed with *All For Me Grog* (Major Minor). This was the stain on a successful 1967 that gave them three hits. Fortunately the next one, *Black Velvet Band* restored the year to something pleasing.

Manfred Mann tried *So Long Dad* (Fontana) in 1967, the year that had *Ha Ha Said The Clown* at 4, and *Sweet Pea* at 36. This, the disastrous third single, meant nothing even though Randy Newman wrote the lyrics. *Mighty Quinn* was to recover declining popularity in 1968.

Peter, Paul and Mary sang *When The Ship Comes In* (Warner). A Dylan composition gave two minor hits in 1964 for PPM, but this was not to give them a 1965 winner. Their next hit was 1970.

Freddy Cannon cried *Action* (Warner). Six hit 1960's Cannon, with one the previous decade, had had nothing showing since *Palisades Park* in 1962 (20), and this high charting US hit made no impression here.

Americans in Britain:
The Music of the US

In the 1950s it was hard to find a really good British record that was not a cover of an existing American hit. The classic rockers came from the States in music thrown up by the likes of Bill Haley, Elvis Presley, Chuck Berry, Jerry Lee Lewis, Carl Perkins, Little Richard, Crickets and Gene Vincent. And there were others of less frenetic disposition, like the great Fats Domino, Everly Brothers, Platters, Ricky Nelson, Eddie Cochran and twanging on guitar with thunderous sound was Duane Eddy.

The American record companies ruled the roost and the charts were full of records from US Columbia on the Philips label, on Capitol, on London American and Brunswick, Vogue Coral and MGM.

There were, of course, British hit artists and they did have considerable following but, as already mentioned, it did seem to be the story of foraging around for UK versions of major US charting records, and though there was some home-grown material which reached the charts it seemed incidental. Teen music depended on the States to export Elvis and Bill Haley and of those UK people thrown up to counteract the US music explosion only a few, like Cliff Richard, proved to be lasting.

But the 1960s saw a major change. Britain found its supergroup in the Beatles and in 1964 the Liverpool foursome knocked America for six and suddenly a vast array of other UK groups made themselves felt. A new blast of fresh air swept through the record market and scene.

But, of course, even with the likes of Beatles, Hollies, Freddie and the Dreamers, Stones, Animals, Moody Blues, etc, the Americans still had a good share of the UK scene. Here I list – in chart entry terms – the successful US acts of the 1960s.

1 Elvis Presley 42
2 Roy Orbison 28
3 Brenda Lee 22
3 Jim Reeves 22
5 Everly Brothers 21
6 Beach Boys 19
7 Supremes 18
8 Gene Pitney 17
9 Frank Sinatra 16
9 Ray Charles 16
11 Duane Eddy 15
12 Four Tops 14
12 Connie Francis 14
12 Del Shannon 14
12 Bobby Darin 12
16 Otis Redding 11
17 Monkees 10
17 Nat 'King' Cole 10
17 Four Seasons 10
17 Stevie Wonder 10

It's interesting to observe how 20 British artists would make the Top 11 and, of course, Cliff Richard narrowly beat Presley by one hit.

In the US list the following artists had their first hits in the UK during this decade, Roy Orbison (1960), Brenda Lee (1960), Beach Boys (1963), Supremes (1964), Gene Pitney (1961), Four Tops (1965), Del Shannon (1961) and Otis Redding (1965).

But what were the classic hits outside of the top scoring chart artists? On an A to Z basis of artist these cuts I suggest either really thrilled people then or then and now:

Fontella Bass – *Rescue Me* (Chess)
Tony Bennett – *I Left My Heart in San Francisco* (CBS)
Chuck Berry – *No Particular Place To Go* (Pye International)
Gary US Bonds – *Quarter To Three* (Top Rank)
Booker T and the MGs – *Time Is Tight* (Stax)

Box Tops – *The Letter* (Stateside)
James Brown – *Papa's Got A Brand New Bag* (London)
Dave Brubeck – *Take Five* (Fontana)
B Bumble and the Stingers – *Nut Rocker* (Top Rank)
Johnny Burnette – *Dreamin'* (London): *You're Sixteen* (London)
Byrds – *Mr Tambourine Man* (CBS)
Canned Heat – *On The Road Again* (Liberty)
Freddy Cannon – *Way Down Yonder In New Orleans* (Top Rank)
Vikki Carr – *It Must Be Him* (Liberty)
Bruce Chanel – *Hey Baby* (Mercury)
Cher – *Bang Bang (My Baby Shot Me Down)* (Liberty)
Chubby Checker – *The Twist* (Columbia)
Chiffons – *He's So Fine* (Stateside)
Perry Como – *And I Love You So* (RCA)
Arthur Conley – *Sweet Soul Music* (Atlantic)
Sam Cooke – *Twistin' The Night Away* (RCA)
Floyd Cramer – *On The Rebound* (RCA)
Creedence Clearwater Revival – *Proud Mary* (Liberty): *Bad Moon Rising* (Liberty)
Crickets – *That'll Be The Day* (Vogue Coral)
Crickets – *Oh Boy* (Coral)
Crystals – *He's A Rebel* (London): *Da Doo Ron Ron* (London): *Then He Kissed Her* (London)
James Darren – *Goodbye Cruel World* (Pye International)
Doris Day – *Move Over Darling* (CBS)
Jimmy Dean – *Big Bad John* (Philips)
Dion – *The Wanderer* (HMV)
Dixie Cups – *Chapel Of Love* (Pye International)
Doors – *Light My Fire* (Elektra)
Lee Dorsey – *Working In A Coalmine* (Stateside): Holy Cow (Stateside)
Drifters – *Save The Last Dance For Me* (London)
Bob Dylan – *Times They Are A-Changin'* (CBS): *Like A Rolling Stone* (CBS)
Shirley Ellis – *The Clapping Song* (London)
Betty Everett – *Getting Mighty Crowded* (Fontana)
Shelley Fabares – *Johnny Angel* (Pye International)

Fifth Dimension – *Aquarius – Let The Sunshine In* (Liberty)
Eddie Floyd – *Knock On Wood* (Atlantic)
Four Seasons – *Rag Doll* (Philips)
Aretha Franklin – *I Say A Little Prayer* (Atlantic)
John Fred and the Playboy Band – *Judy In Disguise (With Glasses)* (Pye)
Bobby Fuller – *I Fought The Law* (London)
Marvin Gaye – *I Heard It Through The Grapevine* (Motown)
Marvin Gaye and Kim Weston – *It Takes Two* (Motown)
Bobbie Gentry – *Ode To Billy Joe* (Capitol)
Stan Getz and Joao Gilberto – *The Girl From Ipanema (Garota De Ipanema)* (Verve)
Don Gibson – *Sea Of Heartbreak* (RCA)
Bobby Goldsboro – *Honey* (United Artists)
Eydie Gormie – *Yes My Darling Daughter* (CBS)
Dobie Gray – *The In Crowd* (London)
Harper's Bizarre – *59th Street Bridge Song (Feeling Groovy)* (Warner)
Edwin Hawkins Singers – *Oh Happy Day* (Buddah)
Jimi Hendrix Experience – *Hey Joe* (Polydor): *All Along The Watchtower* (Track)
Clarence 'Frogman' Henry – *But I Do* (Pye)
Hollywood Argyles – *Alley Oop* (London)
Isley Brothers – *This Old Heart Of Mine* (Motown)
Marv Johnson – *You Got What It Takes* (London)
Jimmy Jones – *Good Timin'* (MGM)
Ben E King *Stand By Me* (London)
Carole King – *It Might As Well Rain Until September* (London)
Lemon Pipers – *Green Tambourine* (Pye)
Ketty Lester – *Love Letters* (London)
Little Eva – *The Locomotion* (London)
Bob Lind – *Elusive Butterfly* (Fontana)
Lovin' Spoonful – *Summer In The City* (Kama Sutra)
Bob Luman – *Let's Think About Living* (Warner)
McCoys – *Hang On Sloopy* (Immediate)
Barry McGuire – *Eve Of Destruction* (RCA)

Scott McKenzie – *San Francisco (Be Sure To Wear Flowers In Your Hair)* (CBS)
Mamas and Papas – *Monday Monday* (RCA)
Marcels – *Blue Moon* (Pye International)
Little Peggy March – *Hello Heartache Goodbye Love* (RCA)
Marvelettes – *When You're Young And In Love* (Motown)
Monkees – *I'm A Believer* (RCA)
Chris Montez – *Let's Dance* (London)
Nashville Teens – *Tobacco Road* (Decca)
Rick Nelson – *Hello Mary Lou* (London)
Nilsson – *Everybody's Talkin'* (RCA)
1910 Fruitgum Company – *Simon Says* (Pye International)
Tony Orlando – *Bless you* (Fontana)
Robert Parker – *Barefootin'* (Island)
Paul and Paula – *Hey Paula* (Philips)
Peter, Paul and Mary – *Blowing In The Wind* (Warner)
Wilson Pickett – *In The Midnight Hour* (Atlantic)
Sandy Posey – *Single Girl* (MGM)
Johnny Preston – *Running Bear* (Mercury)
Ramrods – *Riders In The Sky* (London)
Otis Redding and Carla Thomas – *Tramp* (Stax)
Martha Reeves and the Vandellas – *Jimmy Mack* (Motown)
Righteous Brothers – *You've Lost That Lovin' Feelin'* (London)
Jeannie C Riley – *Harper Valley PTA* (Polydor)
Smokey Robinson and the Miracles – *Tracks Of My Tears* (Motown)
Jimmie Rodgers – *English Country Garden* (Columbia)
Tommy Roe – *Dizzy* (Stateside)
Ronettes – *Be My Baby* (London): *Baby I Love You* (London)
Rooftop Singers – *Walk Right In* (Fontana)
Diana Ross and the Supremes, and the Temptations – *I Second That Emotion* (Motown)
Roy C – *Shotgun Wedding* (Island)

Royal Guardsmen – *Snoopy Vs The Red Baron* (Stateside)

Ruby and the Romantics – *Our Day Will Come* (London)

Jimmy Ruffin – *What Becomes Of The Broken Hearted* (Motown)

Staff Sergeant Barry Sadler – *Ballad Of The Green Berets* (RCA)

Sam and Dave – *Soul Man* (Stax)

Sam The Sham and the Pharaohs – *Wooly Bully* (MGM)

Sandpipers – *Guantanamera* (Pye)

Shangri-Las – Remember (Walkin' In The Sand) (Red Bird): Leader of the Pack (Red Bird)

Allan Sherman – *Hello Muddah Hello Faddah* (Warner)

Shirelles – *Soldier Boy* (HMV): *Will You Love Me Tomorrow* (Top Rank)

Showstoppers – *Ain't Nothing But A Houseparty* (Beacon)

Simon and Garfunkel – *Mrs Robinson* (CBS)

Nina Simone – *Ain't Got No – I Got Life* (RCA)

Nancy Sinatra – *These Boots Are Made For Walkin'* (Reprise)

Nancy Sinatra and Frank Sinatra – *Somethin' Stupid* (Reprise)

Sir Douglas Quintet – *She's About A Mover* (London)

Percy Sledge – *When A Man Loves A Woman* (Atlantic)

Sly and the Family Stone – *Dance To The Music* (Direction)

O C Smith – *Son Of Hickory Holler's Tramp* (CBS)

Steppenwolf – *Born To Be Wild* (Stateside)

Sufaris – *Wipe Out* (London)

Norma Tanega – *Walking My Cat Named Dog* (Stateside)

Felice Taylor – *I Feel Love Comin' On* (President)

R Dean Taylor – *Gotta See Jane* (Motown)

Nino Tempo and April Stevens – *Deep Purple* (London)

Sue Thompson – *Paper Tiger* (Hickory)

Johnny Tillotson – *Poetry In Motion* (London)

The Tokens – *The Lion Sleeps Tonight* (RCA)

Ricky Valance – *Tell Laura I Love Her* (Columbia)

Leroy Van Dyke – *Walk On By* (Mercury)

Vanilla Fudge – *You Keep Me Hangin' On* (Atlantic)

Bobby Vee – *The Night Has A Thousand Eyes* (Liberty)
Ventures – *Walk Don't Run* (Top Rank)
Dionne Warwick – *Do You Know The Way To San Jose* (Pye International)
Mary Wells – *My Guy* (Stateside)
Andy Williams – *Can't Take My Eyes Off You* (CBS)
Stevie Wonder – *I Was Made To Love Her* (Motown)
Young Rascals – *Groovin'* (Atlantic)
Zagger and Evans – *In The Year 2525* (RCA)

But for one reason or another a great many fine records never chart, and the following US record chart hits failed to make their mark here: in random order.

The Band – *The Weight/I Shall Be Released* (Capitol)
Big Brother and the Holding Company – *Piece Of My Heart* (Columbia)
Association – *Cherish* (Valiant): *Along Comes Mary* (Valiant)
Arbors – *The Letter* (Date)
Merilee Rush – *Reach Out I'll Be There* (Bell): *Angel Of The Morning* (Bell)
Buffalo Springfield – *For What It's Worth (Hey What's That Sound)* (Atco)
Gene Chandler – *Duke Of Earl* (Vee-Jay)
The Sensations – *Let Me In* (Argo)
Don Gardner and Dee Ford – *I Need Your Lovin'* (Fire)
Barbara Lynn – *You'll Lose A Good Thing* (Jamie)
Checkmates Ltd, featuring Sonny Charles – *Black Pearl* (A&M)
Iron Butterfly – *In-A-Gadda-Da-Vida* (Atco)
Jan and Dean – *Deadman's Curve* (Liberty)
Jaynetts – *Sally Go Round The Roses* (Tuff)
Jefferson Airplane – *Somebody To Love* (RCA): *White Rabbit* (RCA)
Chris Kenner – *I Like It Like That, Part 1* (Instant)
Frankie Laine – *You Gave Me A Mountain* (ABC)
Led Zeppelin – *Whole Lotta Love* (Atlantic)
Left Banke – *Walk Away Renee* (Smash)

Barbara Lewis – *Hello Stranger* (Atlantic)
Bobby Lewis – *Tossin' And Turnin'* (Beltone)
Gary Lewis and the Playboys – *Save Your Heart For Me* (Liberty)
Darlene Love – *(Today I Met) The Boy I'm Gonna Marry* (Philles): *Wait Til' My Bobby Gets Home* (Philles)
Newsbeats – *Bread And Butter* (Hickory)
Orlons – *South Street* (Cameo)
Rita Pavone – *Remember Me* (RCA)
Playmates – *Beep Beep* (Roulette)
Della Reese – *Not One Minute More* (RCA)
Regents – *Barbara-Ann* (Gee)
Paul Revere and the Raiders – *Kicks* (Columbia)
Johnny Rivers – *Poor Side Of Town* (Imperial): *Baby I Need Your Lovin'* (Imperial)
Rose Garden – *Next Plane To London* (Atco)
Rosie and the Originals – *Angel Baby* (Highland)
Sensations – *Let Me In* (Argo)
Shep and the Limelites (Hull)
Sir Douglas Quintet – *Mendocino* (Smash)
Spanky and Our Gang – *Sunday Mornin'* (Mercury): *Like To Get To Know You* (Mercury)
Spirit – *I Got A Line On You* (Ode)
Gale Storm – *I Hear You Knocking* (Dot)
Strawberry Alarm Clock – *Incense and Peppermints* (Unit)
Johnnie Taylor – *Who's Making Love* (Stax)
Turtles – *It Ain't Me Babe* (White Whale)
Frankie Valli – *Can't Take My Eyes Off You* (Philips)
Charles Wright and the Watts 103rd Street Rhythm Band – *Do Your Thing* (Warner)
Simon and Garfunkel – *Sound Of Silence* (Columbia)
Bob Crewe Generation – *Music To Watch Girls By* (Dyno Voice)
Byrds – *So You Wanna Be A Rock 'N' Roll Star* (Columbia)
Mark Dinning – *Teen Angel* (MGM)
Skip and Flip – *Cherry Pie* (Brent)
Jerry Butler – *He Will Break Your Heart* (Vee-Jay)
Barrett Strong – *Money* (Anna)

Dee Clark – *Rain Drops* (Vee-Jay)
Maxine Brown – *All In My Mind* (Nomar)
Dick and Dee Dee – *The Mountains High* (Liberty)
Ike and Tina Turner – *It's Gonna Work Out Fine* (Sue)
Marvelettes – *Please Mr Postman* (Tamla)
Contours – *Do You Love Me* (Gordy)
Orlons – *The Wah Watusi* (Cameo)
Barbara Lynn – *You'll Lose A Good Thing* (Jamie)
Jay and the Americans – *She Cried* (United Artists)
Etta James – *Something's Got A Hold On Me* (Argo)
Impressions – *It's Alright* (ABC)
Jimmy Soul – *If You Wanna Be Happy* (SPQR)
Angels – *My Boyfriend's Back* (Smash)
Freddie Scott – *Hey, Girl* (Colpix)
Lonnie Mack *Memphis* (Fraternity)
Doris Troy – *Just One Look* (Atlantic)
Dovells – *You Can't Sit Down* (Parkway)
Garnett Mimms and the Enchanters – *Cry Baby* (United Artists)
Rufus Thomas – *Walkin' The Dog* (Stax)
Jackie Wilson – *Baby Workout* (Brunswick)
Little Milton – *We're Gonna Make It* (Checker)
Capitols – *Cool Jerk* (Karen)
Archie Bell and the Drells – *Tighten Up* (Atlantic)
Deep Purple – *Hush (Tetragrammaton)*
Fifth Dimension – *Stoned Soul Picnic* (Soul City)
Kingsmen – *Louie Louie* (East West)
Ronnie Hawkins – *Down In The Alley* (Roulette)
Mountain – *Mississippi Queen* (Windfall)
Guess Who – *No Time* (RCA)
Randy and the Rainbows – *Denise* (Rust)
Aretha Franklin – *Call Me* (Atlantic)
Rascals – *A Beautiful Morning* (Atlantic)

Some of these American hits failed to cross the Atlantic
for sound reason – UK artists made cover versions which
nudged out the original, British companies did not always
release the American hit and sometimes lifted a different
track from an album because they felt it appealed more to

the indigenous market – America created its own stars or general, recorded sound that either created or bounced off the existing home market and prevailing pop culture of the time. There are many reasons, though sometimes not even excuses or explanations suffice to explain why a record of taste and quality fails.

America began the 1960s as self-contained, content to export its music and stars. Rock 'n' roll showed no sign of abating and its chief star Elvis Presley seemed set for another decade of hits. Arguably the most interesting happening was the emergence of Roy Orbison from country and western pastures, and most commendable was his ability to claim attention and resultant success both sides of the Atlantic.

In more general terms everyone was shaken by major Government investigation into payola scandals during 1960. 1961 saw funk enjoy considerable popularity. So-called 'production-line' pop was emerging in a major way, with schools of songwriters supplying hit songs to artists who could not write original tunes. One of America's biggest groups – Dion and the Belmonts split. The same year saw the birth of Motown Records in Detroit from where hits would soon churn out. Elvis was now much quieter, R&B enjoyed good times, and in factual terms singles accounted for less than 10 per cent of industry's sales, but the radio stations played them, and an artist's way into public awareness was through airplay. 1962 saw the States embrace the Twist while things were much cooler toward the dance craze here in Britain. Much more interesting, at least for me, was the emergence of Phil Spector, ex-Teddy Bears, as a producer and creator of a sound that came with a considerable number of groups. Spector formed the Philles label. The Four Seasons emerged as a major new pop group, Booker T and the MGs proved they were more than a fine studio house band by gaining their own hits and accompanying fan support. In 1963 while we wallowed over the Beatles the Americans kept their distance (for twelve months anyway – the Canadians were not so fussy) Motown had a hot year, the Shirelles kept R&B alive and kicking and Steveland Morris Hardaway (Stevie Wonder) appeared as a pre-teen genius, the Beach Boys made surf seem within the reach of everyone and, otherwise, it was a case of asking why Capitol (US) kept saying no to releasing the Beatles. But they changed their minds in 1964.

In 1964 Britannia ruled the US but only after more initial problems for the Beatles. Capitol still expressed doubt, and so four singles were issued on other labels, where their release didn't cause a similiar furore to that experienced in Britain. But someone still thought the Beatles could go places and would do so if the appropriate promotional campaign was mounted, which it was. The view was correct and hot on the heels of the four's amazing success came a flood of other successful UK acts which not even the restrictive attitude of the American Musicians' Union could quell. The Twist had died and soon came the Monkey, the Jerk, the Bird, and the Frug, but as was so often the case these dance floor gyrations meant little in Britain. Of the new US groups the Supremes took the attention. British influence continued until 1966 with The Rolling Stones attracting a huge following in 1965. R&B with Otis Redding, James Brown and Wilson Pickett fared well, Bob Dylan became a household name thanks to his song *Mr Tambourine Man* being taken into the pop charts by folk-rockers The Byrds. Gospel music had a departure in Dionne Warwick and pop gained a future long-lasting star. In 1966 the US government authorities tried to ensure rock songs with drug or similiar lyrical connotations were given no airplay. Meantime The Beach Boys produced *Pet Sounds*, Simon and Garfunkel produced home-grown truths about American life in pleasant musical form; The Stones and Beatles ensured British presence was maintained, and the Monkees arrived. Flower power came in 1967, 'peace-love and freedom' was born, drug-taking influenced groups and cultural life-styles, and amidst it the Americans took Procol Harum under their wing, almost made the Spencer Davis Group as big as The

Stones, liked Van Morrison and themselves produced
The Association, Doors, Jefferson Airplane, Buffalo
Springfield and a host of others. Steppenwolf arrived in
1968; as did Sly and the Family Stone; Janis Joplin after
Monterey success in 1967 made her mark; Aretha
Franklin was named top singles artist of the year by major
music paper *Billboard*; post Otis-Redding's death saw the
artist with six chart hits; John and Yoko indulged in an
album *TwoVirgins*; Britain's Stones hit the top with
Jumpin' Jack Flash; clubs flourished coast to coast and for
the Beatles, *Hey Jude* coupled with *Revolution* proved a
huge seller. Creedence Clearwater Revival bowed in with
Proud Mary and, in America, the first of nine successive
million sellers; the Band had *Music From Big Pink* on the
market; the Woodstock Festival spawned a three record
album set and another bundle to follow; a host of interesting bands came to the fore on the West Coast like It's A
Beautiful Day and Flock; there was Blood Sweat & Tears
and other blues-styled outfits; Three Dog Night; Stones;
late 1968-assembled; 1969-functioning Zeppelin took the
hard-rockers by storm; Britain's Who were one of the
main Woodstock acts and continued to be a giant UK
concern with the Jagger team.

But the US music scene isn't really for compressing
and the past paragraphs have been a rough and ready
instant look at the years through the decade. Where
American music differed radically from Britain was in the
political and social happenings that beset the States
throughout the ten years and influenced the music.
America had famous men assassinated, had Cuban problems, had the 83 crew of an intelligence ship *Pueblo* captured, saw Richard Nixon become its president, sent
teenagers to Vietnam ... a long, long story of events
which were mirrored in much of the music and gave rise
to movements that had, or adopted, rock groups to spread
their reaction and eventual message to forces that, in part
and at times, threatened the peace and survival of the
world.

Obituary Notices

This section lists popular music artists who died during the decade. Where thought appropriate, there is a summary and brief analysis of the artist's career.

Laverne Andrews. Cancer killed the eldest of the Andrews sisters, Laverne, on 8 June, 1967. She was born 1915 on 6 July. The sisters were born in Minneapolis. Patti sang lead and most of the solo passages until 1953. They had hit records selling in the millions during the Thirties and Forties.

The Bar-Kays backed Otis Redding, and the majority of the original line-up perished in the same air crash that took the life of Otis Redding on 10 December, 1967. One member, James Alexander, was booked on another plane and he – with crash survivor Ben Cauley – continued the group's name successfully from 1968 onwards.

Jesse Belvin was a member of US group Earth Angel. He died in 1960.

Bill Black was born 17 September, 1926. He died on 21 October, 1965. Black was a string bass session player for Sun, and played with Elvis for five years. He formed the Bill Black Combo and continued with the insistent bass sound that was so much part of early Presley instrumentation.

Earl Bostic died 20 October, 1965. He is remembered most for the recordings he made for US, King Records. He played clarinet, tenor sax and fronted his own nine-piece combo on alto with Majestic Records at the end of World War Two. He played during his career with Fate Marable, Don Redman and Cab Calloway. His death was due to a heart attack.

Johnny Burnette – born 1934, died 1963 – hit the music business late, he was in his twenties. He was popular on the US rock circuit of the Fifties but initially found success as a songwriter.

At the beginning of the following decade Burnette became a hit artist charting strongly Stateside in 1960 and 1961. He had five UK hits and like in his home country the greatest success was for *You're Sixteen*.

A P Carter of the famed US country music family died on 7 November, 1960. A P, wife Sara and cousin Maybelle, all from South Virginia, were legendary performers with a music career spanning from the early 1920s to their disbanding in 1943. The daughter of Maybelle was June and she it was who married Johnny Cash. The Carter family name has continued through June's singing, and through members appearing in various Cash concerts.

Alma Cogan died 26 October, 1966. She was one of Britain's most popular and successful girl singers of the period. Her songs were corny but undeniably catchy and to go with their performance came a bubbly charisma that was loved by many. Among her hits were *Hernando's Hideway*, *Sugartime* and *Where Will The Dimple Be*. During the Fifties she had more hits than any other woman but just one in the Sixties, *Cowboy Jimmie Joe*. Alma had aspirations to a show-biz career from her early teens. She appeared, albeit briefly, in the film *The Blue Lamp* and sang regularly on the very popular BBC Light Programme comedy show *Take It From Here*, which among others starred Jimmy Edwards and June Whitfield.

Sam Cooke was born 22 January, 1931. He died in a Los Angeles motel on 10 December, 1964. The court verdict on his death was given as 'justifiable homicide'. Cooke achieved the near impossible, by retaining black-audience links where, at the same time, finding a teenage pop market. He had numerous US R&B hits and a particularly bright period in the UK between 1960 and 1962 when three records made the top ten: *Chain Gang*, *Cupid* and *Twistin' The Night Away*. Numerous songs of his were given cover versions by white artists with Rod Stewart being one major artist to owe him much. Cooke also had a list of famous black musician admirers including Marvin Gaye, Smokey Robinson, Al Green and Otis Redding.

Tommy Edwards was best known for his record *It's All In The Game*, in the late 1950s. He had recorded the song in 1951 but it was not until 1958 with a fresh cut and new release that success came. He died in his early forties. The fateful day was 23 October, 1969.

Brian Epstein, among others, managed the Beatles. But the traumas associated with this role, various personal problems and other factors yet to be fully revealed contributed to his suicide attempt in September 1966 through a pill overdose. However, on 27 August, 1967 he was found dead in his London bedroom. Under Epstein's direction the Beatles made a demonstration record which he touted around record companies meeting at least one major company rebuff. With the Beatles' signing to EMI Epstein next guided the group to their record and monetary bonanza, though the latter did not come without problems.

Richard Farina married Joan Baez's little sister Mimi. Half Cuban-Irish, Farina sprang out of the early Greenwich Village scene of the late 1950s. One of his songs *Pack Up Your Sorrows* was much recorded by folkish luminaries. In 1966, Farina had a launching party for his novel *Been Down So Long It Looks Like Up To Me* but during the party frolics Farina got on a motorcycle, an accident happened and Farina was dead.

Alan Freed was known as the first rock 'n' roll disc jockey. Freed, born 1922 Philadelphia, began work in radio at 20 and is credited with inventing the term 'rock 'n' roll'. By the late Fifties he was 'the' jock, with composing credits on numerous US hits and credits in three films, the all-important *Rock Around The Clock*, on *Rock, Rock, Rock* and *Don't Knock The Rock*. Freed was partly responsible in bringing black music to a general audience. Sadly Freed's name was bandied about in payola scandals and he pleaded guilty in the early Sixties to taking bribes and received a fine and suspended prison sentence. He died on 20 January, 1965.

Judy Garland, the legendary show-biz singer, died on 22 June, 1969. With no disrespect to the great and famous artist she is only of passing interest in terms of this volume.

Woody Guthrie was arguably the most important figure in American folk music. The Okemah, Oklahoma singer-songwriter was born 12 July, 1912 and died from Huntington's Chorea in 1967. His son was Arlo and his major popular disciple was Bob Dylan. Guthrie's influence went beyond whatever strictures might be contained in a word like 'folk'. He told Americans what their country should be like; was part of the politically left folk movement; and was much involved with the trade union movement. He made old traditions ever young. Guthrie's contribution was so massive that his influence can never die.

Roy Hamilton was born on 16 April, 1929. He came from Leesburg, Georgia and died on 20 July, 1969, from a severe stroke. Hamilton was a popular US R&B artist and in that music's chart enjoyed a chart number one with *You'll Never Walk Alone*. The Righteous Brothers were among those who owed much to Hamilton and they recorded two of his hits. Hamiton found other success in the gospel music field.

Michael Holliday died 29 October, 1963; and so ended the life of a much loved hit-maker of the previous decade. The 1960s had opened brightly with a chart-topper *Starry Eyed* but *Skylark* barely made the Top 40 and *Little Boy Lost* just held position 50 for one week and a career was over, sad as it seemed, as the new music and groups arrived in force. Holliday's Crosbyish vocal tones first hit the British public with *Nothin' To Do* in 1965. His most famous record was *The Story Of My Life*. He was part of the film *Clowns In Clover* also starring the Crazy Gang and Shirley Eaton. He took his own life.

Johnny Horton the American country rock singer, was killed in a car crash on 5 November, 1960. Horton never realised his full potential in Britain as cover versions of his records took from him sales, possible chart placing and overall popularity. He was born 30 April, 1927. His early career saw him known as the 'Singing Fisherman'. By the end of the 1940s he was amongst the country stars of the time on a variety of top ranking TV shows. His hit success came from rockabilly-flavoured C&W material such as *North To Alaska*, *Battle Of New Orleans* and Stateside, *Honky Tonk Harwood Floor* and *Honky Tonk Man*.

Elmore James was one of the first recording artists for the legendary Chess company of Chicago, also for the Flair label from 1954. James was a legendary Mississippi – born bluesman. He died 24 May, 1963.

Brian Jones. On 2 July, 1969, Stones-hero Brian Jones was no more. It was a death not totally unexpected, though the circumstances could not have been predicted. Jones, billed at London's Marquee on 21 July, 1962, as Elmo Lewis (guitars), was born 26 February, 1944. He and Jagger vied for top marks with the girls and he had his own very large cult following. Close associates describe him as someone who was very tender but a 'mixed-up feller'. He was very intelligent, often charming and good company. Yet he would often get himself into hassles and be his own worst enemy. Jones loved Anita Pallenberg but she eventually left him for Stones man Keith Richard. His death will always be shrouded in mystery. He was found dead in his own swimming pool. Shortly before his death he had left the Stones and announced he would form his own band.

Johnny Kidd died in a Lancashire car crash on 7 October, 1966. Kidd, alias Frederick Heath, formed his much loved – though in chart terms, not as successful as once might have been thought – group in 1958 with a first release in 1959. Kidd's 1960 record *Shakin' All Over* has been seen as a rock classic. Kidd suffered badly with the advent of the beat boom but even if personnel in the backing-group (The Pirates) kept changing Kidd kept going whatever the current music scene.

Martin Lamble was killed in a car crash during June 1969. Lamble played drums and was in the line-up for the albums *Fairport Convention, What Did We Do Our Holidays, Unhalfbricking*. His place was taken by Dave Mattacks.

Frankie Lymon died of a heroin overdose on 30 April, 1968. He'd had drug problems even before he was 16. He was born New York, September 1942. Lymon sang lead with The Teenagers, a group that literally came together on the street corners of Harlem in the mid-1950s. The five group members were schoolmates and lurched into fame through a blockbuster single *Why Do Fools Fall In Love* that spent four months in the high selling US Top 10. Worldwide the single sold in excess of two million. Stateside The Teenagers vied with the greats of the time for top rating. They appeared in Alan Freed's movie *Rock, Rock, Rock*. Lymon went solo in 1956 but, hooked on drugs, saw his career disintegrate. Several times he gave up hard drugs but always came back for more and died penniless.

Edith Piaf the famous French singer, died on 11 October, 1963. Although her music passed by most young people she has remained a general music legend. Her most famous song was *Non, Je Ne Regrette Rien* where she showed vocal artistry and passionate intensity. In 1983 EMI Records issued *The Piaf Album* that gave an hour of highlights from the musical career of the lady often termed the 'little sparrow'.

Otis Redding died in a plane crash, 10 December, 1967, when the aircraft hit frozen Wisconsin Lake. The 9 September, 1941–born artist, son of a Baptist minister, was hero to many black and white artists with his R&B genius. His gruff baritone voice brought huge crowds, high record sales and sell-out concerts. In 1967, Redding was featured at the legendary Monterey Pop Festival, California, and from there his fame spread in general record circles. Arguably his most-highly regarded single in mass terms was *Dock Of The Bay*, that record was sadly a posthumous release, as were a number of other hits.

Jim Reeves, hero of the British pop-country market, died 31 July, 1964. Stateside he had the support of the pure C&W fraternity. Born August 20, 1924, Reeves sold massively in Britain and particularly so after his death. His deep friendly voice charmed many.

Stu Sutcliffe died 10 April, 1962. He was from Liverpool, a great friend of John Lennon and bass player with The Silver Beatles. He played with them in Hamburg club days. When the Beatles returned to Liverpool in June 1961 he virtually relinquished playing in public. He achieved most in the field of art. He had been a pupil at the Liverpool College of Art and from April 1961 to March 1962 he attended Hamburg's chief art school where he profited from the teaching of Eduardo Paolozzi who was a visiting professor. Tragically Sutcliffe died of a brain tumour at the young age of 21.

239

Dinah Washington was born 29 August, 1924, and died in Detroit on 14 December, 1963. She was called the 'Queen of the Blues' and dominated the female R&B singers of the 1950s, and doubtless would have found much honour if she had survived the Sixties decade. She had countless US R&B chart hits in the Fifties. When she came to Britain at the end of that decade she had an uproarious welcome. Her last hit was *September In The Rain*, 1961. She recorded countless albums and was featured in the classic film *Jazz On A Summer's Day*. She died of heart seizure while resting at home during a break in touring.

Sonny Boy Williamson II. Blues man Williamson (Rice Miller) died 25 May, 1965. His father had died on 1 June, 1948.

Golden Oldies:
Those Still Available

Popular records of the 1950s, 1960s, 1970s and some from
the 1980s which are available and are expected to continue being obtainable can be found in the list that has
been compiled by one of the leading UK record whole-
salers and suppliers of what have popularly become called
'golden oldies': records which have provided the music
industry with considerable extra income. The records in
the list can be ordered from most record shops.

The list – *The Old Gold Collection*, Lightning Records
– does not represent all the records available; merely
a high proportion. Many records have not been made
available to Old Gold for release and at the same time they
are not commercially available from the record company
but in some instances they are still in catalogue.

The Sixties Quiz: 500 Questions

This is a fairly easy but hopefully entertaining quiz on the 1960s. Those seeing themselves as knowledgeable should attempt another of my books *Rock Mastermind*, published by Blandford Press, which tests awareness of known data about a range of subject matter that covers the essential musical happenings of decades from the 1950s onwards.

(ANSWERS ON PAGE 259)

1 *What Do You Want* took which artist to the chart top in 1960?
2 *The Big Hurt* was a hit for which Cardiff girl?
3 Who recorded Jerry Lordan's *Apache* in 1960?
4 Who was known as Little Miss Dynamite?
5 The christian name of Ms Atwell?
6 The two Js form the initials of the *Good Timin'* man. Name him.
7 Tony, Denis and Mike constituted which hit trio?
8 For his fans 'the Twang' was 'the Thang'. Name him.
9 *GI Blues* was a hit for whom?
10 *El Paso* was a UK 1960 million seller for which artist?
11 *My Old Man's A Dustman* came from which skiffle king?
12 Born 3 October, 1938 – who died 27 April, 1960?
13 Name the artist who recorded *He'll Have To Go* in 1960?
14 *Love Is Like A Violin* was a first hit for which comedy man?
15 Who recorded Lionel Bart's *As Long As He Needs Me*?

16 Name Dion's first British success.
17 Which American sang *Rubber Ball*?
18 Jerry Lee Lewis returned to the UK charts in May 1961 with what record?
19 *Portrait Of My Love* gave the first hit record to which guy with two Ms?
20 In January of 1961 Jimmy Savile flew to the USA and presented a gold disc to Elvis Presley for which record?
21 Which one-time Indian resident was 21 in 1961?
22 *Halfway To Paradise* was the first top tenner for which major star?
23 Sisters who sang with Frankie Vaughan.
24 His backing group were the Outlaws.
25 Ottilie sang with which jazz band?
26 Britain's Eurovision entry for 1961 came from the Allisons. Title?
27 Wife of bandleader Johnny Dankworth?
28 There were how many in the title of a drink associated name group?
29 *Baby* was a million seller for Dinah Washington in 1961. Who got the minor credits for being on the record?
30 John Barry had how many listed in his group name?
31 Who sang *Let's Get Together*?
32 Brian Bennett joined which group in 1961?
33 Who was just 14 in February 1961 when she had hits?
34 Robert Morley joined which star of *The Young Ones*?
35 Tom, Dusty and Tim made up which trio?
36 Clarence 'what' Henry?
37 The Hurricanes play with whom?
38 *Happy Times* followed *Bless You* for which artist?
39 Shirley Douglas sang with whose skiffle outfit?
40 Who was a 27-year-old guitar-strumming Glaswegian in 1961?
41 *Bobby's Girl* was a hit for which lady?
42 Jimmy Dean told the story of a so-called bad man.

The man?

43 The Locomotion gave which girl a hit?
44 *Ramblin' Rose* was a hit for the King. Who was he?
45 Two Cs in his name and a twist. Who?
46 The Millermen swung with whom?
47 *Hey Baby* sang which artist?
48 Which children marched Kenny Ball into the chart?
49 Who was the chairman of *Juke Box Jury*?
50 A disc jockey with a time name. Who?
51 Which American soul man's name had a kitchen and food feel?
52 *Come Outside* was whose cry?
53 How many people made up Karl Denver's group?
54 Shane sang with which band?
55 'Greetings', said Keith, Brian, Charlie, Mick and Bill in an ad. Who?
56 Chad and Jeremy Clyde, but what was Chad's surname?
57 Honey played drums with whom?
58 Fill out the letters SWJ.
59 The Luvvers were girls or guys?
60 Who did the Luvvers work with?
61 RC played the piano. His name?
62 How many coins made a number one charting group of 1964?
63 MW stood for which young male artist?
64 He played the role of Pickwick. Name him.
65 Who managed the Fab Four?
66 Joe who with *In The Mood*?
67 NP was a man with an orchestra who also produced records. Name him.
68 The duo who wrote most of the Beatle hits. Who?
69 Who crashed into the charts with *I'm Into Something Good*?
70 Name the group involved with the hit man of the last question.
71 Which group with the single male name?
72 The pop star whose film was *What A Crazy World*.

73 Who had his Dreamers?
74 How many guys made up the Migil outfit?
75 The Rebel Rousers sang with which artist?
76 Ray, Les, Norman and Ralph belonged with?
77 The DJ with a column each week in *The People* during the 1960s?
78 Who was ALO who discovered the Stones?
79 Which quality woman jazz singer recorded *Can't Buy Me Love* in 1964?
80 RSG stood for which TV show?
81 Barron, P'nut, Dave, Butch and Duke were which group?
82 Name the short film made by The Shadows.
83 What kind of life provided a film title for Cliff.
84 Who had PJ for his initials?
85 How many people made up The Hollies in 1964?
86 What station broadcast pop on 208?
87 Which DJ had the first Radio One show?
88 What was the name of a dog associated with a certain DJ?
89 Think of 'Highland' and spell the name his way. Who?
90 KK were her initials. Name her.
91 Who was the 'Old Groaner'?
92 He wasn't a doctor though he was a GP. Who?
93 Who was called 'dynamo dusty'?
94 Name the lovely lady with Cliff in *Wonderful Life*?
95 Who was Priscilla White?
96 The man who put poetry into motion. His name?
97 The girl who claimed the party was hers – was called?
98 RSG viewers called her 'the Queen of Blue Beat'. Her name?
99 Kane was part of his name, the other bit had biblical associations. What was it?
100 PPM was which folk group?
101 How many steps to heaven featured in the classic song?
102 Which twelve year-old sang *Fingertips*?
103 *He's So Fine* sang which girl group?

104 How many Seasons?

105 July 1964 saw the first Beatle film. The title?

106 The first UK group to follow in the Beatle success wake was the DC5. Who were they?

107 A number hit utilised by RSG.

108 *I Wish You Would* sang which group?

109 *She's Not There* sang who?

110 He produced The Animals, and many since.

111 Peter Noone appeared on which big TV soap opera?

112 The title had six words the same. What was it?

113 Singer without shoes. Who?

114 Soup for a name. Who?

115 BB wrote with Hal David. Who was BB?

116 A Brazilian lady who teamed up with Stan Getz.

117 Hit song from a Broadway musical for Louis Armstrong. The song?

118 A DJ who was JP but nothing to do with the law.

119 The boy who was remembered by Twinkle?

120 Berry Gordy Jnr founded which famous record company?

121 How many days of the week featured in a Beatle song?

122 Usually they grow on bushes but these ones rocked. The group?

123 Five-piece from Birmingham who sang *Go Now*?

124 A unit with two numbers. Give the right name with the numbers.

125 Carter, Lewis and Ford comprised which group seen as the UK answer to the Four Seasons?

126 Dad was a miner and he sang in the local chapel choir. Name?

127 Name the Elvis 1965 hit with a title of religious association.

128 An Engel, a Maus and a Leeds – and you have which group?

129 Cilla did well with it and so did the Righteous Brothers. What song?

130 Len with numbers. Name the hit.

131 Who had the *Clapping Song*?

132 PPM had a 1964 hit with which Robert Zimmerman song?
133 Whose farm did Dylan sing about?
134 What is the missing word before *Homesick Blues*?
135 Who sang *We Shall Overcome* into the charts?
136 Guy, Woodley, Potger and Durham consituted which band?
137 Who warbled *Tears*?
138 Two girls' names in a Beach Boys hit. The title?
139 *Holy Cow* sang who?
140 The letter after Roy. .?
141 John Sebastian was whose leader?
142 What season in the city?
143 Who went walkin' in boots?
144 The American who scored with Sunny was who?
145 S&G were who?
146 Name the Cher hit with a noise for a title.
147 Which underwater hit for the Beatles?
148 *Michelle* by the Beatles proved a chart topper for which group?
149 David and Jonathan were two writers. Greenaway was one; who was the other?
150 Who replaced Paul Jones?
151 Who were once the Troglodytes?
152 Ex-Animals organist who led his own group. Name him.
153 Spanish group with a colour in one of their hits. Name them.
154 NVB were which band?
155 A St Peter, at least in-part. Give his full name.
156 What dragged by – according to Cliff?
157 Cliff's film of 1966 was titled?
158 Gary Leeds of the Walkers recorded two solo records in 1966 under what name?
159 A friendly animal for his pop christian name. Who?
160 Who recorded *Distant Drums*?
161 A TV special written by the Beatles for Christmas screening?
162 The album with *Mr Kite* was entitled?

163 Nesmith and Dolenz were two of which group?

164 Davy Jones came from which UK city?

165 Brian and the group parted. Who were they?

166 *Gin House Blues* for whom?

167 *Arnold Layne* a hit for which group?

168 Who said 'the wind cries Mary'?

169 Stevie and Muff were two brothers in which group?

170 Robin, Maurice and Barry were?

171 Which hit had a musical reference to Bach's *Air On A G String*?

172 A circus-titled hit from a Kink?

173 Who was the Kink member with the hit of the last question?

174 Who had an amazing dancing bear?

175 What did the clown say according to the Manfreds?

176 A London tube-station was named in which hit of 1967?

177 The Seekers topped the charts with which film song?

178 *Bonnie and Clyde* was a hit for whom?

179 The religious film for Billy from Cliff was?

180 Name the title of the Eurovision Song Contest winner of 1967.

181 Who sang the song of the last question?

182 Lulu topped the US charts with a teacher-title song. Name it.

183 A Charlie Chaplin associated song gave Petula Clark which big hit?

184 He was who else before becoming Engelbert Humperdinck?

185 Which comedian who sang of careless hands?

186 Snoopy fought who?

187 Psychedelic group from the States with an in part 'desert' name.

188 Sam and Dave hit high with a title of two words. *Man* was one word. What was the other?

189 Desmond sang three numbers. What were they?

190 How many drunken nights were in the song title?

191 The group with a sweet name, and a male name in the song hit. Name the group.

192 Name the hit song of the last group.

193 What kind of express is mentioned in a group's name?

194 First hit and chart-topper for *Mony Mony* by whom?

195 The Beatle trade name near the end of the 1960s was?

196 Brasil with a number. What was it?

197 Who jumped like a flash?

198 Mighty who – according to Dylan?

199 *Hello, How Are You* said who?

200 The Love Affair covered which US hit?

201 Two film names for an Equals hit. They were?

202 A name and the Casuals chart debut – title?

203 Who had a crazy world?

204 The Nice adapted a musical's title song. What was it?

205 Dolls without substance – according to the title anyway. Who?

206 Cliff's Eurovision entry for 1968.

207 What position did Cliff reach in that 1968 Contest?

208 Did the same writers of the 1967 Sandie Shaw song also write Cliff's 1968 number?

209 Who were these writers?

210 A biblical girl's name for a Jones hit. The song?

211 A minstrel with a hit. His name?

212 Leapy Lee's hit was entitled?

213 The girl from the Brian Auger Trinity was?

214 The last mentioned group had a hit with a Dylan song. Title?

215 The group with a name that reminds one of moving vehicles.

216 Who sang about *(Sittin' On) The Dock Of The Bay*?

217 His initials were DW: What came next?

218 He left and the group became a trio in 1969. His name?

219 Which was group that became the trio of the last question?

220 Two Bs for their name. Who are they?

221 An airplane with a political name before it.

222 Tin and warmth are the clues to whose name?

223 Who sang with Gary Puckett?

224 Dylan album with a British religious figure for two of the names in its title.

225 What kind of male did Elvis sing of in 1968?

226 French orchestral leader with a colour hit. Title?

227 Group with a death-associated name.

228 *Ain't Got No – I Got Life* came from which musical?

229 Who had a hit with the song mentioned in the previous question?

230 Group with a jammy name. Who were they?

231 The last group had a hit from a double album. Whose album?

232 *The Good* ... and what else featured in the hit title?

233 Who covered *Hey Jude* and hit the charts?

234 The tambourine colour?

235 British film actor with a song that talked of an oven.

236 Smith's initials – the man of Hickory Holler.

237 Recorded in 1966 but a hit for the brothers in 1969. Name the song.

238 The group of the last question?

239 Cement and water give you the clue to a hit group with a flower in at least one of their hits.

240 Who was the MMMMFs speaking DJ on the Radio One roster?

241 What was the name of the Radio One show that ran from 10.00 *pm* to midnight?

242 Gutteral throaty roar from which vocalist from Sheffield?

243 Fields of fruit gives the clue to a hit from Merseyside.

244 Steam was the first of which two words forming this group's name?

245 DJ John Peel had a 'something' garden show. What is the missing adjective?

246 Name the group pleased that they were dead.

247 Name Frank Zappa's group.

248 What was the title of Dylan's double album that, in title at least, had a connection with Marilyn Monroe?

249 On his 1963 album title, Bob was described as doing

what?

250 Who wrote *It's For You*?

251 Who recorded the title of the previous question?

252 Name the 1964 big hit from The Animals that contained in its title at least one hoped-for event every summer's day.

253 Name the Rolling Stone who died at the end of the decade.

254 Who wrote the main film music for *Zabriskie Point*?

255 Who quit the Bee Gees in 1969?

256 *Life With The Lions* was their album. Who were they?

257 Which lead singer was arrested on stage for supposed lewd behaviour?

258 Who had a chart topper with *Albatross*?

259 What kind of way was it according to The Move?

260 Who was the new lead singer of The (Small) Faces, announced for late 1969?

261 Which Beatles song for a Stones hit?

262 Which record company first auditioned the Beatles?

263 Who sang the Beatle song *Hello Little Girl*?

264 *Tip Of My Tongue* for which Merseysider?

265 They sang *Like Dreamers Do* thanks to L&M. Who?

266 Greek Wars surname of US lady on Apple. Who?

267 Who scored for *The Family Way*?

268 Who scored the *Wonderwall* music?

269 Which label for Mary?

270 Give farmyard Stones title?

271 Very young love in which Supremes title?

272 *Either* or *Or* for the Small Faces title.

273 Not the hardback writer – the opposite. Title?

274 Which number nervous breakdown?

275 Awayday song?

276 What was golden?

277 What was on a string?

278 Adjective for flamingo.

279 She was pink. Who was?

280 Who was a rockafella according to the song?

281 Name the Beatle and wife title.

282 *Yesterday* was the third word. The other two?

283 The doomed JJ.

284 A Fish in which group's name?

285 Who had a magic band?

286 *For What's It Worth* sang which Buffalo?

287 CSN were?

288 *Wooden Ships* was whose first album?

289 How high the number for the MC people?

290 Whose farm hosted Woodstock?

291 Who wrote the song *Woodstock*?

292 Which folkish singer with initials JC?

293 If Dylan was the king then some said she was queen. Who?

294 What is Woody's son called?

295 *Rubber Soul* came out when?

296 When was *Revolver* issued?

297 What year saw the death of Brian Epstein?

298 Who directed *A Hard Day's Night* and *Help!*

299 What style neck sweaters were worn by the Fab Four?

300 What year was the famous Dylan motorcycle crash?

301 Name The Band's first album.

302 Brian, Dennis, Carl, Mike and Al constituted which group?

303 What Californian sport gave the Beach Boys their identity?

304 What was the Beach boy hit with the same word three times?

305 Complete *Little Deuce*. :?

306 What was good according to the title?

307 The Beach Boy song about a girl whose name begins with W.

308 What kind of honey did the Beach Boys sing of?

309 ... sort of sounds formed a 1966 album title for the Beach Boys?

310 Which European country features as a Beach Boy album title?

311 The Gibb family came from where in England?

312 What year was the mining distaster – according to

the Bee Gees?

313 What instrument did Colin Peterson play in the first Bee Gees?

314 Name the US-city, Bee-Gee titled hit.

315 *Sweetheart Of The Rodeo* was one of their albums. Who?

316 They had a 1965 hit with *Mr Tambourine Man* but who wrote it?

317 The Byrds fared moderately with *All I Really Want To Do*. Who fared better?

318 Manzarek was keyboards player with what US group?

319 Whose album was *Strange Days*?

320 The number of Dylan's highway?

321 What kind of lady belonged in the lowlands according to Dylan?

322 The Easybeats came from where?

323 Who replaced Judy Dyble?

324 Which group is indirectly referred to in the previous question?

325 With which Stones song did Marianne Faithfull kick off her chart career?

326 The Dimension number?

327 Spring, Summer . . . the four what?

328 Who was the lead singer of the above group?

329 Name the apperitif featured in a song of the last question's group?

330 *Be Sure To Wear Some Flowers In Your Hair* appeared in Parentheses. What was the song's main title?

331 Who sang the song mentioned in the last question?

332 The parent-named group was who?

333 The group with two Ms or two words both beginning with M!

334 Liverpool band who charted with *Wishin' And Hopin'*

335 Who was king of the road?

336 What colour were the apples?

337 What size were the apples?

338 Surname of *Sailor* album inspired man?

339 What did Eric Stewart play in the Mindbenders?

340 What kind of love did the Mindbenders sing of?

341 Name the Marvelettes song about the mail.

342 *Heatwave* and *Dancing In The Street* were hits for whom?

343 Whose name was featured in credits with The Miracles?

344 The Move were from where?

345 *Night Of Fear* from The Move was a pastiche of a classical tune. Who was the classical composer of this piece?

346 The hose-pipe hit?

347 Name Gary Brooker's band.

348 What shade of pale?

349 How many Righteous Brothers?

350 Kenny Rogers sang with whom?

351 Three Liverpudlian humourists. Who?

352 *Sweets For My Sweet* was whose first hit?

353 Needles and what?

354 Jeff Banks married who?

355 What quintet with a title?

356 Percy of snow associations. Who?

357 Who had hit with *Suspicion*.

358 Diana, Mary, Florence and Barbara Martin were?

359 Cindy Birdsong replaced . . ?

360 Who was the British screamin' gentleman?

361 Jonathan's University?

362 Jonathan's University degree subject?

363 Jonathan's first hit?

364 If you can turn his surname, give his full name.

365 He made *Somewhere* from which musical a hit?

366 Proby of question 365 also did well with another song from the musical. What was it?

367 A flower for the surname of Tim? Who?

368 There was a Lord with his name but who was the Tim minus grandiose connection?

369 Who sang *Gimme Little Sign*?

370 Ronnie sang it but Bobby's was the original. The

song?

371 *World Of Broken Hearts* was a second hit for who?

372 The American Breed charted once in the UK with what?

373 The Tuxedos were credited with what artist?

374 *Inside-Looking Out* sang who?

375 How many little words for the Applejacks?

376 Sweet hit for the Archies?

377 Which cut is the deepest?

378 Frankie Avalon said they should not be thrown away. What?

379 The S&G 1966 hit for the Bachelors?

380 *Midnight* where? According to Kenny Ball.

381 The Acapulco date for a Herb Alpert hit?

382 When I'm what age according to the Beatles?

383 What colour stockings for John Barry?

384 First Beatle hit?

385 What can't be bought – said the Beatles?

386 One word 1965 Beatle chart-topper.

387 Other side hit of *Yellow Submarine*?

388 State of health in what 1964 Beatle hit?

389 Where was the hole, Harry?

390 Tony Bennett left his heart where?

391 What kind of love said Cliff Bennett?

392 Who said, 'I've been wrong before?'

393 Colour of the Dover cliffs?

394 Jane and who with *Je T'Aime*?

395 Who was the Mike paying tribute to Buddy Holly?

396 Colour of the fields for the Beverly Sisters?

397 What was happening to the contents of the pot – according to Blue Mink?

398 Who was Boone's speedy song character?

399 Johnny (?) sang Pat Boone.

400 Name fun band who sang *I'm The Urban Spaceman*.

401 *Soul Deep* was their third UK hit. Who?

402 Whose was the ball according to Joe Brown?

403 Where did Canned Heat decide they would go?

404 Pearl Carr sang with whom?

405 According to the Caravelles, in order to cry you do

not have to be what?

406 Theme from which medical serial gave Richard Chamberlain a hit?

407 A perfume-named man with *Keep On*. Who?

408 *Sweet Talkin' Guy* from which US female group?

409 The name came three times in an Eddie Cochran hit. The name?

410 The Cook and Moore 1965 hit?

411 The day of the week which is never?

412 The river colour for Creedence?

413 How did Mary feel for Creedence?

414 The sporting hit of Cream?

415 The girl of Cuff Links?

416 Who was still alive – sang Dave?

417 He had the knife. Who?

418 The instrument man of Johnny Cymbal?

419 Translate *La Mer* and give the Bobby Darin record title in full.

420 Class order for Spencer's title. What was it?

421 Where were the Dennisons from?

422 What sort of teenager was featured by Dion?

423 A famous novelist gave birth to a male vocalist who sang *That's The Way Love Goes*. Who?

424 The musical instrument said to be like love in a 1960 hit?

425 Two numbers of Ken Dodd's fifth hit?

426 Joe Dolan came from which country?

427 Billy sang one 1960s hit with which lady?

428 Time of the train for Paul Evans?

429 Bern Elliott sang with whom?

430 What did Betty Everett say in 1965?

431 What did Betty Everett say in 1966?

432 Billy's letter was full of what?

433 Who fought the law in a 1966-titled song?

434 *Count On Me* sang the *Up On The Roof* girl. who?

435 Lorne sang about which Beatle name?

436 What was the living habit of Joe according to Herman?

437 What kind of traffic according to Jimi?

438 What did Bert say to the blues?

439 The three modes of transport according to Billy J.

440 Mr Loudermilk's language.

441 The sharp method of dance favoured by Love Sculpture.

442 It was goodbye to heartache but the opposite to something else. What was the rest of Little Peggy's message?

443 Where was the cathedral of NVB?

444 How many bells for Brian of Liverpool?

445 The colour of Elvis' Christmas.

446 What was the message from Elvis about backyards?

447 What was Elvis' wish about Christmas?

448 The two guys of a 1966 Elvis hit?

449 The other side of *His Latest Flame*?

450 What were the Elvis kissing instructions of 1963?

451 Elvis promise of 1968?

452 Tommy's girls of 1962?

453 Tommy's girl of 1969?

454 Julie's matrimonial song of 1964?

455 Julie's matrimonial song of 1965?

456 The two characters of Alan Sherman in 1963?

457 Who said someone cried in their sleep last night in a Doug Sheldon hit of 1962?

458 Name the type of school featured by Bobby Rydell in 1960.

459 Staff Sgt with a 1966 hit?

460 Bowie sang of *Changes* in the seventies but who had a hit with a song of this title in 1966?

461 What was the 1963 Top 20 song message title of Chris Sandford?

462 The ring title hit of S&G in 1969?

463 What hit for the Singing Nun?

464 What did Clodagh tell midnight?

465 The wish of Temptations, in 1968?

466 Whose son was the subject of a song from O C Smith?

467 The soldier's description given by the Small Faces?

468 How many reasons said Connie?

469 What was the bird question of Conway Twitty in 1960?

470 Whose return was it according to the Upsetters?

471 Who did Bert Weedon apologise to in 1960?

472 How was Jack in 1966?

473 Who were the pictures of, in a 1967 Who hit?

474 The other side of *The Last Time* from The Who?

475 The animal of a Who hit in 1968?

476 What kind of bus was run by The Who?

477 What game was someone a wizzard at?

478 The first hit of The Who?

479 The town of Roger Whittaker's chart debut, was?

480 1967 and Andy with a chart hit about music for what purpose?

481 What was Andy's song title problem of 1963?

482 Stevie's first hit was?

483 The Dylan song hit for Stevie was?

484 Mark's adjective for his girl hit of 1961?

485 What was Jim's revived hit title of 1964?

486 For the Young Rascals the operative hit word of 1967 was?

487 The Troggs first hit?

488 The Troggs only chart-topper?

489 A Small Faces title but also a minor hit for Doris Troy. Title?

490 First hit for Tremeloes was?

491 First hit for Traffic?

492 What was wrong with the shoe according to Traffic?

493 Double repeated colour of wine for a 1969 hit. The colour?

494 The Doc of Andy Stewart?

495 What was the question to Donald in Andy's hit of 1960?

496 Del's debut hit and a chart topper was titled?

497 What was the 1965 hit that charted in the next decade, twice from a girl group who all-told had just two hits?

498 Helen's first number one in 1961?

499 The request of Malcom Roberts in 1968 was?

500 Johnnie Ray only survived into the 1960s because a record of his, released in 1959, strayed over for a fortnight. The title?

ANSWERS: QUIZ

1 Adam Faith. 2 Maureen Evans. 3 Shadows. 4 Brenda Lee. 5 Winifred. 6 Jimmy Jones. 7 King Brothers. 8 Duane Eddy. 9 Elvis Presley. 10 Marty Robbins. 11 Lonnie Donegan. 12 Eddie Cochran. 13 Jim Reeves. 14 Ken Dodd. 15 Shirley Bassey. 16 Run Around Sue. 17 Bobby Vee. 18 What'd I Say. 19 Matt Monroe. 20 It's Now Or Never. 21 Cliff Richard. 22 Billy Fury. 23 Kaye. 24 Mike Berry. 25 Chris Barber. 26 Are You Sure. 27 Cleo Laine. 28 Temperance Seven. 29 Brook Benton. 30 7. 31 Hayley Mills. 32 Shadows. 33 Helen Shapiro. 34 Cliff Richard. 35 Springfields. 36 Frogman Henry. 37 Johnny. 38 Tony Orlando. 39 Chas McDevitt. 40 Karl Denver. 41 Susan Maughan. 42 Big Bad John. 43 Little Eva. 44 Nat 'King' Cole. 45 Chubby Checker 46 Bob Miller. 47 Bruce Channel. 48 The Siamese. 49 David Jacobs. 50 Pete Murray. 51 Sam Cooke. 52 Mike Sarne. 53 3. 54 The Fentones. 55 Rolling Stones. 56 Stuart. 57 The Honeycombs. 58 Swinging Blue Jeans. 59 Guys. 60 Lulu. 61 Russ Conway. 62 Four Pennies. 63 Mark Wynter. 64 Harry Secombe. 65 Brian Epstein. 66 Loss. 27 Norrie Paramor. 68 Lennon-McCartney. 69 Herman (or Peter Noone). 70 Hermits. 71 Bachelors. 72 Joe Brown. 73 Freddie. 74 5. 75 Cliff Bennett. 76 Swinging Blue Jeans. 77 Jimmy Savile. 78 Andre Loog Oldham. 79 Ella Fitzgerald. 80 Ready Steady Go. 81 Barron Knights. 82 Rhythms And Greens. 83 Wonderful. 84 Proby. 85 5. 86 Luxembourg. 87 Tony Blackburn. 88 Arnold. 89 Brian Hyland. 90 Kathy Kirby. 91 Bing Crosby. 92 Gene Pitney. 93 Dusty Springfield. 94 Susan Hampshire. 95 Cilla Black. 96 Johnny Tillotson. 97 Lesley Gore. 98 Millie. 99 Eden. 100 Peter, Paul and Mary. 101 Three. 102 Stevie

Wonder. 103 Chiffons. 104 4. 105 A Hard Day's Night.
106 Dave Clarke Five. 107 5-4-3-2-1. 108 Yardbirds.
109 Zombies. 110 Mickie Most. 111 Coronation Street.
112 Um. 113 Sandie   Shaw. 114 Heinz. 115 Burt
Bacharach. 116 Astrud   Gilberto. 117 Hello   Dolly.
118 John   Peel. 119 Terry. 120 Gordy,   Motown.
121 8. 122 Rockin' Berries. 123 Moody Blues. 124 Unit
four plus two. 125 Ivy League. 126 Tom Jones.
127 Crying In The Chapel. 128 Walker Brothers.
129 You've Lost That Lovin' Feelin'. 130 1-2-3.
131 Shirley   Ellis. 132 Blowin'   In   The   Wind.
133 Maggie's. 134 *Subterranean* Homesick Blues. 135
Joan Baez. 136 Seekers. 137 Ken Dodd. 138 Barbara
Ann. 139 Lee Dorsey. 140 C. 141 Lovin' Spoonful.
142 Summer. 143 Nancy Sinatra. 144 Bobby Hebb.
145 Simon and Garfunkel. 146 Bang Bang. 147 Yellow
Submarine. 148 Overlanders. 149 Roger Cook. 150 Mike
D'Abo. 151 Troggs. 152 Alan Price. 153 Los Bravos.
154 New Vaudeville Band. 155 Crispian St Peters. 156
Time. 157 Finders Keepers. 158 Gary Walker. 159 Cat
Stevens. 160 Jim Reeves. 161 Magical Mystery Tour.
162 Sgt Pepper's Lonely Hearts Club Band. 163 Monkees.
164 Manchester. 165 Tremeloes. 166 Amèn Corner.
167 Pink Floyd. 168 Jimi Hendrix. 169 Spencer Davis.
170 Bee Gees. 171 A Whiter Shade Of Pale. 172 Death
of a Clown. 173 Dave Davies. 174 Simon Smith. 175
Ha. 176 Finchley Central. 177 Georgie Girl. 178 Georgie
Fame. 179 Two A Penny. 180 Puppet On A String. 181
Sandie Shaw. 182 To Sir With Love. 183 This Is My
Song. 184 Gerry Dorsey. 185 Des O'Connor. 186 The
Red Baron. 187 Electric Prunes. 188 Soul. 189 007.
190 7. 191 1910 Fruitgum Company. 192 Simon Says.
193 Ohio. 194 Tommy James and the Shondells. 195
Apple. 196 66. 197 Jack. 198 Quinn. 199 Easybeats.
200 Everlasting Love. 201 Laurel & Hardy. 202 Jesa-
mine. 203 Arthur Brown. 204 America. 205 Paper Dolls.
206 Congratulations. 207 Second. 208 Yes. 209 Martin-
Coulter. 210 Delilah. 211 Don Partridge. 212 Little
Arrows. 213 Julie Driscoll. 214 This Wheels On Fire.

215 Traffic. 216 Otis Redding. 217 Washburn. 218 Peter Tork. 219 Monkees. 220 Beach Boys. 221 Jefferson. 222 Canned Heat. 223 Union Gap. 224 John Wesley Harding. 225 US Male. 226 Blue (Love is Blue). 227 Scaffold. 228 Hair. 229 Nina Simone. 230 Marmalade. 231 Beatles. 232 The Bad and the Ugly. 233 Wilson Pickett. 234 Green. 235 Richard Harris – McArthur Park. 236 O C. 237 This 'Ole Heart Of Mine. 238 Isley Brothers. 239 Foundations. 240 Jimmy Young. 241 Late Night Extra. 242 Joe Cocker. 243 Strawberry Fields Forever. 244 Packet. 245 Perfumed. 246 Grateful. 247 Mothers Of Invention. 248 Blonde on Blonde. 249 Freewheelin'. 250 Lennon-McCartney. 251 Cilla Black. 252 The House Of The Rising sun. 253 Brian Jones. 254 Pink Floyd. 255 Robin Gibb. 256 Lennon & Yoko. 257 Jim Morrison. 258 Fleetwood Mac. 259 Blackberry. 260 Rod Stewart. 261 I Wanna Be Your Man. 262 Decca. 263 Fourmost. 264 Tommy Quickley. 265 Applejacks. 266 Doris Troy. 267 Paul McCartney. 268 George Harrison. 269 Apple. 270 Little Red Rooster. 271 Baby Love. 272 All Or Nothing. 273 Paperback Writer. 274 19th. 275 Day Tripper. 276 Silence. 277 Puppet. 278 Pretty. 279 Lily. 280 Cinderella. 281 Ballad of John and Yoko. 282 Yester-me-Yester-you. 282 Janis Joplin. 284 Country Joe and the Fish. 285 Captain Beefheart. 286 Springfield. 287 and 288 Crosby, Stills and Nash. 289 5. 290 Max Yasgur. 291 Joni Mitchell. 292 Judy Collins. 293 Joan Baez. 294 Arlo. 295 December 1965. 296 August 1966. 297 1967. 298 Dick Lester. 299 Polo-neck. 300 1967. 301 Music From Big Pink. 302 Beach boys. 303 Surf. 304 Fun Fun Fun. 305 Coupe. 306 Vibrations. 307 Wendy. 308 Wild. 309 Pet. 310 Holland. 311 Manchester. 312 1941. 313 Drums. 314 Massachusetts. 315 Byrds. 316 Dylan. 317 Sonny and Cher. 318 Doors. 319 Doors. 320 61. 321 Sad Eyes. 322 Australia. 323 Sandy Denny. 324 Fairport Convention. 325 As Tears Go By. 326 5th 327 4. 328 Franki Valli. 329 Sherry. 330 San Francisco. 331 Scott McKenzie.

332 Mamas and Papas. 333 Manfred Mann. 334 The Merseybeats. 335 Roger Miller. 336 Green. 337 Little. 338 Miller. 339 Guitar. 340 Groovy. 341 Please Mr Postman. 342 Martha Reeves and the Vandellas. 343 Smokey Robinson. 344 Birmingham. 345 Tchaikovsky. 346 Fire Brigade. 347 Procol Harum. 348 Whiter. 349 Two. 350 First Edition. 351 Scaffold. 352 Searchers. 353 Pins. 354 Sandie Shaw. 355 Sir Douglas Quintet. 356 Sledge. 357 Terry Stafford. 358 Supremes (pre: Primettes). 359 Florence Ballard. 360 Lord Sutch. 361 Oxford. 362 English. 363 Everyone's Gone To The Moon. 364 Jimmy Page. 365 West Side Story. 366 Maria. 367 Rose. 368 Tim Buckley. 369 Brook Benton. 370 Roses Are Red. 371 Amen Corner 372 Bend Me Shape Me. 373 Bobby Angelo. 374 Animals. 375 Three. 376 Sugar Sugar. 377 First. 378 Teardrops. 379 The Sound Of Silence. 380 Moscow. 381 1922. 382 64. 383 Black. 384 Love Me Do. 385 Love. 386 Help. 387 Eleanor Rigby. 388 I Feel Fine. 389 In My Bucket. 390 San Francisco. 391 One Way. 392 Cilla Black. 393 White. 394 Serge. 395 Mike Berry. 396 Green. 397 Melting. 398 Gonzales. 399 Will. 400 Bonzo Dog Doo-Dah Band. 401 Box Tops. 402 Darktown Strutters Ball. 403 Goin' Up The Country. 404 Teddy Johnson. 405 Be A Baby. 406 Dr Kildare. 407 Bruce Channel. 408 Chiffons. 409 Jeannie. 410 Goodbye-ee. 411 Sunday. 412 Green. 413 Proud. 414 Anyone For Tennis. 415 Tracey. 416 Suzannah. 417 Mack. 418 Bass (Mr Bass Man). 419 The Sea (Beyond The Sea). 420 Mr Second Class. 421 UK. 422 Lonely. 423 Charles Dickens (1965). 424 Violin (hit for Ken Dodd). 425 Eight by Ten. 426 Ireland. 427 Sarah Vaughan. 428 Midnight (Midnight Special). 429 The Fenmen. 430 Getting Mighty Crowded. 431 It's In His Kiss. 432 Tears. 433 Bobby Fuller. 434 Julie Grant. 435 Ringo. 436 Sleepy. 437 Crosstown. 438 Bye Bye (title in 1965). 439 Trains, Boats and Planes. 440 Love (Language Of Love). 441 Sabre. 442 Hello To Love. 443 Winchester. 444 Three. 445 Blue. 446 Clean Up

Your Backyard. 447 If Everyday Was Like Christmas. 448 Frankie & Johnny. 449 Little Sister. 450 Kiss Me Quick 451 You'll Never Walk Alone. 452 Sheila – Suzi (Darlin'). 453 Heather (Honey). 454 The Wedding. 455 Hawaiian Wedding Song. 456 Muddah Faddah. 457 Your Ma. 458 Swinging. 459 Staff Sgt Barry Sadler. 460 Crispian St Peters. 461 Not Too Little Not Too Much. 462 The Boxer. 463 Dominique. 464 Goodnight. 465 I Wish It Would Rain. 466 Hickory Holler's Tramp. 467 Tin. 468 Sixteen. 469 Is A Blue Bird Blue. 470 Django. 471 Robbie. 472 Happy (Who hit). 473 Lily. 474 Under My Thumb. 475 Dog. 476 Magic. 477 Pinball. 478 I Can't Explain. 479 Durham. 480 Music To Watch Girls Go By. 481 Can't Get Used To Losing You. 482 Uptight. 483 Blowin' In The Wind. 484 Dream. 485 Unchained Melody. 486 Groovin'. 487 Wild Thing. 488 With A Girl Like You. 489 Whatcha Gonna Do About It? 490 Here Comes My Baby. 491 Paper Sun. 492 Hole In My Shoe. 493 Red Red Wine (Tony Tribe). 494 Findlay. 495 Donald Where's Your Troosers? 496 Runaway. 497 Leader Of The Pack (Shangri-Las). 498 You Don't Know (Helen Shapiro). 499 May I Have The Next Dream With You. 500 I'll Never Fall In Love Again.

Survivors

In chart terms these artists survived into the Sixties after finding success in the *previous* decade.

Paul Anka had first hit with *Diana* in 1957, his only chart-topper.

Louis Armstrong had first hit with *Takes Two To Tango* in 1952 which, like the follow-up in the charts, *Theme From The Threepenny Opera* was a Top 10 hit. But his major chart successes came in the Sixties.

Frankie Avalon, the US teen scream idol, never found the same degree of success here. *Venus* (16) in 1959 was his best pre-1960s record but he had only one other. His first hit was *Gingerbread* (30), 1958.

Avons charted with their cover of *Seven Little Girls Sitting In The Back Seat* almost at the end of the Fifties decade.

Chris Barber's Jazz Band. Trad jazz was popular at the end of the Fifties, and at the beginning of 1959 Barber's band charted with the haunting instrumental *Petite Fleur* (3).

Shirley Bassey started her long career with a cover of the *Banana Boat Song* (8) in 1957, a career that has been punctuated from time to time with hits. Her 1958 *Kiss Me Honey Honey Kiss Me* reached three.

Tony Bennett was the singer's singer, who began his UK chart listing with a chart-topper *Stranger In Paradise* in 1965.

Brook Benton. The summer of 1959 saw his *Endlessly* charting (28).

Chuck Berry, the hero of many a young British musician, first charted in 1957 with *School Day* (24). His classic *Sweet Little Sixteen* was issued in 1958 (16).

Beverly Sisters, a trio of smiling girls, just survived into the new decade. Their first hit was in 1953, *I Saw Mommy Kissing Santa Claus* (11).

Pat Boone was the rave of the well-dressed, with many hits in the 1950s commencing with a cover *Ain't That A Shame* (7) in 1955. *I'll Be Home* was his classic, a chart-topper (1956)

Teresa Brewer just made the 1960s. First hit, 1955, *Let Me Go Lover* (9).

Max Bygraves launched himself with *Cowpuncher's Cantata* in 1952, reaching number six in 1953.

Freddie Cannon had a latish summer hit with *Tallahassee Lassie* which charted in 1959 (17).

Pearl Carr and Teddy Johnson charted in 1959 with the Eurovision ditty *Sing Little Birdie* (12).

Ronnie Carroll, the ballad singer, began with a cover of *Walk Hand In Hand*, 1956 (13).

Champs launched with *Tequila* in 1958 (5).

Petula Clark had her first hit, *The Little Shoemaker*, in 1954 (12). But she sold records long before then as a child star.

Alma Cogan. The British favourite. First hit *Bell*

Bottom Blues, 1954 (4).

Nat 'King' Cole was a musical legend. *Somewhere Along The Way*, 1952 (3), was his first UK recorded hit, but around before then.

Perry Como, who was helped to success by huge TV audiences for his show began UK charts with *Don't Let The Stars Get In Your Eyes*, 1953 (1).

Russ Conway had *Party Pops*, with Russ at piano, to start things off, 1957 (24).

Sam Cooke, a favourite of musicians, had *You Send Me* in 1958 as his first UK hit (29).

Frank Cordell had one 1950s hit, *Sadie's Shawl*, 1956 (29).

Crickets backed Buddy Holly and then carried on under own steam, in 1950s with Buddy, *That'll Be The Day* the first hit, 1957 (1).

Johnny Dankworth, the long-lasting UK jazz man, had one hit in 1950s – *Experiment With Mice*, (7) 1956.

Bobby Darin began with *Splish Splash* (cover here for Charlie Drake among others) in 1958 (28).

Sammy Davis Jnr. 1955, *Something's Gotta Give* (19) was the first one.

Doris Day was a big hit of past decade, most famous *Secret Love* (1) 1954. First hit, 1952, *My Love And Devotion* (10).

Fats Domino had *I'm In Love Again* (28) 1956, the first of many fine cuts.

266

Lonnie Donegan, the UK skiffle king, covered *Rock Island Line*, 1956 (8), the first of many.

Craig Douglas just made the 1950s with his cover of *A Teenager In Love*, 1959 (13).

Charlie Drake the comedian with occasional releases had *Splish Splash* a 1958 cover (7).

Billy Ekstine and Sarah Vaughan survived with a re-issue of *Passing Strangers* in Sixties, but first (22) 1957.

Duane Eddy. Twanging deep-sounding guitar from Eddy first with *Rebel Rouser* 1958 (19).

Paul Evans. US version, November 1959, with *Seven Little Girls* (25).

Everly Brothers sang *Bye Bye Love*, 1957 (6), the first hit of their huge 50s/60s success story.

Adam Faith just made the 1950s with *What Do You Want*, 1959 (1).

Ella Fitzgerald, the famous jazz lady, had *Swingin' Shepherd Blues*, 1958 (15), and others in the decade.

Clinto Ford. His weepie *Old Shep* charted, 1959 (27).

Emile Ford and the Checkmates had first chart topper with *What Do You Want To Make Those Eyes At Me For* which charted Autumn 1959.

Four Preps, the bouncy US college favourites, had *Big Man*, 1958 (2).

Connie Francis began long series of hits with *Who's Sorry Now*, 1958 (1).

Billy Fury became a UK teen rave, *Maybe Tomorrow* began it in 1959 (22).

Bill Haley, the legendary rock 'n' roller, survived in 1960s with re-issue of you know what!

Ronnie Hilton. British balladeer, *I Still Believe*, 1954 (3), was one of many 1950s hits.

Michael Holliday was a UK singer with deep Crosbyish voice. *Nothin To Do*, 1956 (20), was first.

Buddy Holly, first marvellous solo hit *Peggy Sue*, 1957 (6).

Johnny and the Hurricanes began their hits with *Red River Rock*, 1959 (3).

Johnny Kidd and the Pirates. Dummer 1959 promised a new star with *Please Don't Touch* (25).

Frankie Laine, a great man of the 1950s was still so as artist in next decades, *High Noon* the first in Fifties, 1952 (7), but hits before charts began.

Little Richard, the legendary rocker and gospel maker began his legend with *Rip It Up* 1956 (30).

Manuel and his Music Of The Mountains – alias Geoff Love – his *Theme From Honeymoon*, Autumn 1959 (22), just squeezes him in 1950s.

Wink Martindale Survived in 1960s for re-entry and re-issue of *Deck Of Cards*, the story card song, first 1959.

Al Martino, a rich-toned US vocalist, had his first here with *Here In My Heart* (1).

Johnny Mathis was a singer's singer. First here, *Teacher*

Teacher, 1958 (27).

Gary Miller, a UK singer with numerous covers, began with *Yellow Rose Of Texas*, 1955 (13).

Rick Nelson had *Stood Up*, 1958 (27), to begin hit trail for heart throb.

Anthony Newley began with *I've Waited So Long*, 1959 (3).

Nina and Frederick launched with a cover of *Mary's Boy Child*, 1959 (26).

Platters, the famous US vocal outfit, just survived into 1960s but had plenty of hits the previous decade. *The Great Pretender/Only You* 1956 (5), a great double-sider launched them here.

Elvis Presley was pop's top history man. He began here with great *Heartbreak Hotel*, 1956 (2).

Mike Preston, a UK artist, had late-Autumn-1959 hit with *Mr Blue* (12), cover of US hit.

Joan Regan, the popular UK lady balladeer, first charted with *Ricochet*, 1953 (8).

Cliff Richard undoubtedly the UK's top hit-man, began with that classic *Move It* 1958 (2).

Jimmie Rodgers had *Honeycomb* as his first in 1957 (30).

Al Saxon. In 1959 *You're The Top Cha* (17) began it for popular pop TV show star Al.

Jack Scott a deep-voiced Canadian, started with *My True Love* in 1958 (9).

Harry Secombe, the Goon man with fine voice, had *On With The Motley*, 1955 (16).

Neil Sedaka had *I Go Ape* in 1959 (9). It was first UK hit for UK, famed singer-songwriter.

Ann Shelton was one of UK's most loved in the 1950s, with *Arrivederci Darling* as her starters, 1955 (17).

Harry Simeone Chorale began with much covered *Little Drummer Boy*, 1959 (13).

Tommy Steele sang *Rock With The Caveman*, 1956 (13), and gave UK-thought of our hero as UK Elvis, but Steele Soon into show-biz.

Conway Twitty began with distinctive *It's Only Make Believe*, 1958 (1).

Frankie Vaughan, a pop hero for millions in 1950s, started with *Istanbul*, 1954 (11), but purple patch from *Green Door*, 1956 (2).

Sarah Vaughan had *Broken Hearted Melody*, 1959 (7), as first hit for an exquisite US jazz lady.

Gene Vincent found success over here with *Be Bop A Lula* 1956 (30).

Bert Weedon, thought of as UK's Duane Eddy, though much respected guitarist and session man, had **Guitar Boogie Shuffle**, 1959, to begin it all. Reached ten.

David Whitfield was a ballad hero of the 1950s, just one hit 1960s.

Marty Wilde had US covers at the end of Fifties, five hits before 1960s.

Andy Williams, a favourite with ladies, opened with catchy *Butterfly*, 1957 (1).

Jackie Wilson sadly died 1984 after long-time coma, was rock 'n' roll hero for many, opened with *Reet Petite*, 1957 (6).

Jimmy Young had successful covers of US ballads, six years between last hit of 1950s (1957) before *Miss You*, Top 20 in 1963.

The Next Decade

The Seventies – *how the Sixties ended, and how people viewed the coming decade.*

Marmalade topped the charts at the beginning of 1969 with *Ob-La-Di-Ob-La-Da*. The much praised Beatle *white* album *The Beatles* headed the album listings, and in the R&B singles it was *Love Child* from Diana Ross and the Supremes.

Engelbert Humperdinck told music paper readers of a recent American trip and why he preferred England. A *Jeffrey* Lynne talked about *Idle Race* and the later star of ELO (now as *Jeff*) was described as someone 'who looks very like "CW" of Bonnie and Clyde fame' The Caravelles, Solomon Burke, Des O'Connor, Petula Clark, The Showstoppers, Monkees, Fleetwood Mac, Gun and Georgie Fame were among others to receive feature copy in the first issue of *Record Mirror* for the decade's last year.

By December *Record Mirror* itself had become a colour glossy, Woodstock and the Isle of Wight had passed, the Beatles were in disarray, the Stones were to suffer the chaos of Altamont, California on the 6th.

The Archies' *Sugar Sugar* topped the first chart of December and in the album listing it was *Abbey Road* from the Beatles. Jnr Walker and the All Stars with *What Does It Take* was the number one R&B single.

Charlie Gillet let loose some provocative words by saying, 'Britain is destined to be two years behind the taste of the United States, and it would be more efficient if our record industry was geared to this situation. Either record companies should keep their US singles catalogue 'live' for three years, repromoting them about two years after their first issue or, if they must delete them after eighteen months, they should revive them a year after that.'

Gillet decried the number of fine US psychedelic records that had become lost and, at the same time, was irritated by the fact that 'here, we get nothing but synthetic stuff.'

Let It Bleed from the Stones had recently been released; as had the soundtrack of *Easy Rider*; *Recollections* from Judy Collins; *To Our Children's Children* from The Moody Blues; the self-titled *Plastic Ono Band*; and *Scott 4* from Scott Walker.

Two previously un-released tracks – one by the Beatles and the other by the Hollies – were part of an album *No-One's Gonna Change Our World* with the Beatle cut giving the Royal Wildlife charity album its title.

Sinatra was announced for May 1970. One-time chart name Jess Conrad made his comeback with President Records. Tiny Tim had just departed after a six-week visit, Delaney & Bonnie and Friends, with Eric Clapton, had impressed at the Royal Albert Hall, London. Zeppelin's Robert Plant counteracted statement of being a sex symbol by saying, 'I don't do a Tom Jones.' Reviewers talked eloquently about the 'magic of David Bowie' as the *Space Oddity* man had an album issued on Philips.

Pete Townshend told *Record Mirror* readers, 'I think young people are going the right way. There is a mental revolution going on . . . it is one step nearer the spiritual revolution which will follow.' The Kinks issued their third single from their *Arthur* opera – *Victoria*.

Robin Gibb said he was free from the Robert Stigwood Organisation. Chicago Transit Authority, or plain Chicago, arrived in Britain for the first time, Tony Palmer of *All My Loving* fame was announced as producer for *Groupie*, Sid Bernstein in the States offered the Beatles $1 million per night to perform. The film *Magic Christian* fetched good reviews and a David 'Kid' Jensen said he was quitting Luxembourg where he had been a staff announcer. The station was left with four regular DJs, Paul Burnett, Tony Prince, David Christian and Bob Stewart. Noel Edmonds had left earlier in 1969.

The BBC announced *Top Of The Pops* would have extra time in 1970, to become a 45-minute show that would now take records from the Top 30 and not just Top 20. January 22nd was the date that another off-shore radio project, Radio 266 (four miles off the Frinton, Essex coast) was announced; the station was scheduled for 14 February launch; Programme Director was a Mancunian Paul King; and people wondered whether 1970 would see the 'pirates' return.

It would be invidious to suggest that a mere review of the December 1969 scene could reflect the total possibilities of the coming decade, but at least it mentions people who would last, Robert Plant and Zeppelin, Jeff Lynne post-*Idle Race*, (eventually) a new David Bowie, more and better financial inducements for getting the Beatles together, Stones and Who to continue faring well, the Moody Blues with increasing popularity, Chicago to find life hard here while being amazingly successful back home in the States, and Charlie Gillet to emerge as one of rock's most knowledgeable commentators.

The end of the 1960s set the scene for greater BBC TV pop coverage, changes at Radio One and Luxembourg.

January 1970 saw John and Yoko planning a 1970 Peace Festival for Toronto; Hendrix was forming a new group Young Gipsy; Ginger Baker's Airforce was destined for London take-off on the 15th; while ex-Traffic man Dave Mason was rumoured to be getting a new group together. And the year's beginning saw Love Affair, the Bonzo Dog Band and King Crimson calling it a day. There were the usual predictions and chatterings about 'new' hit bands – one of the early named was the Notting Hill Gate, London-based Quintessence. The BBC announced a new plan for 12 local radio stations for 1971, so bringing the total number to 20. John and Yoko exhibited themselves and their love in 14 lithographs at the London Arts Gallery; Motown issued 12 albums on 23 January; a US Senate committee began investigating the Stones gig at Altamont of 6 December, 1969. Vertigo, the Philips progressive label, underwent a change of heart and began issuing singles with *Who Do You Love* from Juicy Luicy (led by Californian guitarist Glenn *Fernando* Campbell); the Bee Gees denied they had split; Alan Freeman and Pete Murray returned to the Luxembourg schedules; Family issued the album *A Song For Me*; Radio Nordsee began test transmissions; and, in Lancaster, on 23 January there was an Arts Festival with Duster Bennett, Jack Bruce, Colosseum among the highlights. 1970 was UNDERWAY.

Great Singles and Albums:
A Personal Selection

This is a personal choice of the great records that came out of the 1960s, U.K. and Stateside. For some time I toyed with the idea of putting them into preferential order but it proved, not unexpectedly, a nightmare so this slightly random list – in the order they came to me – is 200 singles and 100 albums, that's all!

SINGLES
1 Bob Dylan – *Like A Rolling Stone* (CBS)
2 Bob Dylan – *She Belongs To Me* (CBS)
3 Bob Dylan – *Maggie's Farm* (CBS)
4 Dusty Springfield – *I Close My Eyes And Count To Ten* (Philips)
5 Dusty Springfield – *I Just Don't Know What To Do With Myself* (Philips)
6 Merilee Rush – *Reach Out, I'll Be There* (Bell)
7 Arbors – *The Letter* (Date)
8 Beatles – *Penny Lane/Strawberry Fields Forever* (Parlophone)
9 Beatles – *Hey Jude* (Parlophone)
10 Beach Boys – *Good Vibrations* (Capitol)
11 Canned Heat – *On The Road Again* (Liberty)
12 Jane Birkin and Serge Gainsbourg – *Je T'Aime* (Major Minor/Fontana)
13 Byrds – *Eight Miles High* (CBS)
14 Jefferson Airplane – *Somebody To Love* (RCA)
15 Jefferson Airplane – *White Rabbit* (RCA)
16 Righteous Brothers – *You've Lost That Lovin' Feelin'* (London)
17 Rolling Stones – *(I Can't Get No) Satisfaction* (Decca)
18 Rolling Stones – *Little Red Rooster* (Decca)
19 Rolling Stones – *It's All Over Now* (Decca)

20 Cliff Richard – *The Young Ones* (Columbia)
21 Cliff Richard – *Lucky Lips* (Columbia)
22 Wilson Pickett – *In The Midnight Hour* (Atlantic)
23 Moody Blues – *Ride My See Saw* (Deram)
24 Moody Blues – *Nights In White Satin* (Deram)
25 Shadows – *Apache* (Columbia)
26 Carole King – *It Might As Well Rain Until September* (London)
27 William Bell and Judy Clay – *Private Number* (Stax)
28 Carla Thomas – *B-A-B-Y* (Stax)
29 Box-Tops – *The Letter* (Stateside)
30 R Dean Taylor – *Gotta See Jane* (Motown)
31 Simon Dupree – *I See The Light* (Parlophone)
32 Thunderclap Newman – *Something In The Air* (Track)
33 Shirley Bassey – *Something* (Columbia)
34 Chuck Berry – *No Particular Place To Go* (Pye)
35 Françoise Hardy – *Et Même* (Pye)
36 Doors – *Light My Fire* (Elektra)
37 Johnny Ray – *I'll Never Fall In Love Again* (Philips)
38 Brenda Lee – *Speak To Me Pretty* (Brunswick)
39 Little Eva – *The Locomotion* (London)
40 John Leyton – *Son This Is She* (HMV)
41 Brook Benton – *Fools Rush In* (Mercury)
42 Spencer Davis Group – *When I Come Home* (Fontana)
43 Spencer Davis Group – *Gimme Some Loving* (Fontana)
44 Doris Day – *Move Over Darling* (CBS)
45 Joe Cocker – *With A Little Help From My Friends* (Regal Zobophone)
46 Four Tops – *Reach Out I'll Be There* (Motown)
47 Elvis Presley – *In The Ghetto* (RCA)
48 Roy Orbison – *Oh Pretty Woman* (London)
49 Mamas and Papas – *California Dreamin'* (RCA)
50 Mamas and Papas – *I Saw Her Again* (London)
51 Traffic – *Hole In My Shoe* (Island)
52 Who – *My Generation* (Brunswick)
53 Who – *Substitute* (Brunswick)

54 Who – *I Can See For Miles* (Track)
55 Smokey Robinson and the Miracles – *Tracks Of My Tears* (Motown)
56 Ronettes – *Be My Baby* (London)
57 Ronettes – *Baby I Love You* (London)
58 Ike and Tina Turner – *River Deep Mountain High* (London)
59 Otis Redding – *My Girl* (Atlantic)
60 Otis Redding – *(Sittin' On) Dock of the Bay* (Stax)
61 Pink Floyd – *Arnold Layne* (Columbia)
62 Pink Floyd – *See Emily Play* (Columbia)
63 Procol Harum – *A Whiter Shade Of Pale* (Deram)
64 Johnny Preston – *Running Bear* (Mercury)
65 P P Arnold – *First Cut Is The Deepest* (Immediate)
66 P P Arnold – *Angel Of The Morning* (Immediate)
67 Merilee Rush – *Angel Of The Morning* (Bell)
68 Association – *Pandoras Golden Heebie Jeebies* (Valiant)
69 Darlene Love – *(Today I Met) The Boy I'm Gonna Marry* (Philles)
70 Crystals – *Da Doo Ron Ron* (London)
71 Crystals – *Then He Kissed Me* (London)
72 Shirelles – *Will You Love Me Tomorrow* (Top Rank)
73 Shirelles – *Soldier Boy* (HMV)
74 Crosby, Stills and Nash – *Suite: Judy Blue Eyes* (Atlantic)
75 Yardbirds – *Shapes Of Things* (Columbia)
76 Reparata and the Delrons – *Captain Of Your Ship* (Bell)
77 Martha Reeves and the Vandellas – *I'm Ready for Love* (Motown)
78 Mary Wells – *My Guy* (Stateside)
79 Steppenwolf – *Born To Be Wild* (Stateside)
80 The Crests – *16 Candles* (Coed)
81 Jody Reynolds – *Endless Sleep* (Demon)
82 The Penguins – *Earth Angel* (Dootone)
83 Chris Kenner – *I Like It Like That* (Instant)
84 Friend And Lover – *Reach Out Of The Darkness* (Verve Forecast)

85 Frankie Avalon – *Bobby Sox To Stockings* (Chancellor)

86 Bobby Lewis – *Tossin' And Turnin'* (Beltone)

87 Chiffons – *Sweet Talking Guy* (Stateside)

88 Chiffons – *He's So Fine* (Stateside)

89 Chiffons – *One Fine Day* (Stateside)

90 Kinks – *Dedicated Follower of Fashion* (Pye)

91 Kinks – *Dead End Street* (Pye)

92 Johnny Kidd and the Pirates – *Shakin' All Over* (HMV)

93 Drifters – *Save The Last Dance For Me* (London)

94 Drifters – *Up On The Roof* (Atlantic)

95 Drifters – *On Broadway* (Atlantic)

96 Scott McKenzie – *San Francisco (Wear Some Flowers In Your Hair)* (CBS)

97 Joannie Sommers – *Johnny Get Angry*

98 Ronettes – *Walking In The Rain* (London)

99 Crystals – *He's A Rebel* (London)

100 Shangri-Las – *Give Him A Great Big Kiss* (Red Bird)

101 Shangri-Las – *I Can Never Go Home Anymore* (Red Bird)

102 Shangri-Las – *Leader Of The Pack* (Red Bird)

103 Shangri-Las – *Remember (Walkin' In The Sand)* (Red Bird)

104 Walker Brothers – *My Ship Is Coming In* (Philips)

105 Walker Brothers – *The Sun Ain't Gonna Shine Anymore* (Philips)

106 John Lennon – *Give Peace A Chance* (Apple)

107 John Lennon – *Cold Turkey* (Apple)

108 Dixie Cups – *Chapel Of Love* (Pye)

109 Delfonics – *Ready Or Not, Here I Come* (Phillygroove)

110 Marvin Gaye – *I Heard It Thru The Grapevine* (Motown)

111 Betty Everett – *Getting Mighty Crowded* (Fontana)

112 Frankie Laine – *You Gave Me A Mountain* (ABC)

113 Beach Boys – *I Can Hear Music* (Capitol)

114 Beatles – *Get Back* (Apple)

115 Johnny Taylor – *I Wanna Testify* (Stax)

116 Neil Diamond – *Brother Loves Travelling Salvation Show* (Uni)

117 Bob Dylan – *Lay Lady Lay* (CBS)

118 Dells – *Oh What A Night* (Cadet)

119 Creedence Clearwater Revival – *Bad Moon Rising* (Liberty)

120 Jimi Hendrix Experience – *Hey Joe* (Polydor)

121 Jimi Hendrix Experience – *All Along The Watch-tower* (Track)

122 Don Gibson – *Sea Of Heartbreak* (RCA)

123 Four Seasons – *Rag Doll* (Philips)

124 Four Seasons – *Walk Like A Man* (Stateside)

125 Gene Chandler – *Duke Of Earl* (Vee-Jay)

126 James Darren – *Goodbye Cruel World* (Pye)

127 Manfred Mann – *Mighty Quinn* (Fontana)

128 Jimmy Dean – *Big Bad John* (Philips)

129 Norma Tanega – *Walking My Cat Named Dog* (New Voice)

130 Lovin' Spoonful – *Summer In The City* (Kama Sutra)

131 Association – *Cherish* (Valiant)

132 Simon and Garfunkel – *Sound of Silence* (US Columbia)

133 Left Banke – *Walk Away Renee* (Smash)

134 David Bowie – *Space Oddity* (Philips)

135 George Martin – *Radio One Theme* (Parlophone)

136 Sonny and Cher – *The Beat Goes On* (Atco)

137 Marianne Faithfull – *Is This What I Get For Loving You Baby?* (Decca)

138 Lovin' Spoonful – *Darling Be Home Soon* (Kama Sutra)

139 Eddie Floyd – *Knock On Wood* (Stax)

140 Janis Ian – *Society's Child* (Verve)

141 Aretha Franklin – *I Say A Little Prayer* (Atlantic)

142 Aretha Franklin – *Respect* (Atlantic)

143 Stevie Wonder – *I Was Made To Love Her* (Motown)

144 Vanilla Fudge – *You Keep Me Hangin' On* (Atlantic)

145 Scott Walker – *Jackie* (Philips)

146 Sam and Dave – *Soul Man* (Stax)

147 Erma Franklin – *Piece Of My Heart* (London)
148 Tony Orlando – *Bless You* (Fontana)
149 James Darren – *Her Royal Majesty* (Colpix)
150 Elvis Presley – *Can't Help Falling In Love* (RCA)
151 Dion – *The Wanderer* (HMV)
152 Everly Brothers – *Crying In The Rain* (Warner)
153 Everly Brothers – *Temptation* (Warner)
154 Shelley Fabres – *Johnny Angel* (Colpix)
155 Four Seasons – *Big Girls Don't Cry* (Stateside)
156 Aretha Franklin – *Since You've Been Gone* (Atlantic)
157 Sam and Dave – *I Thank You* (Stax)
158 The Equals – *Baby Come Back* (President)
159 Eric Burdon and the Animals – *Sky Pilot* (MGM)
160 Eric Burdon and the Animals – *Monterey* (MGM)
161 Bee Gees – *I've Gotta Get A Message To You* (Atco)
162 Cream – *Badge* (Polydor)
163 Cream – *I Feel Free* (Reaction)
164 Cream – *Sunshine Of Your Love* (Polydor)
165 Arthur Brown – *Fire* (Track)
166 Big Brother and the Holding Company – *Piece Of My Heart* (US Columbia)
167 Dion – *Abraham, Martin And John* (Laurie)
168 Dusty Springfield – *Son Of A Preacher Man* (Philips)
169 Sir Douglas Quintet – *She's About A Mover* (London)
170 Sir Douglas Quintet – *Mendocino* (Smash)
171 Frank Sinatra – *Strangers In The Night* (Reprise)
172 Them – *Here Comes The Night* (Decca)
173 Them – *Gloria* (Decca)
174 Cilla Black – *I've Been Wrong Before* (Parlophone)
175 Petula Clark – *Downtown* (Pye)
176 Animals – *Don't Let Me Be Misunderstood* (Columbia)
177 Animals – *The House Of The Rising Sun* (Columbia)
178 Shirley Ellis – *The Clapping Song* (London)
179 Yardbirds – *Heart Full Of Soul* (Columbia)
180 Anthony Newley – *If She Should Come To You* (Decca)

181 Joan Baez – *It's All Over Now Baby Blue* (Fontana)
182 Beatles – *Day Tripper/We Can Work It Out* (Parlophone)
183 Percy Faith – *Theme From A Summer Place* (Philips)
184 Mary Johnson – *You Got What It Takes* (London)
185 Eddie Cochran – *Three Steps To Heaven* (London)
186 Cliff Richard – *Fall In Love With You* (Columbia)
187 Mahalia Jackson – *The Lord's Prayer* (Philips)
188 Aretha Franklin – *I Never Loved A Man (The Way I Loved You)* (Atlantic)
189 John Fred and the Playboy Band – *Judy In Disguise (With Glasses)* (Pye)
190 Sam Cooke – *Twistin' The Night Away* (RCA)
191 Simon Dupree – *Reservations* (Parlophone)
192 Rooftop Singers – *Walk Right In* (Fontana)
193 Lorraine Ellison – *Stay With Me Baby* (Warner)
194 The Great Awakening – *Amazing Grace* (London)
195 Gladys Knight and the Pips – *Take Me In Your Arms And Love Me* (Motown)
196 Hollies – *I'm Alive* (Parlophone)
197 Troggs – *I Can't Control Myself* (Fontana)
198 Traffic – *Here We Go Round The Mulberry Bush* (Island)
199 Tymes – *People* (Direction)
200 Various – *All The Records I've Forgotten!* (Variety)

ALBUMS

1 Love – *Forever Changes* (Electra)
2 Beatles – *Sgt Pepper's Lonely Hearts Club Band* (Parlophone)
3 Beatles – *White Album* (Parlophone)
4 Jefferson Airplane – *Surrealistic Pillow* (RCA)
5 The Who – *Tommy* (Track)
6 Bob Dylan – *John Wesley Harding* (CBS)
7 Bob Dylan – *Bringing It All Back Home* (CBS)
8 Bob Dylan – *Blonde On Blonde* (CBS)
9 Bob Dylan – *Freewheelin'* (CBS)
10 Country Joe and the Fish – *I-Feel-Like-I'm-Fixin'-To-Die* (Vanguard)

11 It's A Beautiful Day – *It's A Beautiful Day* (CBS)
12 Tim Buckley – *Tim Buckley* (Elektra)
13 Cream – *Wheels Of Fire* (Polydor)
14 Judy Collins – *In My Life* (Elektra)
15 Judy Collins – *Who Knows Where The Time Goes* (Elektra)
16 Big Brother and the Holding Company – *Cheap Thrills* (CBS)
17 Joni Mitchell – *Joni Mitchell* (Reprise)
18 The Incredible String Band – *The Hangman's Beautiful Daughter* (Elektra)
19 Crimson King – *In The Court Of The Crimson King* (Island)
20 Jimi Hendrix – *Electric Lady Land* (Track)
21 Doors – *The Doors* (Electra)
22 Doors – *Strange Days* (Elektra)
23 Blind Faith – *Blind Faith* (Polydor)
24 The Band – *Music From Big Pink* (Capitol)
25 Joan Baez – *Joan Baez* (Fontana)
26 Joan Baez – *Joan Baez Volume 2* (Fontana)
27 Joan Baez – *Farewell Angelina* (Fontana)
28 Beatles – *A Hard Day's Night* (Parlophone)
29 Beatles – *Magical Mystery Tour* (Parlophone)
30 Beatles – *Rubber Soul* (Parlophone)
31 Beatles – *Revolver* (Parlophone)
32 Spirit – *Spirit* (CBS)
33 Dusty Springfield – *Dusty In Memphis* (Philips)
34 Beach Boys – *Pet Sounds* (Capitol)
35 Beach Boys – *All Summer Long* (Capitol)
36 Captain Beefheart – *Safe As Milk* (Pye)
37 Leonard Cohen – *Songs of Leonard Cohen* (CBS)
38 Crosby, Stills and Nash – *Crosby Stills And Nash* (Atlantic)
39 Crosby, Stills, Nash and Young – *Deja Vu* (Atlantic)
40 Roberta Flack – *First Take* (Atlantic)
41 The Grateful Dead – *Anthem Of The Sun* (Warner)
42 Iron Butterfly – *In-A-Gadda-Da-Vida* (Atco)
43 Jefferson Airplane – *Crown Of Creation* (RCA)
44 Led Zeppelin – *Led Zeppelin* (Atlantic)

45 Mamas and Papas – *If You Can Believe Your Eyes And Ears* (RCA)

46 MC5 – *Kick Out The Jams* (Elektra)

47 Steve Miller – *Sailor* (Capitol)

48 Steve Miller – *Brave New World* (Capitol)

49 Steve Miller – *Your Saving Grace* (Capitol)

50 Moby Grape – *Moby Grape* (CBS)

51 Moody Blues – *On The Threshold Of A Dream* (Deram)

52 Van Morrison – *Astral Weeks* (Warner)

53 Velvet Underground and Nico – *Velvet Underground and Nico* (Verve)

54 Laura Nyro – *Eli And The Thirteenth Confession* (CBS)

55 Pentangle – *Pentangle* (Transatlantic)

56 Rolling Stones – *Beggars Banquet* (Decca)

57 Jimi Hendrix – *Are You Experienced* (Track)

58 The Who – *The Who Sell Out* (Track)

59 The Who – *My Generation* (Track)

60 Electric Prunes – *Mass In F Minor* (Reprise)

61 Love – *Love* (Elektra)

62 Velvet Underground – *White Light/White Heat* (Reprise)

63 Tim Hardin – *Tim Hardin* (Verve)

64 Pete Seeger – *The Best Of* (CBS)

65 Odetta – *Odetta At Town Hall* (Vanguard)

66 Family – *Music In A Dolls House* (Reprise)

67 Byrds – *Turn! Turn! Turn!* (CBS)

68 Brian Auger/Julie Driscoll – *Open* (Marmalade)

69 Cream – *Fresh Cream* (Reaction)

70 Françoise Hardy – *Françoise Hardy* (Pye)

71 Françoise Hardy – *Fragile* (Disques Vogue)

72 Françoise Hardy – *François Hardy* (Discques Vogue, not same as release on Pye)

73 Beatles – *Abbey Road* (Apple)

74 Captain Beefheart and his Magic Band – *Trout Mask Replica* (Straight)

75 Beach Boys – *Smiley Smile* (Capitol)

76 The Soft Machine – *The Soft Machine* (Probe)

77 Traffic – *Mr Fantasy* (Island)
78 Traffic – *Traffic* (Island)
79 Cliff Richard – *Best Of Cliff* (Columbia)
80 Frank Zappa: The Mothers Of Invention – *We're Only In It For The Money* (Verve)
81 James Taylor – *Sweet Baby James* (Warner)
82 Pink Floyd – *Ummagumma* (Harvest)
83 Simon and Garfunkel – *Bookends* (CBS)
84 Simon and Garfunkel – *Sounds of Silence* (CBS)
85 Judy Collins – *Wildflowers* (Elektra)
86 Jimi Hendrix – *Axis: Bold As Love* (Track)
87 Various – *Woodstock* (first set of three) (Cotillion)
88 Johnny Cash – *At Folsom Prison* (CBS)
89 Chuck Berry – *His Latest And Greatest* (Pye)
90 Fairport Convention – *What We Did On Our Holidays* (Island)
91 Aretha Franklin – *Amazing Grace* (Atlantic)
92 Aretha Franklin – *I Never Loved A Man (The Way I Loved You)* (Atlantic)
93 Various – *The Rock Machine Turns You On* (CBS)
94 Soundtrack – *West Side Story* (Philips)
95 Johnny Mathis – *Tender Is The Night* (Mercury)
96 Various – *Cruisin'* (Increase, a history of rock and roll radio, with US release only, and covering each year of the Sixties)
97 Phil Spector – *Christmas Album* (Polydor)
98 Walker Brothers – *Walker Brothers Story* (Philips)
99 Supremes – *Supremes A-Go-Go* (Motown)
100 Various – the many great albums (forgotten), by equally great artists ...